STRUCTURED PROGRAMMING AND PROBLEM-SOLVING WITH PASCAL

RICHARD B. KIEBURTZ

DEPARTMENT OF COMPUTER SCIENCE
STATE UNIVERSITY OF NEW YORK AT STONY BROOK

D1523053

PRENTICE-HALL, INC.
Englewood Cliffs, New Jersey   07632

Library of Congress Cataloging in Publication Data

Kieburtz, Richard B. (date)
    Structured programming and problem-solving
with PASCAL.

    Includes index.
        1. Problem solving—Data processing.
2. Structured programming.   3. PASCAL (Computer
program language)   I. Title.
QA63.K53   001.6'42   78-2381
ISBN   0-13-854877-3
ISBN   0-13-854869-2 pbk.

TO MY FATHER, J. RICHARD KIEBURTZ

Printed in the United States of America

10 9 8 7 6 5 4 3 2 1

Prentice-Hall International, Inc., *London*
Prentice-Hall of Australia Pty. Limited, *Sydney*
Prentice-Hall of Canada, Ltd., *Toronto*
Prentice-Hall of India Private Limited, *New Delhi*
Prentice-Hall of Japan, Inc., *Tokyo*
Prentice-Hall of Southeast Asia Pte. Ltd., *Singapore*
Whitehall Books Limited, *Wellington, New Zealand*

CONTENTS

PREFACE

This book is an introduction to problem solving by computational methods. If it helps you to learn how to specify the requirements for a solution, how to formulate, one step at a time, a procedure to follow in generating a solution, and how to describe that procedure so that it may be understood by others, then it will have succeeded in its purpose.

In browsing through the book, you can get some idea of the types of problems for which people have found computational solutions to be useful. These encompass many more activities than one might suspect at first, and of course, only a sampling can be presented here. It is no surprise that many problems arising in science, engineering and applied mathematics are susceptible to solution by computation. One is also prepared to believe that computing systems are useful for keeping business records, although the computation that is done is of a somewhat different nature than is the case in scientific applications. It is perhaps more surprising that activities requiring complex decisions can be analyzed as computational problems, and it certainly is not obvious without considerable study how computation is able to create pictures, translate languages, predict outcomes of elections, do medical diagnosis or discover proofs of theorems in mathematics. It would require more and thicker volumes than this one to investigate all of the applications mentioned, but this book will introduce you to the principal computational techniques used in all of these applications.

You will also discover that this book is not much concerned with computing machines themselves, although you will certainly learn to run programs on some digital computer if you use this book as the text for a course. If your curiosity is aroused about what lies behind the panels on the box, (and it very likely will be) you can jump ahead to Chapter 12, which contains a brief description of some functional modules commonly used in digital computers, and a very sketchy description of how they are put together. This chapter is only a concession to your curiosity, however. If you really want to learn more about how computers work, you will have to read another book on that subject after you finish this one.

One of the principal ways in which this book differs from most introductory computer texts is that it emphasizes a more disciplined approach to the design of computational procedures. There are good reasons for this, although they are not always immediately apparent until your experience with computing gets beyond an introductory course. As in other endeavors, it is pretty easy in computing to discover satisfactory solutions to simple problems. That is what we mean when we say that a problem is simple. But when one is called upon to solve a problem that is not simple, the computational procedure required may be lengthy, complex, and therefore difficult to understand or to describe. It is at that point that the problem solver will see the need for some discipline to guide the organization of his effort, and to help divide the problem into simpler parts. If you learn such an approach to designing computational procedures at the outset, it will become a habitual tool, available for use when needed.

Since this book will require a slightly larger investment of your time to learn a disciplined approach to computing, it will not be the right introduction for everybody. It fact, the quickest and easiest way to gain the ability to use a computer is to teach yourself to use an interactive computing system using the BASIC language, or something similar. And this is quite satisfactory for the computing needs of many people. But if you ever have the occasion to tackle complex computational problems, or large problems which require the coordinated effort of several persons to design a computational procedure, the effort spent in learning a computing discipline will be well rewarded.

This book has been designed for use by readers of differing backgrounds, and should not be used in exactly the same way by everyone. Let me offer the following guide.

For the novice, Chapters 1 through 4 should be read in sequence, although Example 3.8.2 can be passed over in a first reading. Chapter 5 should be read, at least through Section 5.4.

In Chapter 6, the topics begin to cater to specialties of interest to different readers; the novice should read Section 6.1 and at least one from the remaining three sections. Chapter 7 is compulsory through Section 7.4, but the remainder may be read at any time. Chapter 8 should also be digested, although Example 8.4.2 can be skipped if the reader becomes weary. With this background, the various examples of Chapters 9, 10, and 11 can be selected for study according to the interest of the reader. Chapter 12 will interest the novice, but can be read at any time.

For the reader with some experience in computing, who seeks an introduction to the notation of Pascal, Chapters 2 through 8 will satisfy his needs, although the programming techniques and applications of the remaining chapters should also be of interest.

For the student of computing whose interests are not mathematical, Section 6.2, Example 8.4.2, and Chapter 11 may be skirted. However, the examples of Chapters 7, 9 and 10 should be worthwhile.

The science or engineering student has not been forgotten, either. Numerical computation is the topic of Chapter 11, and in addition, he should seek out those sections and examples that others have been warned to avoid.

A decision to be made by the author of any textbook on computing is the choice of a suitable language in which to describe computational procedures. English seems at first to be a good choice since anybody who is able to read this book already knows it. But attempts to describe computations in English have not been totally successful. It lacks precision, contains ambiguities and is therefore not easily translatable into a program for a computer. And a program for a computer is required, eventually, if the computational procedure is to yield a solution to the original problem. On the other hand, there are many languages designed for the specific purpose of programming computers. These languages have precision, are unambiguous, and are more or less intelligible to human beings. They are easily translatable into computer programs; in fact, the translation is done by the computer itself! But there are so many of them; FORTRAN, COBOL, ALGOL, BASIC, PL/1, SNOBOL, LISP are the names of but a few of the most widely used. And every computer programmer has his own personal favorite. If the author selects one of these, then his text will only be used by other instructors who favor the same programming language.

As you will see, this author has decided in favor of a particular programming language, called Pascal. It will be used as a communication language to describe procedures, and as a the means by which you will actually transmit your computational procedure to the computer. In order to render computations more readily understandable, the programming language will be freely augmented with comments in English. Also, English will be used in the preliminary stages of describing a problem and in considering alternate strategies for its solution. In preliminary stages, lack of precision is no handicap, as the concepts themselves remain to be clarified as well as the language.

Pascal has facilities that are needed to support a disciplined approach to program structure, and this is the principal reason for its choice here. In particular, Pascal provides better facilities for the description of data representation than do any of the older programming languages. Many of the examples in this book attempt to show you how to exploit these facilities.

Since this is principally a book about problem solving with the aid of a computer, the body of the text does not contain many digressions on the details of usage of the programming language. To help you with the grammar, punctuation and idiomatic expressions that you will need to write programs in Pascal, this book contains diagrams, called syntax charts, that will help you to learn the rules by which to compose acceptable Pascal sentences.

A dialect of flowchart language is also introduced as an aid to visualization of the logical structure of programs. This language, called iteration graphs, helps one to see clearly what choices must be made in the course of a computation as well as indicationg program steps which are to be repeated a number of times. Iteration graphs are a useful way to represent programs in their inception, allowing one to fill in the details as needed.

Another principal goal of this book is to teach you to compose procedures and to program them for the computer in such a way that another intelligent human being can read and understand your programs. A benefit of investing some effort to make programs intelligible is that you are more likely to understand them yourself. This may sound facetious, but it is asking too much of a computer to expect it to produce correct answers by following directions about which the programmer is also uncertain.

Since this book attempts to do much more than just to teach you a programming language, the ideas presented in it have been gathered from many sources. It is typical after one has been introduced to a new idea and has thought about it for awhile to adopt the idea as one's own, as if it were orphaned from its original source. At the time of this writing, the author still recalls that many of his ideas about programming were gleaned from the work of Robert S. Floyd, Edsger Dijkstra and Niklaus Wirth. With the passage of time, I suppose the ideas will seem to become my own, and I hope that you also will see fit to adopt some of them for your own.

Richard B. Kieburtz
Stony Brook, N.Y.

GLOSSARY
OF COMPUTING TERMS

accumulator -- a register in the arithmetic unit of a computer

accuracy -- in numerical computations, accuracy refers to the
closeness with which a calculated value approximates the
exact result one is trying to compute

algorithm -- a list of instructions for performing a task or
computing a result; it is given in elementary steps that
can be carried out without further instruction

array -- an indexed set of variables, possibly multiply indexed

assignment -- an elementary computational step that gives a new
value to a variable

binary -- having only two possible values

bit -- a single, binary unit of information

block -- in a programming language, a bracketed segment of program text containing declarations of variables and a
sequence of statements

Boolean -- taking a value of either True or False

byte -- an information storage unit corresponding to a single
character

character -- an element of a designated set of symbols, usually
consisting of the letters of the Roman alphabet, the
Arabic numerals, and a number of punctuation symbols

comment -- annotation within the text of a computer program, that
is not interpreted by the computer as part of the program

compound group -- a bracketed sequence of statements in a
program, to be executed as a single unit

computation -- the process of executing a computer program

computer -- an electronic, digital computer

conditional -- depending on the computed value of a Boolean
expression

data structure -- an ensemble of data items with a prescribed
mechanism for reference of a component item

declaration -- annotation in a program that is interpreted as
defining attributes of variables or of a procedure

dimension -- the number of elements along each coordinate of an
array

execution sequence -- in a specific computation by a computer
program, the sequence of steps actually carried out

expression -- in the text of a program, a string of identifiers
and operator symbols, describing an evaluation

floating-point number -- a number represented by a modulus, and
an exponent of the radix of the number system. This
representation allows the point in a fractional number to
be shifted, by adding or subtracting from the exponent
the number of places shifted

grammar -- a set of formal rules used to describe the syntax of a
language

identifier -- in the text of a program, any sequence of characters used to name a variable, constant, label, or
procedure

initialization -- the process of giving initial values to program
variables

instruction -- one of a specified set of orders that can be
interpreted by a computer

invocation -- the process of beginning execution of a program or
        procedure

iteration -- repetition. However, the meaning is generalized to
        include sequential execution of a list of instructions,
        and to include conditional execution

iteration graph -- a graphical notation developed to describe
        algorithms that use repetition or conditional execution

machine language -- not a language at all, but the use of machine
        instruction codes to specify a program

memory -- the internal data storage of a computer

nested -- textually embedded within a surrounding context

operator -- any of a specified set of computational operations

precedence -- an order of priority of application that can be
        defined upon a set of operators

precision -- the amount of information (number of bits or number
        of decimal digits) that is given in the approximation of
        a real number

procedure - a subsidiary algorithm declared in a program text

program -- an algorithm given as a sequence of instructions that
        can be interpreted by a computer

programming language -- a formally defined language for the
        specification of algorithms, and which can be translated
        or interpreted by a computer

record -- a package of one or more items of data in a specified
        format

recursion -- the computational process of re-invoking a program
        or procedure prior to its completion. Intermediate
        results of computation are stacked up so that they will
        not be lost

register -- a cell for storage of data in a computer

relation -- a binary relation defined on the possible values of a
        type of data

scope -- the textual context in which a definition or declaration
is valid

statement -- an imperative sentence in a programming language,
interpreted as one or a sequence of instructions by a
computer

stepwise refinement -- the process of algorithm composition by
specification in successively finer levels of detail

string -- a sequence of characters

type, or data type -- a defined class of data objects

variable -- a named object that can hold a value from a designated data type, and can receive new values by assignment

verification -- the process of establishing the correctness of an
algorithm

word -- a unit of data corresponding to the capacity of a register of the memory of a computer

1 INTRODUCTION: WHAT IS COMPUTING?

Every person today knows of the existence of large computers and knows enough of their application that he has in mind some opinion as to what computing is all about. If pressed for an answer, our man on the street might tell you that computing is "the way they make out paychecks. You know, they put all the numbers into the computer and it figures out how much to deduct for income tax, how much for social security, for health insurance, for union dues, and it makes out your paycheck for the amount that's left." Or he might tell you, "Computing is the way they design things these days. If an engineer is designing a bridge, he has all of his complex calculations done on a computer instead of using a slide rule as he used to." Another interviewee may reply, with a tone of bewilderment, "Computing? Why computing is how everything is controlled nowadays. When I get in my car in the morning, the engine is run by a computer. My telephone calls are routed by another computer. The company I work with makes men's clothing. All of the patterns are produced by computers, and the cloth is cut by computer controlled machines. You know, they even sent a computer to the moon with the astronauts. Why, the world just wouldn't run without computing!" Yes, nearly everyone has some idea about the applications of computers today, but many fewer people would be able to give you a very clear picture of just how computing is brought to bear on all of these diverse applications.

Just what is computing all about? First of all, it is concerned with elementary operations which are very simple indeed. In fact, the simplicity of the elementary operations performed by a computer sometimes leads people to underestimate the complexity of computing. One opinion sometimes heard from

1

scientists (usually grey-haired ones) who know very well how computers work, is that "A computer is really no more than a very large, very fast calculating machine." In view of the sophisticated applications of computing of which even the layman is vividly aware, one cannot believe that this characterization as a large, fast calculator tells the whole story. Yet there is an element of truth to it, for on the level of the tiny components of which a computer is made, the individual operations performed are each very simple, as we shall see in Chapter 12 (which you may read at any time you are interested).

But the level of the elementary operations is too primitive a place to start if we want to gain an understanding of computing as quickly as possible. For the immense capabilities of computers are gained by the organization of these elementary operations; by composing simple functions to obtain capabilities of very much greater complexity. We shall do better to begin our study on much higher and somewhat more abstract conceptual level dealing with the logical organization and composition of familiar operations.

1.1 Algorithms

Computer science is the study of computational procedures and of methods by which to design and apply these procedures to real problems. An <u>algorithm</u> is a computational procedure, which is unambiguous, deterministic, finite and given in terms of elementary instructions that can themselves be carried out. In addition, we usually desire that our algorithms should be effective, that is that they should accomplish the goal originally set out for them, but it turns out that the question of determining whether or not an algorithm is effective is so difficult that we would not want to make that requirement part of our definition. To illustrate the requirements imposed by the definition, we shall consider a few examples.

Example 1.1.1--Recipe for buckwheat pancakes

a. Place in a large bowl 1 cup of buckwheat flour, 1 teaspoon baking soda, and some salt.

b. Add 1 tablespoon of melted shortening and 1 egg, and mix with the dry ingredients.

c. Add some water and mix into a thick batter.

d. Put two tablespoons of shortening in a frying pan and heat until the shortening begins to smoke.

e. Pour some batter into the hot frying pan and cook until bubbles appear through the pancake. Turn, and cook until golden brown.

Now this recipe might well be sufficient to guide an experienced cook to success in making buckwheat pancakes, but to a novice it is just not specific enough and his pancakes will very likely prove to be inedible. Most recipe books contain recipes given very much like this one, however, and the reason that people are able to use them is that a common bond of knowledge exists between the writer of the recipe book and the cook who uses it. This knowledge is gained by having been taught to cook, or else by years of experience in cooking, remembering successes and failures and the means by which they were achieved. In communicating recipes and procedures for doing other tasks, we usually take for granted that the person with whom we are communicating has a "common knowledge" of the rudiments of the task we are explaining, and do not give instructions in sufficient detail to be followed by an absolute novice. When you start communicating with a computer, you will be shocked to discover that the computer is an absolute novice, has learned nothing from past experience, and that computational algorithms must be specified in every detail, leaving nothing to be interpreted by "common knowledge".

Example 1.1.2-- Instructions for finding a summer cottage

a. Go north on Route 3 for about six miles until you pass the general store on your left; then turn off at the next intersection.

b. Go along until you pass a big, spreading oak tree by the road; then in about a quarter of a mile, look for a dirt road on the right.

c. Follow the dirt road until the third, or maybe it's the fourth mailbox, and turn down the driveway.

d. Go down the driveway about 400 yards. It's a white cabin with green shutters -- you can't miss it.

These instructions are ambiguous at several points. In (a) they fail to mention which way to turn from the main road. In (b) there is no assurance that the large oak tree specified as a lankmark will be unique; the countryside may be an oak forest. In (c), our guide is specifically ambiguous when he cannot remember which mailbox marks the driveway. The recipe ends with a comment at the end of (d) -- "you can't miss it". This comment accompanies many lists of ambiguous directions. While the human searching for his friend's summer cottage may rely on his past experience, knowledge of the area or other aids not explicitly given in the list of instructions, the computer would not be able to do so, and a computational procedure containing ambiguities such as the ones in the example would not be sufficient. The human may also have difficulty, but he is adaptable to unexpected situations and will fall back on other methods such as exploration or asking for more specific directions if he cannot successfully resolve the ambiguities in the directions he was originally given.

Example 1.1.3-- A procedure for becoming a millionaire

a. Withdraw all your money from your bank account.

b. Do step (c) each day until you become a millionaire or a pauper.

c. Go to the local racetrack and bet all your money on the daily double combination paying the highest odds.

This is an example of a procedure which is nondeterministic. That is, if the procedure is executed at different times, it will not necessarily produce the same outcome even though the instructions are explicit and unambiguous. We do not wish to consider nondeterministic procedures as algorithms, although they are sometimes entertaining to contemplate.

Example 1.1.4 -- A procedure for drying out a leaky rowboat

a. Get a two-gallon plastic bucket.

b. Stand in the rowboat and bail the water out as fast as you can until less than two gallons remains in the bottom.

This procedure is unambiguous, deterministic, and the elementary steps can be readily carried out. But in carrying it out, there will be some cases in which you never finish bailing, namely if the boat is swamped to begin with, or if it has such a large leak that the water runs in faster then you can bail it out. One would say that this procedure was not finite because there are some cases to which it applies where its execution would never halt. This characteristic is also true of some computational procedures, and it is often difficult to detect. However, we would like to require of an algorithm that it should be finite, for only after its execution has halted can one talk about the result given by the procedure.

You should now have an idea as to what we shall study about computation. In order to apply computation to the solution of problems, we compose algorithms, specific computational procedures which are unambiguous, deterministic, finite in their execution and which are carried out in simple steps. If we are successful and our algorithms accomplish the tasks they were designed to do, then we will say they are effective. Remember that to be effective, an algorithm must work correctly on all initial values of the data for which it was designed, and not only for one particular test case.

1.2 How are algorithms formulated?

When faced with a problem to be solved or a task to be performed, how does one go about developing an algorithm for its solution? Will the algorithm as formulated always satisfy the conditions of unambiguity, determinism, finiteness and the ability to be carried out in simple steps? Naturally, there will be opportunities to make mistakes, but a few examples may help to give an idea as to how we go about the formulation of algorithms.

Example 1.2.1 -- Given a non-negative integer, list all pairs of non-negative integers which sum to the given integer.

This is the type of problem that one encounters in school at age six or seven, which is about the age that most children first seem to develop algorithms for the solution of problems. The principal source of difficulty in this problem is that the pupil is asked to list all pairs that sum to the given integer, rather than just one pair or some pairs. So if he just puts into his list those pairs which immediately come to mind as having the required sum, he will not be certain of having listed them all. He must adopt a systematic approach. But he has some information to guide him. By the time he is given a problem of this type, he will know that addition is commutative, so that by listing only ordered pairs he may still be sure of meeting the require- ments of the problem. He will also know that of the pairs

5

which sum to a given number, the pair containing the largest integer will consist of the given integer and zero. So an algorithm that he may discover or which may be suggested to him by his teacher is the following:

a. Begin the list with the pair consisting of the given integer and zero.

b. For as long as the two integers in the last pair listed differ by more than one, repeat the sequence of steps (c--d)

c. Subtract one from the first integer of the last pair listed and enter the result as the first integer of the next pair.

d. Find an integer which, when added to the number found in the previous step, sums to the integer given originally.

Of course, our first-grade pupil does not state his algorithm this formally, but he will learn to go through a sequence of steps such as those listed above, in the course of solving problems of this type.

Example 1.2.2-- An algorithm for long division

Everyone has learned how to do long division of integers, accumulating the quotient one numeral at a time. We can give an algorithm for this procedure, perhaps not quite in the same form that you have learned it.

a. Call the dividend by another name, remainder. If the divisor is larger than the remainder, then write zero for the quotient and stop, otherwise go on to the next step.

b. Count the number of decimal places in the divisor and in the remainder. Form a decimal number consisting of the numeral 1 followed on the right by a number of zeros equal to the number of decimal places by which the remainder is longer then the divisor. Call this number the multiplier.

c. For as long as any numerals at all remain in the multiplier, repeat steps (d--e).

d. Multiply the divisor by the multiplier, and determine how many times this product can be successively subtracted from the remainder. Write the number of subtractions as the next numeral of the quotient (immediately to the right of any previously written partial quotient) and discard the old value of the remainder, replacing it by the result of the successive subtractions.

e. Erase the rightmost numeral of the multiplier.

This algorithm probably differs from the one you learned in elementary school in that it does not specify the positions in which various numbers are to be written on a piece of paper. Instead, the algorithm refers to various numbers by name, and the actual values of the numbers attached to some of the names will change from one step to another during the course of the calculation. The algorithm does not even have to be done with pencil and paper, but could also be carried out using an adding machine or an abacus. Incidentally, as given here, the algorithm may produce a non-zero quotient having a zero as the leftmost digit. Can you see why?

Example 1.2.3-- Looking up a word in a dictionary

This is an example of a searching operation, one of the most common functions performed in any information retrieval system. We shall consider several algorithms for this example.

Version 1 -- Sequential searching

a. Given any word to be looked up, begin by opening the dictionary to the first page of entries.

b. For as long as the desired word does not appear on the page to which the dictionary is opened, and the page is not the last one, repeat step (c). Otherwise, proceed to step (d).

c. Turn to the next page.

d. If the word appears on the page, then give its definition, otherwise report that the word as given was not found in the dictionary.

This algorithm is correct, but it is not one that most of us would choose to use because of the number of individual page searches required. The large number of words listed in a dictionary makes it important to us to use an efficient search procedure. The efficiency can be improved by making use of the alphabetical ordering relation which is defined on words, and of the fact that words are listed in the dictionary according to this order.

Version 2 -- Binary searching

a. Given any word to be looked up, make a sheaf of all the pages of the dictionary and hold them with your left hand. Open the sheaf to an arbitrarily chosen page.

b. For as long as the desired word does not appear on the page to which the dictionary is opened, repeat step (c). When the word does appear, proceed to step (d).

c. If the desired word occurs in order before the first word on the open page, then select all the pages in the sheaf before the open page, and hold them with your left hand as a new sheaf. Otherwise, if the desired word occurs after the last word on the open page, select as the new sheaf all the pages of the sheaf following the open page. Open the newly selected sheaf of pages to an arbitrarily chosen page.
In the event that neither of the above conditions is satisfied, but instead the desired word follows the first word and precedes the last word on the open page (but does not appear on that page), then stop and report that the word is not to be found in the dictionary.

d. Give the definition of the word found on the open page.

In comparison to the algorithm of Version 1, this algorithm can be much faster on the average. If N stands for the number of pages in the dictionary, then the average number of pages to be inspected in a search can be reduced by the ratio of

$$N/2 : \log_2 N \ ^\dagger$$

Another interesting feature of the version 2 algorithm is that although it appears to be nondeterministic, it is not. The eventual outcome of either finding the word and giving its

---

$\dagger$ Achievement of the reduction depends on the rule used to select an arbitrary division of the sheaf. Dividing it exactly in two each time enables the search reduction to be realized; so does a uniformly random selection of the division point.

definition, or of reporting that the word is not in the dictionary, is completely independent of the particular choices of page sheaves made in steps (a) and (c).

Some dictionaries furnish still more information to guide an efficient search, in the form of index tabs. For a tabulated dictionary, one might use the following algorithm:

Version 3 -- Indexed binary searching

a. Given any word to be looked up, select as a sheaf the pages starting with the tab corresponding to the first letter of the desired word, and extending up to the following tab. Open the sheaf to an arbitrary page.

Steps (b--d) are the same as version 2.

We see that the benefit of the index tabs is only to reduce the size of the initially chosen sheaf of pages to be searched. If there are R tabs and the number of pages between adjacent tabs is approximately the same for all tabs, then the number of pages to be searched will be reduced by approximately log R. This is only an improvement by a constant, and so is not nearly so important as the improvement obtained in going from sequential searching in Version 1 to binary searching in Version 2.

The reason for referring to Versions 2 and 3 as binary searching algorithms is that in step (c) a binary choice is made to determine which of the two alternatives to use as the next sheaf. It is the division of the search space into two parts at each repetition which makes the algorithm efficient and which leads to the estimate of approximately $\log_2 N$ as the average number of pages to be searched.

Example 1.2.4-- The missionaries and the cannibals

In the wilderness of the island of New Guinea, three missionaries and three cannibals are traveling together when they encounter a broad river. They have with them a small canoe which can carry a maximum of three people at a time. The missionaries do not trust the cannibals and so they establish the following conditions for the river crossing.

i) A missionary must occupy the canoe on each trip across the river.

9

ii) On either bank of the river, cannibals must not outnumber missionaries (unless there is no missionary on a particular bank).

Can you help the missionaries devise a scheme for ferrying the party across the river?

This is an example of a decision-making problem, in which there are several constraints imposed at each step of a solution. It is not obvious at the outset that there exists even one solution satisfactory to the missionaries, or whether there may be several.

A starting point for analysis might be to list all the possible configurations of missionaries and cannibals on the two banks of the river. In this problem, the number of configurations is finite. The order in which they are enumerated is arbitrary; it merely furnishes us with a means of indexing the configurations. We use "X" to stand for a cannibal and "O" to stand for a missionary.

Index	Right bank	Left bank
1	XXXOOO	–
2	XXXOO	O
3	XXXO	OO
4	XXX	OOO
5	XXOOO	X
6	XXOO	XO
7	XXO	XOO
8	XX	XOOO
9	XOOO	XX
10	XOO	XXO
11	XO	XXOO
12	X	XXOOO
13	OOO	XXX
14	OO	XXXO
15	O	XXXOO
16	–	XXXOOO

Of the sixteen possible configurations, only numbers 1, 4, 5, 6, 8, 9, 11, 12, 13, and 16 are acceptable to the missionaries. Configuration 1 is the one from which the problem starts, and number 16 is the desired goal.

Possible loadings of the canoe can also be enumerated. We give only those boatloads that contain at least one missionary, since that condition has been made a requirement.

Load index	Canoe loading
a	O
b	OO
c	OOO
d	XO
e	XOO
f	XXO

What is really of interest in this problem is the dynamic behavior of the configurations, that is, the way in which they can be changed from one to another by prescribing sequences of canoe loads back and forth across the river. To keep track of all possibilities, we shall require two tables, one to determine the changes of configuration resulting from right bank to left bank trips, and the other to account for transportation in the opposite direction. The columns of each table represent configurations, specified by an index from one to sixteen, and the rows of each table represent the possible canoe loadings, indexed from a to f. In each square of each table may appear a result if the initial configuration corresponding to the column was modified by making a canoe trip in the specified direction, using the loading corresponding to the row. The entries given in the tables can easily be checked by drawing little diagrams on paper. However, the use of the tables will help us to keep track of this information without figuring it out all over again each time we may wish to simulate a river crossing.

TABLE RL

	Configuration index															
	1	2	3	4	5	6	7	8	9	10	11	12	13	14	15	16
a	2	3	4	–	6	7	8	–	10	11	12	–	14	15	16	–
b	3	4	–	–	7	8	–	–	11	12	–	–	15	16	–	–
c	4	–	–	–	8	–	–	–	12	–	–	–	16	–	–	–
d	6	7	8	–	10	11	12	–	14	15	16	–	–	–	–	–
e	7	8	–	–	11	12	–	–	15	16	–	–	–	–	–	–
f	10	11	12	–	14	15	16	–	–	–	–	–	–	–	–	–

	Configuration index															
	1	2	3	4	5	6	7	8	9	10	11	12	13	14	15	16
a	-	1	2	3	-	5	6	7	-	9	10	11	-	13	14	15
b	-	-	1	2	-	-	5	6	-	-	9	10	-	-	13	14
c	-	-	-	1	-	-	-	5	-	-	-	9	-	-	-	13
d	-	-	-	-	-	1	2	3	-	5	6	7	-	9	10	11
e	-	-	-	-	-	-	1	2	-	-	5	6	-	-	9	10
f	-	-	-	-	-	-	-	-	-	1	2	3	-	5	6	7

Tables RL and LR give all possible configurations, but we already know that some of them are unacceptable to the missionaries. Since we have no wish to generate unacceptable solutions, the tables could be pared down somewhat by listing only those columns corresponding to the acceptable configurations. Also, those table entries indicating unacceptable configurations may just as well be replaced by an "x". The pruned tables are:

TABLE RLA

	1	4	5	6	8	9	11	12	13	16
a	x	-	6	x	-	x	12	-	x	-
b	x	-	x	8	-	11	-	-	x	-
c	4	-	8	-	-	12	-	-	16	-
d	6	-	x	11	-	x	16	-	-	-
e	x	-	11	12	-	x	-	-	-	-
f	x	-	x	x	-	-	-	-	-	-

TABLE LRA

	1	4	5	6	8	9	11	12	13	16
a	-	x	-	5	x	-	x	11	-	x
b	-	x	-	-	6	-	9	x	-	x
c	-	1	-	-	5	-	-	9	-	13
d	-	-	-	1	x	-	6	x	-	11
e	-	-	-	-	x	-	5	6	-	x
f	-	-	-	-	-	-	x	x	-	x

At this point, we have not yet made any attempt to formulate an algorithm for the missionaries, but have developed a systematic way to represent the various possibilities that are available in the generation of a solution. And in the course of developing this systematic representation it has been possible to discover a surprising amount about the form that a solution might take. From tables RLA and LRA one can see, for instance, that canoe loading f (one missionary and two cannibals) will never be used, and that there are two possible configurations (4 and 13) from which only a single canoe loading can enable the constraints to be satisfied.

A solution, if one does exist, could be expressed in the form of a sequence of canoe loadings to be utilized on successive trips back and forth across the river. Thus, dacccb would represent the following sequence: a missionary and a cannibal cross from right bank to left; the missionary returns alone; three missionaries cross from right to left; all three return; they cross again; two missionaries return. This example illustrates something about these sequences that may be useful in developing an algorithm. When a letter appears doubled in a sequence, it indicates that a canoe load has crossed the river in one direction, then returned with exactly the same load. Such trips are redundant and will contribute no progress toward a solution. Therefore, we could restrict our attention to sequences containing no doubled letters.

A brute force algorithm by which to search for a solution would be the following. Enumerate all possible river crossing sequences somehow or other. Then, testing each sequence in turn, determine whether or not the sequence is acceptable, by seeing if it leads to legal configuration transformations according to tables LRA and RLA. The search would continue until a sequence was found which produced a transformation from configuration 1 to configuration 16.

For instance, to test the sequence dad, first apply loading d to configuration 1 using table RLA, which tells us that configuration 6 will result. Next, using the table for return crossings, LRA, apply loading a to configuration 6, obtaining configuration 5. Lastly, when loading d is applied to configuration 5 in table RLA, it is found to produce an unacceptable configuration, and so the sequence dad is rejected.

The astute reader will see that if some sequence, such as dad, fails to produce a transition to an acceptable configuration, then no other sequence having dad as its first three letters can be an acceptable sequence either. As soon as it is determined that dad is not an acceptable sequence, one can

13

proceed to cross out of the enumeration all untried sequences having this beginning. The amount of effort spent in testing sequences can be reduced drastically by this simple expedient.

Finally, if an enumeration of sequences is to be used to guide the search for a solution, how might one give such an enumeration? An easy way is to first give all sequences one letter long, in alphabetical order a, b, c, d, e. (Note that canoe load f has already been found not to lead to acceptable configurations.) Next all two-letter configurations are given: aa, ab, ac, . . . ed, ee; then three-letter sequences, and so on. By searching an enumeration of sequences ordered by length, one will be assured of finding a solution involving the minimum number of canoe trips, if one exists.

Completing the specification of an algorithm to solve the missionaries and cannibals problem will be left as an exercise. If you attempt to carry out the algorithm yourself, you will soon discover that one can save much time by generating only those sequences of a given length that have already been found to have acceptable prefixes, instead of generating all sequences of that length, and deleting the very large number of unacceptable ones.

This last example is typical of many complex decision-making problems. Solutions involve the generation of a succession of seemingly plausible candidate configurations and a series of tests imposed on each candidate to determine whether or not it is actually acceptable. It is characteristic of such problems that the number of conceivable candidates for solution is very large, so the key to an effective algorithm is often to discover some means of limiting the generation of proposed solutions. In the example just given, a first step towards an algorithm was to determine a means of enumerating proposed solutions, even though they seemed not to possess any natural order, or means of enumeration.

We have considered four examples of algorithm composition to gain some idea of what might be the essential constructions used in algorithms. One can observe that each made use of the ability to test conditions and to determine further action on the basis of the outcome of the test. Each used repetition or iteration of some sequence of basic steps. The second and third, at least, made use of a name for some entity (the remainder, a sheaf of pages) whose value changed during the course of executing the algorithm, but which was treated in the same way each time the basic steps were repeated. These constructions will be formalized and used repeatedly when we begin programming computations for a computer.

Algorithms constitute systematic procedures that can be used to solve whole classes of problems, rather than being restricted to obtain specific, one-time-only answers. From the examples given, it should be evident that nearly everyone makes use of algorithmic methods in carrying out tasks at least some of the time, and some people make use of algorithmic methods in nearly everything they do. These persons are referred to by their acquaintances as being "highly organized". The reason they we are not more aware of the use of algorithmic methods in carrying out everyday tasks is that people seldom bother to write down the algorithms they have learned or devised for their own use; they only know them informally. It is only when we are dealing with a formal system, and can rely on no common bond of experience or ingenuity to interpret informal algorithms, that we are faced with the need to write down algorithms in a formal notation.

Up to now, the algorithms we have been using as examples have concerned tasks carried out by humans, so it has been possible to state them in informal English, readily understoood by humans. Faced with the prospect of communicating with a computer, it will be necessary to learn a new language, a formal notation in which meanings are precise and unambiguous and which can, therefore, be translated by a computer into the myriad electrical signals which govern its own internal workings. Fortunately, many years of development have provided us with formal programming languages that are relatively intelligible and easy to learn.

Self-check questions

1. Why must an algorithm for a computer be detailed and specific?

2. By what criterion do you decide whether an algorithm step is "elementary"?

3. How can the tables RLA and LRA be used in developing a solution to the Missionaries and Cannibals problem of Example 1.2.4?

4. Give some requirements of a language in which to state algorithms.

1.1 Give an algorithm for selecting items in a supermarket from your grocery list. This can be thought of as a matching problem, for the sequence in which items appear on the grocery list will not agree with the sequence in which they are shelved along the aisles of the store.

1.2 An exercise given to elementary school children is that of matching lists of words to form compound words. For instance, given the list:

     1. break   a. plane
     2. air   b. fold
     3. hard   c. bird
     4. blind   d. ware
     5. blue   e. fast

the corresponding list of conpound words would be indicated by the pairs of indices, 1e, 2a, 3d, 4b, 5c. Give an algorithm for matching lists of this kind, giving as a result a list of pairs of indices corresponding to the compound words formed.

Notice that the algorithm you have constructed is very likely unable to handle cases in which some of the constructions are not unique. For instance, suppose we dissect the words bargain, peacock, horsefly, doughnut, and carboy to make this pair of lists:

     1. bar   a. nut
     2. pea   b. fly
     3. dough   c. gain
     4. horse   d. boy
     5. car   e. cock

Unless you have composed an algorithm that can back up to try other choices than the first ones that seem to make sense, it will probably fail to complete the resynthesis of these lists. An elementary school child would also have trouble, but if you were asked to match the lists yourself, you would employ a more sophisticated algorithm, possibly augmented by ad hoc methods.

16

1.3   Give an algorithm for the addition of two decimal integers.
       Next give an algorithm for the addition of a list of
       decimal integers. How do you keep track of the carry? Is
       your algorithm for adding a list the same one you would
       actually use with pencil and paper?

1.4   Give an algorithm for checking the accuracy of
       multiplication of decimal numbers, by the sum-of-nines
       method. (The sum-of-nines method forms a check numeral from
       each of the multiplicand and multiplier. The check numeral
       is the modulo 9 sum of the digits of the given number. To
       form this check numeral, you merely accumulate the sum,
       retaining only the excess over 9. For example, the check
       numeral formed from 78 is 6, since 7 + 8 = 15, which is
       greater than 9, and 15 - 9 = 6. The product of the check
       numerals, modulo 9, must agree with the check numeral of
       the product.)

       Will the same algorithm be effective when the digits of
       the numbers are summed modulo some digit other than nine,
       such as seven? Explain why the algorithm works.

1.5   Give an algorithm for making change for a customer in a
       store. The result of the algorithm should tell how many
       bills or coins of each denomination to return, and should
       return the fewest possible pieces of money. Thus, an
       algorithm that always gives only pennies in change is not
       acceptable.

1.6   Give an algorithm for locating a house in a strange city if
       you have the street address. Try to include all details
       that are actually significant, such as determining which
       way along the street the house numbers increase.

1.7   Complete the specification of an algorithm for the mission-
       aries and cannibals problem (Example 1.2.4) by giving a
       sequence of steps by which trial solutions are to be gener-
       ated and tested until a satisfactory solution is found.

2 USING COMPUTATIONAL VARIABLES

The language that we are going to use the describe algorithms for the computer is called Pascal. It was designed by Professor Niklaus Wirth, and its genesis is in the line of the programming languages ALGOL 60 and ALGOL W. Pascal incorporates several mechanisms for controlling the sequence of steps executed by a program and for describing the data on which it works. The combination of these mechanisms make the language relatively simple for students to learn and to use. Even if you might use another programming language sometime in the future, you will find that the basic concepts you will learn in order to compose programs in Pascal will also apply to the other language. Of course, the specific notation may be different, but learning a new notation is not a difficult task.

In this programming language, one can write ordinary decimal numbers and expressions of arithmetic, such as 3.1416, 7 + 5, 1/2, and 9.3*18. The arithmetic operations of addition, subtraction, multiplication and division are represented by the symbols +,-,* and /. Parentheses can be used, just as in expressions of ordinary arithmetic, to indicate the scope of the operators. The expression 2 * (3-(4+4)) will make sense in this language, and the computer will evaluate the expression to the number -10. Negative numbers are indicated by placing a minus sign before the number.

The examples of the last chapter showed that one also wants to be able to express <u>variables</u>, which may take different values at different steps during the course of a computation, just as is done in mathematical notation. In Pascal, variables can be given names. We shall write names as capitalized, proper names throughout this book, although you will more likely see them printed entirely in capital letters when your programs are listed by the computer. The names may be as long or as short as you like, and may contain numerals as well as letters, but each name must begin with a letter and must not contain any blanks or punctuation marks. Thus, "Frank", "Harry", "X", "A1", "A2", "A3", "December25", and "LargestFactor" are all acceptable names, but "2by2", "U.R.Stuck", and "First of January" are not. A name is attached to a variable and a variable can have a value, but how can it be given one?

2.1 Assigning values to variables

The most direct way to give a value to a variable is by assignment. Assignment is the operation you are familiar with from algebra, when you say "let x have the value 2" or "let S be the square root of 5." In Pascal, we don't use the word "let" to denote assignment, but there is a special symbol, ":=" which is used for the assignment operator. We would write X := 2, or S := Sqrt(5). The symbol ":=" can be read as "is assigned the value", in reading Pascal programs. Once a value has been assigned to a variable, that value may be used again in subsequent expressions just by referring to the variable by name. The variable will retain the same value until another assignment is made to it, or until it receives a new value by one of the other means to be discussed. Thus, if we write C := (7-4) / 2, followed subsequently by the expression C * 8, the latter expression will be equivalent to 1.5 * 8, and will be evaluated to 12.

Assignment of a value to a variable is a way by which you can specifically state that you want to have an expression evaluated now and to remember this value for reference later. The assignment statement implies a certain order in which its component operations are to be done. The expression to the right of the ":=" is first evaluated, then the variable on the left receives the new value. It is important to keep this order in mind.

Not only can values be used over again by making repeated references to the variables, but the variables themselves can be reused by making subsequent assignments of new values. Sometimes this is a good idea, and sometimes it is not. As was seen in the examples of the last chapter, it is very helpful to be able to assign a succession of values to a variable in a repeated step of an algorithm. Each value that the variable receives is processed in exactly the same way. It is a potential source of confusion, however, to use the same variable name to represent values of completely unrelated entities which are referred to in different parts of a computation. In fact, it usually helps our understanding of an algorithm given as a program, if distinct variable names are used to represent conceptually distinct quantities, and if the variables are given descriptive names rather than abstract, symbolic names. This is particularly true if the algorithm involves the use of a large number of quantities that must be represented by variables. Consider the following simple example.

Example 2.1.1 -- Computation of sales tax.

Version 1: using abstract names for variables

```
A1 := 0.07;
A2 := A1 * X;
Y := X + A2;
```

Version 2: using descriptive variable names

```
TaxRate := 0.07;
SalesTax := TaxRate * NetPrice;
TotalPrice := NetPrice + SalesTax;
```

It sometimes happens that after initially composing an algorithm, one may put it aside for several days in order to do other work, and upon returning to the task of completing and checking the algorithm, is faced with the problem of trying to recall his thoughts of the previous few days. Imagine having to do this if you have written your algorithm in the cryptic style of the first version of the example, and imagine how much easier the task might be if you had made use of the descriptive power available to you by giving variables names such as those used in version 2.

2.2 Some distinctions between algorithmic and algebraic notations

In conventional algebraic notation, there is no notion of immediate evaluation of expressions and so it is possible to state equations or other relations involving variables which represent unknown quantities. For example, the pair of simultaneous linear algebraic equations

$$5x + 8y = -1$$
$$3x - 2y = 13$$

is such an example, in which the variables x and y represent unknowns. The equations can be satisfied if there exist real numbers to substitute for the variables x and y in each equation, such that the resulting arithmetic expressions on the two sides of each equation evaluate to common values. The order in which evaluation is to be carried out is not prescribed.

In algorithmic notation, there is no such notion of an unknown or an unevaluated variable. Evaluation proceeds by a prescribed sequence, and each expression must be capable of being evaluated at the step in the algorithm at which it is encountered. In an algorithm, we do not state the conditions of a problem in hope that a solution exists; instead, we state an explicit procedure for constructing a solution. Thus, if a solution to the pair of simultaneous equations given above is desired, we must first perform some algebraic manipulation to separate variables. We can obtain a pair of equations , each containing only a single variable:

$$5x + (4*3)x = -1 + (4*13)$$

$$(3*8)y - (5(-2))y = (3*(-1)) - (5*13)$$

Collecting terms in the same variable and dividing by the coefficient of each variable, we obtain

$$x = \frac{-1 + (4*13)}{5 + (4*3)}$$
$$y = \frac{(3*(-1)) - (5*13)}{(3*8) - (5*(-2))}$$

From explicit equations such as these, we obtain values for the unknowns x and y which will solve the equations by the simple operation of assignment. Thus, an algorithm for solving the original pair of simultaneous equations is arrived at:

$$X := (-1 + (4*13) / (5 + (4*3));$$
$$Y := ((3*(-1)) - (5*13)) / ((3*8) - (5*8-2)))$$

In the notation of Pascal, there is no convention of implied multiplication if a numerical coefficient is written immediately to the left of the variable name. Thus, 5y has no meaning in Pascal, although in algebraic notation the meaning of 5y is understood to be shorthand for 5*y. Also, one can only use linear notation in Pascal. Fractions cannot be expressed by writing the numerator above the denominator, but instead must be written as a numerator followed by the division operator followed by a denominator.

2.3 Getting values in and out of the computer

Quite obviously, if a computer is to do anything more interesting than to execute fixed computations and to keep the outcome a secret unto itself, there must be some way to communicate values of data items to a computer, and to have the results reported back. In Pascal programs, input and output of values to the computer can be called for by using the built-in procedures Read and Writeln. Values to be read must be supplied on a sequence of punched cards to follow a program deck (assuming that your computer uses card input) and the values to be output will be printed following the listing of your program.

To utilize a Read instruction, the program must contain variables which are to hold the values to be read from the input stream. The effect of a Read is very much like the effect of one or more assignment statements, except that the values to be assigned are not obtained by evaluation of expressions appearing in the program, but instead by interpretation of the data cards supplied to the card reader. For instance,

Read (A, B, C)

will direct the computer to examine the input data until it locates three values, assigning the first value found to variable A, the second to B, and the third to C. In case three appropriate values are not found, the computer will be unable to complete the instruction, and will print an error message on your output.

A Writeln instruction is less likely to cause trouble, for it does not depend on the availability of data supplied at the input device, and can fail only if a program has become so verbose that the number of lines written exceeds the maximum number specified by you, the programmer. In the list of items to be written, one can include not only variables, but any expression that can have a value, including constants and messages. Thus one might give the instruction

Writeln (A, B, ' PRODUCT =', A*B)

22

This statement would cause four items to be printed in a single line across a page of the output: the value currently held by A, the value currently held by B, the message PRODUCT = and the value of the expression A*B. For instance, the sequence of Pascal statements

```
A := 7;
B := 3;
Writeln (A, B, ' PRODUCT =', A*B)
```

could produce the line of output:

```
7              3 PRODUCT =            21
```

For more details on such matters as how the spacing is controlled, look ahead to Chapter 7.

2.4 Programming versus calculating

The examples that we are about to consider are essentially trivial computations which could easily be done on a hand-held electronic calculator (or more painfully, without one), with perhaps a pencil and scratchpad handy in order to record intermediate values. Yet the computations as we shall describe them illustrate some of the aspects of programmed computation that make it so powerful. First of all, the use of program variables eliminates the need for the scratchpad; this form of memory is replaced by the data storage capability of the computer. Also, one does not have the problem that sometimes arises when the scratchpad becomes crowded with figures, that of recalling which figure to use in the next step of calculation. Since each variable is identified by a unique name, rather than by its currently held value, the values held in the computer's memory cannot become confused during the execution of a particular calculation.

Secondly, the sequence of instructions executed by a hand calculator must be remembered by the user if the calculation is to be repeated on some additional set of data. To use the computer, the sequence of instructions is written down once and given to the computer before the calculation is done the first time. The set of instructions constitutes a program for the computer, and is a particular representation of an algorithm. It can be remembered by the computer in order to do the programmed calculation on one set of data after another, without intervention by the programmer.

There is a price to be paid by the human for the use of this powerful capability of a computer to store programs. Programming requires a greater level of intellectual abstraction than does the use of a hand-held calculator. When using a calculator, each instruction is interpreted immediately, and its result is available to help the user decide what should be the next step of the calculation. But in composing a program, the user must anticipate what the computer will do when it executes his program sometime in the future. He does not have intermediate results at hand to guide his choice of the next program step, but must be able to grasp the significance of each program step that he has written, as it may be applied to any data he may wish to provide.

Example 2.4.1--Currency conversion

As every tourist who has visited a foreign country has discovered, during the first week away from home he is troubled by the difficulty of translating prices given in the local currency into an equivalent price in his 'home' currency. Suppose, for instance, that one wishes to program a computer to convert Japanese yen to American dollar values. This program requires the ability to obtain a value, the price in yen that is to be converted, then to multiply by a constant conversion factor, and to output the result. In Pascal such a program segment would be

```
Read (Price);
Writeln ('PRICE IN YEN IS', Price);
Writeln ('EQUIVALENT DOLLAR VALUE IS', 0.00358*Price)
```

where 0.00358 is the yen-to-dollar conversion factor.

The capability to do this trivial sort of programmed calculation, multiplication by a stored constant, has been built into many of the electronic hand-held calculators, earning their manufacturers the everlasting gratitude of countless American tourists.

In the program of Example 2.4.1 it appears that a redundant statement has been included, namely the instruction which calls for the value of Price to be written on the output record immediately after it has been input. However, the statement is not at all redundant. First, remember that a hand-held calculator does the same; a value entered on the keyboard is displayed so that the user can confirm that the entry was made correctly. Also, the output may contain the only record of the computation

24

that a user, or the client of a user has to show. If the input data used in a computation are unavailable, then the only way to relate a result to the values that were input will be to have called for the input values to be printed on the computation record. This should always be done.

A somewhat less trivial sort of calculation is one which requires the generation of intermediate values, and the use of these values in several different parts of the ensuing calculation. By using a program variable, an intermediate value can be computed once and saved for multiple future references, and need not be recomputed each time that it is needed.

Example 2.4.2-- Calculating the per unit cost of manufactured
                items

A small business manufactures bookshelf kits for installation on a wall. A kit in its product line consists of 3 shelves, each 6 feet long, and 15 wall mounting brackets. The manufacturer employs a labor force of three persons, with a payroll of 150 dollars per day; he buys shelving and brackets in large lots at a fixed price per lot. His problem is to calculate from his labor cost, material costs, and the number of kits produced in one day, the cost of manufacture per kit.

Let us introduce program variables to be used a follows:

ShelvingLength will represent the number of linear feet of
                shelving purchased,
ShelvingCost will represent the price paid for the lot of
                shelving,
Nbrackets will be the number of brackets purchased,
BracketCost will be the purchase price of the lot of
                brackets,
LaborCost will be the daily payroll of the business,
Nkits will represent the number of kits produced in one day.

A few other variables will also be introduced, but their use will be clear from the context of the program segment.

The amount and cost of materials purchased may vary from one purchase to the next, so these quantities will be input as data. After reading these values, the remaining program steps evaluate the per unit costs of materials and labor, then sum these to obtain a cost per kit produced.

```
Read (ShelvingLength, ShelvingCost, Nbrackets, BracketCost);
Writeln (ShelvingLength, ShelvingCost, Nbrackets,
     BracketCost);
CostperFoot := ShelvingCost / ShelvingLength;
CostperBracket := BracketCost / Nbrackets;
LaborCost := 150;
Read (Nkits);
Writeln ('DAILY PRODUCTION IS', Nkits);
LaborCostperUnit := LaborCost / Nkits;
CostperKit := 3 * 6 * CostperFoot + 15*CostperBracket
                                  + LaborCostperUnit;
Writeln ('MANUFACTURING COST PER KIT IS', CostperKit);
```

In the program segment, the variables CostperFoot, CostperBracket, and LaborCostperUnit are used to hold intermediate values. In this particular algorithm, these intermediate values are used only once, but in more involved computations, they might be referred to several times. By assigning the values to named variables, they can be reused without being recalculated.

The program segment above, while correct, will not be accepted by the computer as it stands, for it is not a complete Pascal program. In the chapters ahead, we shall learn how to add declarative information to the list of program statements, so that the algorithm can be properly interpreted for the computer.

Self-check questions:
1. Suppose the following sequence of Pascal statements was executed

```
Read (A, B);
B := 1;
C := 2;
D := 3;
Read (C);
```

and that the input data contained the sequence of values

10 20 30

What will be the final values held by the variables A, B, C and D?

What has happened to the other values?

2. If the following sequence of statements is executed, what value will be printed?

```
K := 1;
K := K + K;
K := K + K;
Writeln (K);
```

2.5 Syntax charts

As a visual aid to mastering the syntax of Pascal, Professor Wirth has introduced a set of graphs that describe the phrases of the language. These graphs, which we call syntax charts, will enable you to answer your own questions about how sentences in Pascal should be constructed, and to answer them quickly, once you have learned to read the graphs. Each labeled box on a syntax chart gives the name of a word or a phrase that can be used in Pascal. Rectangular boxes, such as identifier contain generic names that may represent a number of distinct words or phrases, all of the same syntactic type. Circles and oval shaped boxes, such as (NOT) contain keywords and operator symbols of Pascal, written literally as they must appear if used in a program. The boxes are connected by lines with arrowheads, to indicate which words or phrases may follow one another in a syntactically correct sentence. For instance, the syntax for an assignment statement is described by

statement

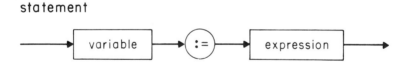

in which variable is one type of phrase, itself described by a syntax chart, and expression is another.

Many of the phrases that can be formed in Pascal have more possible variations of form than does the assignment statement. The syntax charts enable variation to be described by allowing the lines to branch. The rules governing branches on a syntax chart are very simple, but must be followed rigorously, otherwise misinterpretation of the charts is possible. At a branch, any of the paths may be followed, but the lines must only be traversed in the sense indicated by the arrowheads. Thus, if there are

27

branches away from a line, and other branches leading back into the same line, the order in which these branches appear along the line is highly significant.

Let us apply the syntax charts to the description of the expressions that we have encountered in this chapter. The simplest component of an expression, that involving only the highest precedence operator, is called a ⌐factor⌐. Its chart is:

factor

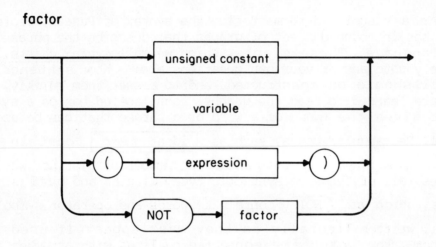

This syntax chart has an interesting feature, one that is common to many others. It contains as one of its component phrase names, its own ⌐factor⌐ . We call this a recursive phrase, for its definition contains a description of itself. The significance of the recursive phrase is not greatly different form that of any other, insofar as its use in composing a correct sentence. According to the chart, any well-formed example of ⌐factor⌐ may be substituted for the occurrence of the box bearing that name in the template for a factor. In particular, this instance of a recursive phrase allows us to form an instance of factor with as many occurrences of <u>not</u> as we may wish to write;

    <u>not</u> <u>not</u> <u>not</u> <u>not</u> <u>not</u> <u>not</u> <u>not</u> <u>not</u> <u>not</u> <u>not</u> True

is a valid instance of a ⌐factor⌐. (What is the value of this expression?)

There are ways other than recursive definition to indicate that a subphrase may be repeated. The simplest way is to draw the lines of the syntax chart so that a cycle, or loop may occur along some path through the chart. For example, the next simplest component of an expression, called a ⎴ term ⎴ has the chart:

term

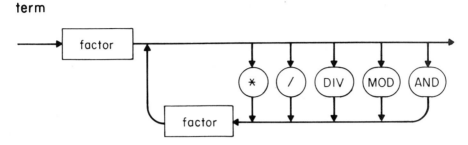

By following a cycle in the chart, you can trace out the formation of the term

A * B * C * D * E * F * G * H * I * J * K * L

There are also cases in which the optional occurrence of a phrase or word is to be specified. This is illustrated by the optional unary plus or minus sign in the chart for simple expression . The fact that the sign is optional is indicated because there is a line that may be followed to bypass both of the circles containing these symbols.

simple expression

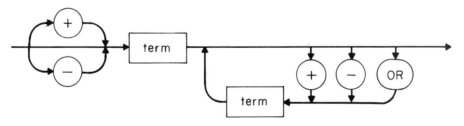

To complete the syntax for expressions, we have only to incorporate the relational operators, whose use will be discussed in Chapter 3. Note that in the chart that follows, there is no cycle. Since no line is directed back toward a previously traversed point on the chart, it expresses only the optional occurrence of a relational operator and second simple expression following the first.

expression

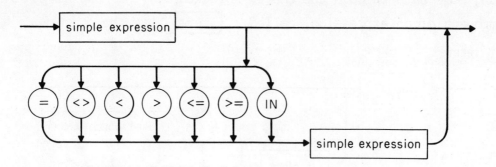

Except for some omissions in the possible variations of factor these syntax charts contain the entire description of expressions that can be formed in standard Pascal. Note that the precedence of operators is implicit in the syntax charts. This is of course, not an accident.

Throughout the rest of the book, syntax charts for other phrases of Pascal will be introduced, often in simplified form when first encountered. In some implementations of Pascal, modifications to the character set may be necesary, but these are not to be regarded as altered syntax, merely as altered symbols for the same phrases. A complete set of syntax charts for standard Pascal is given in the Appendix.

EXERCISES FOR CHAPTER 2

In each of the following problems, identify the computational variables that will be needed, give them appropriate names and compose an algorithm in the form of a Pascal program segment.

2.1 An hourly employee is paid at the rate of $4.37 per hour, for the number of hours actually worked each week. From his gross pay, 6% is deducted for payment of social security tax, and 14% is withheld as income tax. He also has union dues of $3 per week deducted from his pay. Give an algorithm to determine the gross pay, social security tax payment, withholding tax payment, and take home pay of an hourly employee. The number of hours worked during a week is to be supplied as data to the algorithm.

2.2 One form of consumer loan is the discounted installment loan. It works this way. On a loan of $1000 face value, at 6% annual interest, for a duration of 18 months, the interest is calculated in advance by multiplying 1000 by .06, then by the period of the loan, 1 1/2 years. This yields the interest owed, $90, and it is immediately deducted from the face value; the borrower never sees it. He instead receives the difference of $910 as the principal amount of the loan. Repayment is made in equal monthly payments whose amount is the face value of $1000 divided by duration of the loan in months.

a) Devise an algorithm which takes as data the face value, interest rate in percent, and duration in months, and which calculates the total amount of interest to be paid, and the actual principal amount of a discounted installment loan.

b) Since the face value of a discounted installment loan is repaid in equal monthly payments, the balance outstanding declines each month. It is not hard to show that the average balance over the duration of the loan is given by the formula

Average unpaid balance =

$$\text{Face value} * \frac{(1 + \text{Duration in months})}{2 * \text{Duration in months}}$$

Calculate the rate at which simple interest would be paid on the average balance over the duration of the loan in order to produce the same total dollar amount of interest as is produced by the discounted installment loan.

2.3 The plot plan for situating a building on a lot is shown below. All corners are right angles except for the two front corners of the lot. The zoning regulations decree that not more than 30% of the area of the lot can be built upon. Can you devise a computational algorithm to determine what fraction of the area of the lot will be occupied by the building?

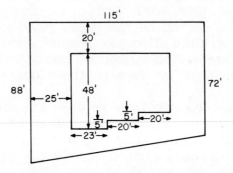

2.4 When rational numbers are expressed as fractions, it is often difficult to compare them. (Is it obvious by inspection that 24/91 is greater then 17/65?) Devise a computational algorithm to determine which of two rational fractions is the larger.

2.5 A mathematician is out for a walk when it begins to rain. He realizes that while he remains outside, the amount of rain falling on his head will be proportional to the density of raindrops in the air, to the velocity with which they are falling, to the upwards projected area of his head, and to the duration of his exposure. If he runs for shelter, he can reduce the length of time he remains outdoors. On the other hand, if he runs, he will be struck on the front by raindrops and will receive a wetting from his own action that is proportional to the density of raindrops, his running speed, his projected frontal area, and to the time it takes him to reach shelter.

The time to reach shelter is proportional to the distance to reach it, and inversely proportional to his speed afoot. Can you help him by giving a computational algorithm to compute the total amount of rain he will encounter, if given the initial values of the other parameters as inputs? (This simple problem can, of course, be solved analytically; it is complicated to some extent if you add a wind that gives the raindrops a horizontal component of velocity.)

2.6   Corporate and municipal bonds are issued under the following terms. Each bond carries a redemption value, an amount of money to be paid upon maturation of the bond. In addition, the bond pays interest in equal amounts to be collected quarterly. The nominal rate of interest is the sum of four quarterly interest payments divided by the redemption value of the bond.

However, bonds are traded like other securities, and the nominal interest rate may differ from the prevailing rate of interest for comparable securities at the time a bond is sold. To compensate for this, bonds are bought and sold at values discounted or increased relative to the redemption value. Thus, the net worth of the bond, which is the sum of all remaining interest payments plus its redemption value, is equivalent to the net worth of a hypothetical bond whose redemption value is the sale price, and whose nominal interest rate is the interest rate prevailing at the time of the sale.

Define algebraic variables to stand for (a) redemption value, (b) nominal rate of interest, (c) sale price, (d) prevailing rate of interest, (e) time until maturation, (f) net worth. Give an algebraic equation equating the net worth of an actual bond to the net worth of a hypothetical bond. Solve the equation for the sale price.

Give a computational algorithm to calculate the selling price of a corporate bond, given its redemption value and nominal interest rate, and the prevailing rate of interest on bonds at the time of sale. Use the algorithm to determine the sale price of a $1000 bond collecting interest at 6% per year, which is 12 years from maturation, if the prevailing rate of interest is 9%.

3 PROGRAMMING THE COMPUTER TO MAKE DECISIONS

In the last chapter we saw that computer programming languages allow one to evaluate expresssions and to assign values to variables. An algorithm may consist partly of sequences of assignment statements giving a succession of values to individual program variables. But there will be many problems for which the algorithm we wish to use will contain several alternatives for evaluation. In such cases, the computer must make decisions as to which algorithm steps to execute, based on conditions of the data. The programming language must provide means for stating the conditions governing such decisions.

3.1 Conditional assignment

The most obvious way to employ decision-making capability in an algorithm is by formulating an expression whose evaluation depends on some condition of the data. This is common practice in mathematics as, for instance, in the definitions of the simple functions,

Maximum:
$$max(x,y) = \begin{cases} x, & \text{if } x > y, \\ y, & \text{otherwise} \end{cases}$$

Minimum:
$$min(x,y) = \begin{cases} y, & \text{if } x > y, \\ x, & \text{otherwise}; \end{cases}$$

Modified Difference:

$$x - y = \begin{cases} x - y, & \text{if } x > y, \\ 0, & \text{otherwise.} \end{cases}$$

In Pascal, we can simulate the conditional evaluation of an expression by executing alternative assignments to a variable, depending on the outcome of a test:

max:
```
if X >= Y then
    Max := X
else
    Max := Y
```

min:
```
if X >= Y then
    Min := Y
else
    Min := X
```

modified difference:
```
if X > Y then
    PositiveDifference := X - Y
else
    PositiveDifference := 0
```

We can represent the syntax of the conditional assignment statement by adding to the syntax chart given in Chapter 2 for the assignment statement alone. The extended chart is:

statement

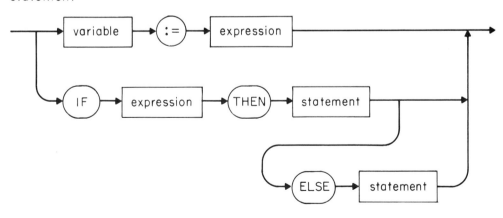

3.2 Relational and boolean expressions

The condition tested in making a decision as to which of a pair of alternative assignments to make in a conditional assignment statement is given by an expression. This expression, appearing between the keywords if and then must take on one of the values True or False; we call this set boolean values, after the English mathematician George Boole, who investigated the properties of an algebra in which to embed logic.

The simplest kind of boolean expression states a relation which may or may not hold between two quantities. If the quantities are numeric, then the possible relations are strict inequalities, '<', '>', reflexive inequalities '<=', '>=', equals '=' and does not equal '<>'. If the quantities are non-numeric but are defined over a totally ordered set of values, as for instance, the letters of the alphabet, then the same set of relations have meaning. For quantities that are not totally ordered, like the addresses of houses, it makes no sense to talk about inequalities "greater than" or "less than", but one can still use the relations "equals" and "does not equal" meaningfully. Pascal defines additional relations on set types, but for now, we shall make use of only the relational operators given above.

A relational expression is evaluated by first evaluating the pair of subexpressions that appear on both sides of the relational symbol, then comparing these values. If these subexpressions depend on variables, then they may not always yield the same values, for their values will depend on the data. Therein lies the power of conditional evaluation, for the choice of algorithm steps can be made to depend on the data at any desired step. Relational expressions are the most obvious form of boolean expression, but not the only form. One sometimes wants to base a decision on whether at least one of several possible conditions holds. Notice that the syntax chart above implies that a conditional statement may be substituted for ⌐statement⌐ as well as an assignment can be. Consider the following:

Example 3.2.1 -- Parcel post dimensions

The United States Postal Service imposes restrictions on the maximum size and weight of a package to be sent by parcel post. The weight must not exceed 44 pounds, and the sum of the length plus the girth must not exceed 72 inches.

Suppose that for parcels of rectangular cross-section, the dimensions are given as the values of variables A, B, and C, and the weight is given is the value of Wght, in units of inches and pounds, respectively. However, the dimensions are not necessarily given in order of greatest length. Give an algorithm to determine whether or not a parcel is acceptable.

To calculate the postal dimension, one needs to know which of the three dimensions is the largest, for the formula penalizes girth more than it does length. We can compute a value for the postal dimension by making use of conditional assignment.

```
if (A >= B) and (A >= C) then
    PostalDimension := A + 2*(B+C)
else if B >= C then
    PostalDimension := B + 2*(A+C)
else
    PostalDimension := C + 2*(A+B)
```

In the first line of the statement, two conditions are tested to find out whether A is the largest of the three dimensions. If it is, then the expression A + 2*(B+C) is evaluated and assigned to the variable. Otherwise, if one or the other of the conditions tested in the first line is false, the assignment on the second line is not performed, but instead control passes beyond the first else.

This second alternative is only tried after having determined that A cannot be the largest dimension. In the statement following the first else, it is only necessary to compare B and C to find the largest dimension. This statement is not simply an assignment, but is another conditional statement nested within the larger one:

```
if B >= C then
    PostalDimension := B + 2*(A+C)
else
    PostalDimension := C + 2*(A+B)
```

Notice that out of the three possible assignments to the variable PostalDimension that appear in the large conditional statement, only one is actually executed. The values of the relational expressions are used in the if clauses to determine which one it is to be.

Finally, a second step involving a test of two conditions will determine the acceptability of the parcel:

if (PostalDimension <= 72) and (Wght <= 44) then
    Accept
else
    Reject

In Pascal it is possible to form expressions that combine logical quantities such as relational expressions by the use of three logical operators. These are the symbols not, and, and or. Of these, not is a unary operator, meaning that it acts on a single value. It negates the truth value of the logical constant, variable, or relational expression immediately following it. and and or are binary operators. The rules defining the actions of these operators are most easily given in terms of the constants, True and False:

        not True = False
        not False = True

        True and True = True
        True and False = False
        False and True = False
        False and False = False

        True or True = True
        True or False = True
        False or True = True
        False or False = False

We see that the domain of values on which these operators act, and the range of values that they can compute is limited to the set {False, True}. These are the constants of the Pascal type Boolean, a predeclared scalar type. Note the order implied by listing False before True. These constants are ordered, just as are the constants of any scalar type. We call the operators not, and, or the Boolean operators.

Values of Boolean expressions can be assigned to variables for reference in a later step. A variable can in turn be used as a term in a Boolean expression, or can be tested in an if clause. When the value of a relational expression is assigned to a variable, the variable should not be thought of as shorthand for the expression, but merely as a record of the value that the relation had at a particular point in execution of the program.

38

For instance, consider the sequence of statements,

```
N := 10;
IsPositive := N > 0;
Read (N);
if IsPositive then . . .
```

At the second statement, the relation N > 0 is evaluated and found to be satisfied, so that IsPositive will receive the value True. At the third statement, N receives a new value, which might be positive, negative, or zero. At the fourth statement, the if clause tests the value held by the variable IsPositive, which no longer has anything to do with the current value of N. The value of IsPositive at the fourth statement is a record of the condition N > 0 at the second statement. A variable used to store the Boolean value of a condition for use in governing a decision to be made in a subsequent algorithm step is called a flag.

Self-check questions:

1. In each of the following conditional assignment statements, which assignments will actually be executed?

    a) ```
       if (1 < 2) and (2 < 3) then
          A := 1
       else
          A := 0
       ```

    b) ```
       if (1 < 2) or (2 > 3) then
          B := 1
       else
          B := 0;
       ```

    c) ```
       if not (1 < 0) then
          C := 1
       else
          C := 0;
       ```

    d) ```
       if ((1 < 2) or (3 < 2)) and (1 < 0) then
          D := 1
       else
          D := 0
       ```

3.3 Precedence of operators

When an expression involves more than a single operator, its evaluation may be ambiguous unless we introduce rules by which to resolve possible ambiguities. The simplest such rule is a rule of association. In evaluating the expression

A + B + C + D

we do not have to specify whether evaluation is to be done left-to-right, right-to-left, from both ends inward, or in some other order, because the addition operation is associative. Subtraction is not, however, and if we write

A - B - C - D

the order in which the subtractions are performed makes a difference. Custom dictates that we should impose a rule of association to the left, that is, left-to-right evaluation, in order to resolve an ambiguity involving multiple instances of the same operator. If left association is not what is intended, then parentheses can be introduced to make the association explicit. Right-to-left evaluation would be specified as

A - (B - (C - D))

When different operators are mixed in an expression, there is some cause to argue that left association is not the best rule to apply uniformly. For instance, if one writes in conventional algebraic notation

x + 2y

it is more likely that what he means is

x + (2*y)

than

(x + 2)*y

Many programming languages, including Pascal, have therefore adopted a notational scheme called the precedence of operators by which to specify a hierarchy of association rules. Operators of the same precedence are evaluated left-to-right, but if two consecutive operators in an expression have unequal precedence then the one of higher precedence is applied first. Association of operators can always be explicitly specified by the use of parenthesized notation, so the precedence rules do not make it impossible to form a desired expression. In Pascal, the precedence classes of operators, from highest to lowest are:

not

* / div mod and

+ - or

= <> <= >= < > in

In the examples we have seen so far, we have occasionally made use of the precedence of operators. For instance, in the expression

A + 2*(B+C)

the sum B+C had to parenthesized in order to specify its evaluation prior to multiplication by 2. However, multiplication of (B+C) by 2 occurs in preference to addition of 2 to A, because the multiplication operator has higher precedence than does addition.

The Boolean expression

(A = B) and (A = C)

required the use of parentheses in order to secure the desired association, because and has higher precedence than do the relational operators. Had the expression been written as

A >= B and A >= C

then the first operation that would have been performed would have been

B and A

which was not desired.

Self-check questions:

1.   Evaluate the following expression, keeping in mind the precedence of operators defined for Pascal:

3 * 3 * 2 - 3 * 5 + 1

2. Given the following assignments of values to the Boolean
    variables,

            A := False;   B := True;   C := False

    evaluate each of the following Boolean expressions:

    a) A or B and not C
    b) not ((A or B) and C))
    c) not (C and (A or B))
    d) not C and B or A

3.4 Describing conditional alternatives

Boolean expressions can be used not only to control the choice of which assignment to make, but of which subsidiary algorithm to execute. Identification of the choices to be made is so important in composing algorithms that there have been invented several informal notational aids to help keep track of the alternatives when one is in the pencil-and-paper stage of algorithm composition.

One such scheme, called iteration graphs[†] will be presented in this and the following chapter, and then used in the remainder of the book. An iteration graph is composed of several types of rectangular boxes, with informal descriptions of algorithm steps written inside. The basic box is simply a rectangle

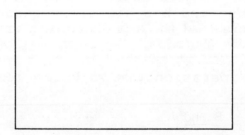

in which is written the description of a single step, or a sequence of several steps.

[†] The form of iteration graph presented here is due to I. Nassi and B. Schneiderman, ACM SIGPLAN Notices, vol. 8, No. 8, pp. 12-26, August, 1973.

A binary choice of steps is designated by a rectangle containing a triangle at the top, in which is written the Boolean expression upon whose outcome the the choice is to be made.

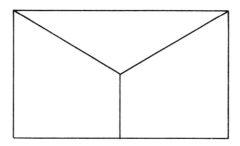

The lower part of the rectangle is divided into two boxes. In the leftmost is written the algorithm step to be performed in case the condition is satisfied, in the rightmost the step to be performed in case the condition fails. A simple example will illustrate the scheme.

Example 3.4.1 -- The shopper's dilemma

A music lover, shopping during his lunch hour, discovers a turntable on sale that is just what he needs to complete his stereo system. However, it is a few days until his next payday, and he is uncertain as to how to pay for the purchase. If the balance in his checking account is sufficient, he would prefer to write a check in payment, but otherwise he will have to charge the purchase to an account on which he must pay carrying charges.

An informal description of the choice of action that will be made by our shopper can be given by a decision box in the notation of iteration graphs:

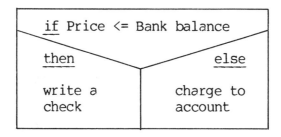

If we were to try to describe the consequence of the shopper's purchase on his financial records, we might be able to make use of a Pascal program segment. For instance,

43

if the consequence of writing a check is reduction in the balance of the checking account, and the consequence of charging a purchase is an increase in indebtedness, a program describing these effects could make use of a conditional assignment statement,

```
if Price <= Balance then
      Balance := Balance - Price
else
      Debt := Debt + Price
```

Notice that the conditional statement corresponds directly to the decision box, once the two actions to be governed by the specified condition have been expressed as Pascal statements.

3.5 Devising algorithms to solve problems

The payoff of our study of algorithms will come when we are able to invent algorithms to obtain solutions to real problems. It would be nice if there were some straightforward, easily explained procedure to follow so that one could move from the statement of a real-world problem to the construction of an algorithm for its solution. Life is not so easy. Problem solving requires considerable application of intelligence, careful attention to details, and often a sequence of trials and errors. There is, however, a method for developing an algorithm by means of a sequence of partial specifications, proceeding from a description of the solution, in intellectually manageable steps. This process has been given a variety of names by various authors. We shall call it stepwise refinement†. The best way to illustrate the process may be by example, and the only way to learn it is to try for yourself.

Example 3.5.1-- Shall I rent or buy a house?

A man and his wife have just been transferred to a new locality, and his is faced with the choice of whether to buy or to rent a home. After consulting a real estate agent, he finds two possibilities which interest him. There is a comfortable apartment for rent, including utilities, for $300 per month. Alternatively, there is a house for sale for

---

† N. Wirth, "Programming by Stepwise Refinement", Communications of the ACM, vol. 14, No. 4, p. 221, April, 1971.

which he will have to put up a down payment of $6000, monthly payments of $290, and a utilities bill which will average $60 a month. He would prefer to buy the house, but it appears at first glance to be too expensive. However, he consults his accountant who advises him that of the monthly house payment, $110 goes to pay local property taxes and $140 goes to pay the interest on the mortgage. Under federal income tax law, the amounts he pays in interest and in local taxes may be deducted from his gross income before he figures his federal tax. His problem is now more complicated than before, and the answer to the question of which alternative is more economically advantageous is by no means obvious. Can we devise an algorithm to help the man figure out the net cost of owning a house?

At first glance, if the income tax is not considered, it looks as though our friend will pay $50 per month, or $600 more per year to purchase a house than to rent an apartment, when the utilities payments are taken into account. In addition, he will lose the interest he could get if the amount of his down payment were invested in a savings bank -- 6% of $6000, or $360 per year.

Now, let us develop an algorithm to compute the net cost of buying, relative to that of renting, when the income tax is taken into account. What we will do is to calculate the expendable income that the man will have left over after taxes and after paying his housing expenses under each option. The man's salary will have to be known, as will other information required to calculate his income tax. The parameters used in making the calculation under each of the alternate options will be:

Savings interest -- the interest he expects to receive from his savings account;

Local tax -- the local property taxes he expects to pay each month which are a deductible expense under the income tax law;

Mortgage interest -- the interest paid on his mortgage each month, which is also a tax deductible expense;

Payments -- monthly payments for housing;

Utilities -- anticipated monthly payment of utilities bills.

45

Next, let us describe the tasks to be performed. Our client is basically interested in knowing what will be his expendable income remaining after taxes and after deducting his housing expense. This can be specified as

<u>Principal task</u>: compute expendable income;

this is to be done in case of
  a) purchase of a house,
  b) rental of an apartment.

Before expendable income can be computed, however, the gross income and the income tax must be known. These requirements lead us to define

  <u>subtask 1</u>: compute GrossIncome; and
  <u>subtask 2</u>: compute IncomeTax.

Subtask 1 can be carried out directly, since the constituent parts of gross income are known,

GrossIncome :: Salary + SavingsInterest

Subtask 2, on the other hand, is somewhat more complicated. Income tax is not computed directly as a function of gross income, but instead is a function of the so-called taxable income obtained by subtracting authorized exemptions and deductions from the gross income. This leads us to decompose Subtask 2 into

  <u>subtask 2.1</u>: compute TaxableIncome; and
  <u>subtask 2.2</u>: compute IncomeTax from TaxableIncome.

Let us develop an algorithm segment to accomplish subtask 2.1, the computation of taxable income. A married couple is allowed a personal exemption of 750 dollars for each person, to be deducted from gross income.

AdjustedIncome := GrossIncome = 2*750

Certain expenses are also allowed as deductions from income prior to tax computation. Two alternative methods are provided for the computation of deductions, one based on an itemization of actual expenses, and the other based on a standard estimate. The taxpayer may employ whichever method yields him the greater advantage.

46

```
ItemizeDeduction := 12*(LocalTax + MortgageInterest)
                    + OtherDeductions;

StandarDeduction := .15 * GrossIncome
```

A conditional statement is used to indicate the choice to be made on the basis of the relative values obtained in the two preceding statements.

```
if ItemizeDeduction > StandarDeduction then
    Deduction := ItemizeDeduction
else
    Deduction := StandarDeduction
```

Finally, subtask 2.1 will be completed by

```
TaxableIncome := AdjustedIncome - Deduction
```

Now that we know how subtask 2.1 will be carried out, calculation of income tax is to be done according to a graduated schedule, as shown in the diagram of Fig. 3.1. Those who earn more are expected to pay a higher percentage of their income in taxes (unless they have claimed very large deductions). Therefore, the computation of tax must take into account the rate of taxation, depending on income. Let us assume that the taxable income is at least as great as the value of Base 1 but not as great as Base 3. Since income in the range from Base 1 to Base 2 is taxed at a lower rate than is income in the range from Base 2 to Base 3 it is necessary first to determine which tax formula applies, and then to do the appropriate computation. Pascal provides the conditional statement as a means of designating such a choice. A statement that will accomplish the tax computation is

```
if TaxableIncome <= Base2 then
    IncomeTax := BaseTax + Rate1*(TaxableIncome - Base1)
else
    IncomeTax := BaseTax + Rate1*(Base2 - Base1) +
                 Rate2*(TaxableIncome - Base2)
```

This will complete the algorithm segment for subtask 2.2, and therefore for subtask 2 as well.

In terms of the results of performing the subtasks, the algorithm steps required to complete the principal task

47

under conditions of either purchase or rental can be given by a pair of assignment statements,

```
NetIncome := GrossIncome - IncomeTax;
ExpendableIncome := NetIncome - 12*(Payments + Utilities)
```

These statements will be the final steps of an algorithm.

Having now completed the composition of program segments to perform each subtask as well as the principal task, all that remains is to assemble the program segments into the required sequence. The sequence is dictated by the order in which the various subtask results are required. If the program segment for each subtask is substituted into the sequence in place of its specification, each required value will be computed before needed in another step. Upon doing this substitution, the following program segment is obtained for the accomplishment of the principle task:

```
GrossIncome := Salary + SavingsInterest;
AdjustedIncome := GrossIncome - 2*750;
ItemizeDeduction := 12*(LocalTax + MortgageInterest) +
                    OtherDeductions;
StandarDeduction := 0.15 * GrossIncome;
if ItemizeDeduction > StandarDeduction then
    Deduction := ItemizeDeduction
else
    Deduction := StandarDeduction;
TaxableIncome := AdjustedIncome - Deduction;
if TaxableIncome <= Base2 then
    IncomeTax := BaseTax + Rate1*(TaxableIncome - Base1)
else
    IncomeTax := BaseTax + Rate1*(Base2 - Base1) +
                 Rate2*(TaxableIncome - Base2);
NetIncome := GrossIncome - IncomeTax;
ExpendableIncome := NetIncome - 12*(Payments + Utilities);
```

If values are now supplied for the constants which determine the amount of income tax, and initial values are supplied for the variables which represent data concerning our friend's personal finances, then we can carry out the steps of the algorithm to help him calculate his expendable income for each of the two alternate housing arrangements. Suppose that the following assignments of values are made:

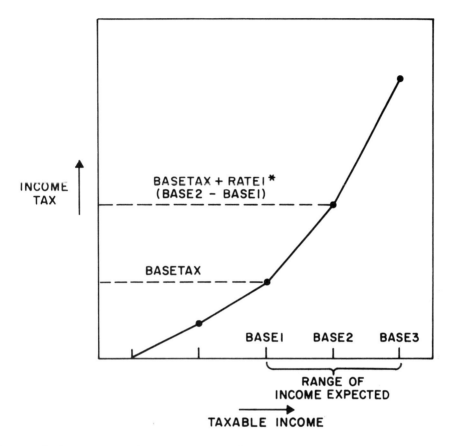

Figure 3.1   Relation between income tax and taxable income when
the tax rate is graduated.

```
Base1 := 8000;
BaseTax := 1280;
Rate1 := 0.22;
Base2 := 12000
Rate2 :=0.26;
```

and that our friend's salary is

```
Salary := 16000;
```

He is able to justify tax-deductable expenses other than the interest on a mortgage or local property taxes of

```
OtherDeductions := 500;
```

and the $6000 which he had available to use as a down payment on a house represents his entire savings.

Option 1 -- to rent an apartment

If the man decides to rent his apartment, then his $6000 will remain in the savings bank, drawing interest at 6%, and he will have

```
SavingsInterest := 360;
LocalTax := 0;
MortgageInterest := 0;
Payments := 300;
Utilities := 0;
```

as initial values of the data to use in calculating his expendable income. If the steps of the algorithm are executed using the initial values given above, the successive values calculated and assigned to each of the variables will be

GrossIncome	16360
AdjustedIncome	14860
ItemizeDeduction	500
StandarDeduction	2000
Deduction	2000
TaxableIncome	12860
IncomeTax	2483.60
ExpendableIncome	10276.40

Option 2 -- to buy a house

In the event that the man should choose to purchase the house, then his savings must be invested as a down payment on the purchase; however, his monthly payments become partially tax deductible. The initial values of the parameters are assigned as

```
SavingsInterest := 0;
LocalTax := 110;
MortgageInterest := 140;
Payments := 290;
Utilities := 60;
```

Upon execution of the algorithm, the following values will be calculated

GrossIncome	16000
AdjustedIncome	14500
ItemizeDeduction	3500
StandarDeduction	2000
Deduction	3500
TaxableIncome	11000
IncomeTax	2040
ExpendableIncome	9760

Before going on, follow the computational steps of the example, carrying out the indicated calculation by hand, to see if you can verify the values above.

From the results of the two calculations, it is seen that it will still be less expensive for the man to rent than to buy, but the difference it will make to his expendable income is only $516.40 rather than the apparent difference in cost of $960. Furthermore, our model has not attached any value to the fact that of the monthly house payment, $40 goes towards retirement of the mortgage, increasing the net worth of the man, if not his expendable income, by $480 in the course of one year. On a net worth basis, the added cost of purchasing his own house would amount to only $36.40 per year.

Even on this basis, the model we have used is over-simplified, for it should take account of a probable rate of economic inflation of between 2 and 20 per cent per year. Inflation will increase the attractiveness of purchasing a house when properly accounted for. However, the example has already achieved its immediate purpose, which was to demonstrate that a seemingly complicated problem can often be solved algorithmically by simply breaking down the analysis of the problem into a sequence of small steps. You can gain experience in doing this yourself by trying some of the exercises at the end of the chapter.

A final comment is in order. Since any expression appearing in a step of an algorithm must be evaluated when that step is executed, it is important that steps of an algorithm are listed in proper order. The order in which steps are evaluated should ensure that each variable is assigned a value before it is referred to in any expression. In this way, because it is to be executed in sequence, an algorithm differs from a definition which is not to be executed.

3.6 Comments and their use

Even when a programmer is careful to give descriptive names to the variables he uses, it is often difficult to read an algorithm given as a Pascal program and understand its function completely without some hints. There is a means of providing hints in the form of comments in the text of a program. Comments are distinguished from statements or expressions of the language by being enclosed in comment brackets (* ... *). The left and right comment brackets are each two-character symbols. Many Pascal implementations also allow curly brackets { ... } as comment brackets, but many line printers won't print them.

Example 3.5.1 -- A comment

    (* comments in Pascal are not part of the algorithm,
       and are ignored by the computer.*)

Of course, you must be careful not to forget to place the terminating bracket at the end of a comment, for the computer will then ignore the text of your algorithm from that point on until it encounters the end of the next comment!

In reading a long program, it should be made easy for a reader to distinguish comments from the text of actual Pascal statements. While the comment brackets allow the computer to make the distinction without difficulty, this convention is not always adequate for the human reader. Therefore, we prefer a convention in which some additional visual identification is embedded within

52

a comment, in order to catch the eye of a reader and alert him to the fact that he is not reading program but prose. The text of short, one-line comments can be bracketed by a string of four or five asterisks,

(***** short comments look like this *****)

Longer comments, which have the status of explanatory paragraphs, can be enclosed in a box of asterisks. The asterisks must appear between the opening and closing brackets.

```
(***********************************************************
* MULTI-LINE COMMENTS ARE NOT EASILY CONFUSED WITH THE SUR- *
* ROUNDING PROGRAM TEXT, EVEN IF THEY SHOULD CONTAIN ALGE-  *
* BRAIC EXPRESSIONS -- SUCH AS                              *
*          X*(X*A + B) + C = 0                              *
* WHEN THE ENTIRE COMMENT IS BOXED IN ASTERISKS             *
**********************************************************)
```

There are some places in the text of a computer program where the insertion of comments is ordinarily very helpful. At the beginning of a program, comments can be used to describe the functions that the algorithm is designed to perform, and to give a general description of the method of the algorithm. Next, it is very helpful to use comments describing the program variables and their intended uses. Within the body of the program text, comments are often helpful in describing the alternative courses of action whenever a conditional statement indicates that a decision is to be made in execution of the algorithm.

3.7 Compound statements

Often, one of the alternatives that is to be executed, depending on the outcome of a conditional test, cannot easily be expressed by a single statement. It is convenient to have some means by which to package together a whole sequence of statements to be executed as a group whenever that decision is indicated. Pascal provides this capability with a pair of reserved words, begin and end. When these words bracket a sequence of statements, the entire sequence is called a compound statement, and is executed as an indivisible unit. The use of statement brackets, begin ... end to indicate the association of statements is analogous to the use of parentheses to indicate the association of expressions.

<u>Example 3.7.1</u> --Exchanging the values of a pair of variables

    As a simple application of the use of a compound
statement, suppose that there are two variables, called Max
and Min, whose relative values are unknown, and that we wish
to establish that Max will hold the larger of the two
values, and the Min the smaller. A conditional test will
establish whether or not an exchange of their values is
needed. If it is, then it will be necessary to save one of
the two values in a temporary variables while the other is
being copied. A sequence of three assignment statements will
be required. These can be put into a compound statement so
that if the test calls for the interchange of values, all
three assignments will be executed.

```
if Max < Min then
    begin
        Temporary := Max;
        Max := Min;
        Min := Temporary;
    end
```

    Once again, we can extend the syntax chart for a ⎹ statement ⎹
so that it will include the compound statement:

statement

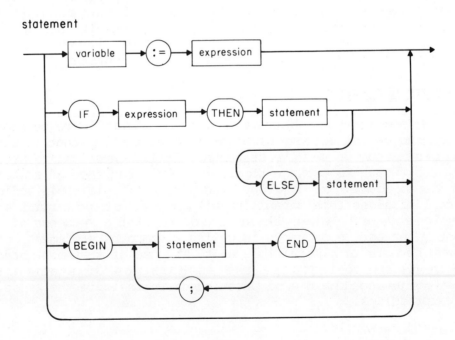

54

The line at the bottom of the chart implies that a statement may consist of nothing at all! This so-called empty statement has been introduced in order to allow greater freedom in the placement of semicolons. Without it, a semicolon could not appear immediately before the keyword end. With it, the `statement` that appears between a semicolon and end is accounted for by the syntax for an empty statement.

At this point we should like to clear up a potential source of ambiguity in the syntax introduced so far. The syntactic description of a statement such as

> if C1 then if C2 then X := Y else X := Z

fails to specify whether the else clause is to be associated with the first or the second if clause. In Pascal, the ambiguity is resolved by defining the else clause to associate with the immediately preceding if clause. In case a programmer wished to have the else clause associate with the first if clause, he would be forced to express this by enclosing the intervening conditional statement in compound statement brackets, as

```
        if C1 then
            begin
                if C2 then X:=Y
            end
        else X:=Z
```

Self-check question

1. In example 3.7.1, if the exchange had been programmed without the use of a temporary variable, by the program segment

```
        if Max < Min then
            begin
                Max := Min;
                Min := Max;
        end
```

and the initial values of Max and Min had been 1 and 3, respectively, what would be their final values?

55

3.8 The structure of a Pascal program

In order to apply what we have so far learned about the composition of algorithms and their expression in the programming language Pascal, we must learn to embed our program segments into a complete Pascal program. A program consists of a heading, followed by a block, and terminated by a period; its syntax is given by the chart below.

program

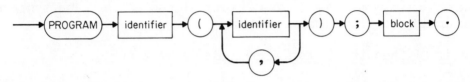

Within the heading, the first identifier is the name of the program. Following the program name is a parenthesized list of names of the external file variables used by the program. These files are the means by which your program communicates with the outside world, and the list must contain at least one file name. Initially, your programs may refer only to the file whose name is Output, where your results will be sent, or to the file Input, from which the program may read data.

The block contains a statement list, bracketed by begin ... end, but this may also be preceded by a list of declarative statements, or declarations. Later chapters will elaborate further on the variety of forms that declarations may have, but for our first program we shall need only to declare the names and types of our variables. Pascal incorporates four elementary value types, given the names Integer, to designate integer numbers; Real, to designate decimal-fraction approximations to the continuum of real numbers, and the non-numeric scalar types Boolean and Char. The type Char has as its values the finite set of characters that can be read or printed by the computer. Let's see how to put together the various pieces we have been given, the assignment statement, conditional statement, Read and Writeln statements, compound statement, expressions, program heading and block, to form our first complete Pascal program.

Example 3.8.1 -- Personal finance

In this example, we return to the simple decision that was discussed in Example 3.4.1, that of the shopper's dilemma. Here, we shall embed the program segment that makes the decision into a complete program. You will notice that a program consists of paragraphs. First comes the heading, followed by a paragraph in which the variables are declared. Then comes the body of the program in the form of a compound statement. This too, may be broken into paragraphs, three in the example program given below. The first allows us to obtain initial values for the variables by reading them from the Input file. The second paragraph makes the decision (and writes the check for the purchase, if need be), and the third prints the final values obtained.

```
program Shopper (Input, Output);
    var
        Balance, Debt, Price : Real;
    begin
        Read (Balance, Debt, Price);
        Writeln ('INITIALLY, BALANCE =', Balance,
                ' DEBT =', Debt, ' PRICE =', Price);

        (**** decide how to pay for a purchase ****)
        if Price < Balance then
            begin
                Writeln('PAY TO THE ORDER OF HI-FI STORES, INC',
                        Price);
                Balance := Balance - Price;
            end
        else
            Debt := Debt + Price;

        Writeln ('FINAL BALANCE =', Balance, ' DEBT =', Debt);
    end.
```

For our next program, we can choose a less trivial computation. Still, the program will have in common with the one above the same kind of paragraph structure, and will use exactly the same kinds of statements.

Example 3.8.2 -- Finding the intersection
                of a pair of line segments

Given a pair of straight line segments, how might we find out whether or not they intersect? One way would be to plot both line segments on a piece of graph paper and solve the problem by inspection. However, we can also represent a line by a linear algebraic equation, and we can devise a mathematical algorithm to test for intersection of the line segments. A suitable form for the equation of a line involves three coefficients,

$$Ax + By = C \qquad\qquad (1)$$

where the variables x and y represent coordinates of points in a plane. Given any set of three coefficients, the pairs of points (x,y) which satisfy the equation lie on a straight line. If a line segment is specified by giving the coordinates of its endpoints $(\underline{u},\underline{v})$ and $(\underline{x},\underline{y})$, then substitution of these points into equation (1) gives us a pair of simultaneous equations that must be satisfied by any set of coefficients A, B, C which describe the line.

$$A\underline{u} + B\underline{v} = C,$$
$$A\underline{x} + B\underline{y} = C.$$

Since there are only two equations and three parameters are to be determined, one of the parameters may be chosen arbitrarily. We shall choose C to be the determinant of the matrix formed by the endpoint coordinates,

$$\text{Let } C = \begin{vmatrix} \underline{u} & \underline{v} \\ \underline{x} & \underline{y} \end{vmatrix} = \underline{u}\underline{y} - \underline{v}\underline{x}.$$

This choice makes C equal to the square of the distance from the origin of coordinates to the point on the line nearest the origin.

When this choice is made for C, solution of the equations for A and B yields

$$A = \underline{y} - \underline{v}, \text{ and } B = \underline{u} - \underline{x}.$$

Once the equations of two lines have been obtained, it is easy to locate their intersection. If there is a point (x,y) that lies on both lines, then the coordinates of that point must satisfy the equations of both lines. Therefore, to solve for the intersection, we must solve another pair of simultaneous, linear equations. In case the lines are parallel, however, the simultaneous equations will have no solution. Once an intersection of two lines has been found, we determine whether two line segments intersect by asking whether the point of intersection of the lines lies within both line segments.

Utilizing the method of stepwise refinement, let us first specify the major algorithm steps that are to be carried out, in the informal notation of an iteration graph.

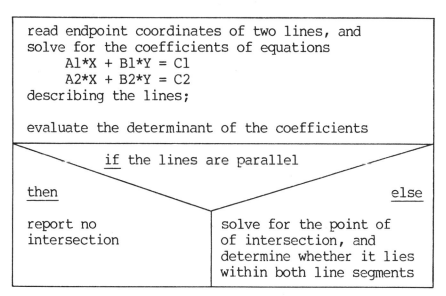

We shall now translate the iteration graph into a Pascal program. First comes the program heading, followed by a comment that tells in general terms, what the program is intended to accomplish. Then there appear the declarations of all variables to be used in the program. This is followed by a compound statement which is the direct interpretation of the iteration graph. We can get started by writing a program heading,

program Intersection (Input, Output);

and an explanatory comment. But at that point, we may be stuck, for it is usually not possible to anticipate all of the variables that we might find useful in the composition of a program. Let's postpone giving the declarations until after we've defined the statement list. A good start is to read the required data, and to print a copy of the input data on the output listing:

```
Read (Ul, Vl, Xl, Yl);
Writeln ('ENDPOINTS OF LINE 1:', Ul, Vl, Xl, Yl);
Read (U2, V2, X2, Y2);
Writeln ('ENDPOINTS OF LINE 2:', U2, V2, X2, Y2);
```

Next, the solutions for the A, B, C coefficients of the equation for each line can be given the form of a sequence of assignment statements:

```
Al := Yl - Vl; Bl := Ul - Xl; Cl := Ul*Yl = Vl*Xl;
A2 := Y2 - V2; B2 := U2 - X2; C2 := U2*Y2 = V2*X2;
```

The determinant is also evaluated and its value assigned to a variable, since we shall need it again.

```
Determinant := Al*B2 - A2*Bl;
```

We have now translated the upper box of the iteration graph.

The test for parallel lines is made on the value of the determinant; the program step to be taken if the lines are parallel is just to print a message. If the lines are not parallel, a more complicated action must be taken, so we shall employ a compound statement.

```
if Determinant = 0 then
    Writeln ('THE LINES ARE PARALLEL')
else
    begin
        .
        .
    end
```

Within the compound statement, we must compute the value of a pair (x,y) that solves the equations

$$A_1 x + B_1 y = C_1$$
$$A_2 x + B_2 y = C_2$$

The values can be given in terms of the previously computed determinant, and the values of the A, B, C coefficients, and assigned to variables X and Y representing the coordinates of the intersection.

```
X := (B2*Cl - Bl*C2)/Determinant;
Y := (Al*C2 - A2*Cl)/Determinant;
```

Finally, we must determine whether the intersection lies between the endpoints of each line segment. This determination is a bit complex, because the relative values of the endpoint coordinates of each line segment are not known in advance. Therefore, we need to construct a Boolean expression that considers all possible cases. If it were known that U1 were the larger of the endpoint coordinates of line 1 along the x-axis, then we could test that the value of X was no larger than U1 and no smaller than X1. On the other hand, if U1 were the smaller of the endpoint coordinates along this axis, then the parity of the test for X would be reversed. The test for containment of the x-coordinate of the intersection point within the endpoint coordinates of line 1 becomes

$$(U1 > X1) \text{ and } (X <= U1) \text{ and } (X >= X1)$$
$$\text{or } (U1 < X1) \text{ and } (X >= U1) \text{ and } (X <= X1)$$

Unfortunately, while this test will answer the question about containment of the intersection within line segment 1 for nearly all cases, it is not yet complete. If the line segment is parallel to the y-axis in the plane, its x-coordinate will be constant at all points and testing it will yield no information. Therefore, we must also test the possible containment of the y-coordinate of the intersection.

Although we need not have done so in this algorithm, we have chosen to assign to a variable the value of the large, Boolean expression that determines whether the intersection lies within a line segment. The expression could have been used directly in a conditional statement, but it seems more intuitive to utilize a flag variable with the mnemonic name OnLine1 to represent this condition.

After having translated the iteration graph we are nearly through with the composition of our program. Two important steps remain. First, we must read over what we have written with care, to make sure that it is complete and does not contain obvious errors. It may help to make a clean copy of it on a fresh sheet of paper. As we re-read the program, we can make a list of the names of all of the variables that we have used. The second step is to give declaration statements to associate a data type with each of the variables that appears on our list. The complete Pascal program, including comments and declarations, appears as follows:

61

```
program Intersection (Input, Output);
(*****************************************************
* This program tests two line segments, specified by *
* the coordinates of their endpoints, and determines *
* whether or not they intersect.                     *
*       Line 1: From (U1, V1) to (X1, Y1)            *
*       Line 2: from (U2, V2) to (X2, Y2)            *
* Both lines are represented by equations of the form*
*       A*X + B*Y = C                                *
*****************************************************)

var
    U1, V1, X1, A1, B1, C1, U2, V2, X2, Y2, A2, B2, C2,
      X, Y, Determinant : Real;
    OnLine1, OnLine2 : Boolean;

begin
    (***** Obtain A, B, C coefficients for both lines *****)
    Read (U1, V1, X1, Y1);
    Writeln ('ENDPOINTS OF LINE 1:', U1, V1, X1, Y1);
    Read (U2, V2, X2, Y2);
    Writeln ('ENDPOINTS OF LINE 2:', U2, V2, X2, Y2);
    A1 := Y1 - V1; B1 := U1 - X1; C1 := U1*Y1 - V1*X1;
    A2 := Y2 = V2; B2 := U2 - X2; C2 := U2*Y2 - V2*X2;

    (***** Evaluate the determinant of the coefficients ****)
    (***** A zero determinant indicates parallel lines *****)
    Determinant := A1*B2 - A2*B1;
    if Determinant = 0 then
        Writeln ('THE LINES ARE PARALLEL')
    else
        begin
            (*********************************************
            * Find the point of intersection, and determine*
            * whether it lies on both line segments.     *
            * The Boolean variables OnLine1 and OnLine2  *
            * are used to represent the condition that the *
            * intersection lies between the endpoints of  *
            * Line 1 or Line 2, respectively.            *
            *********************************************)
            X := (B2*C1 - B1*C2)/Determinant;
            Y := (A1*C2 - A2*C1)/Determinant;
            OnLine1 := (U1 > X1) and (X <= U1) and (X >= X1)
                   or (U1 < X1) and (X >= U1) and (X <= X1)
                   or (V1 > Y1) and (Y <= V1) and (Y >= Y1)
                   or             (Y >= V1) and (Y <= Y1);
```

62

```
OnLine2 := (U2 > X2) and (X <= U2) and (X >= X2)
           or (U2 < X2) and (X >= U2) and (X <= X2)
           or (V2 > Y2) and (Y <= V2) and (Y >= Y2)
           or              (Y >= V2) and (Y <= Y2);
    if not OnLine1 then
        Writeln ('INTERSECTION FALLS OFF LINE SEGMENT 1')
    else if not OnLine2 then
        Writeln ('INTERSECTION FALLS OFF LINE SEGMENT 2')
    else
        Writeln ('THE LINE SEGMENTS INTERSECT AT ', X, Y);
    end
end.
```

One final caution concerning the example must be mentioned. The test Determinant = 0 will not yield the expected result in all cases. This is because the computer cannot actually handle real numbers, but only finite rational approximations to them. A better test would be

```
Determinant < (A1*B2 + A2*B1)*1E-6
```

For an explanation, see Chapter 11.

3.9 Handling multiple alternatives

Now that conditional execution has been introduced as a means of programming a computer to make decisions, this tool can easily be generalized to cases involving multiple decisions. One technique is simply to cascade the use of conditional tests.

Example 3.9.1 -- Computing income tax from a graduated scale

A page from the 1975 Federal Income Tax Forms contains the table given in Figure 3.2. How might we program an algorithm to perform the computation indicated by the table? A straightforward method would be to compose a conditional expression testing successively whether taxable income falls within each of the ranges specified by the table.

```
if Taxableincome <= 500 then
    Incometax := 0.14*Taxableincome
else if Taxableincome <= 1000 then
    Incometax := 70 + 0.15*(Taxableincome - 500)
else if Taxableincome <= 1500 then
    Incometax := 145 + 0.16*(Taxableincome - 1000)
else if Taxableincome <= 2000 then
    Incometax := 225 + 0.17*(Taxableincome - 1500)
```

```
            else if Taxableincome <= 4000 then
               Incometax := 310 + 0.19*(Taxableincome - 2000)
            else if Taxableincome <= 6000 then
               Incometax := 690 + 0.21*(Taxableincome - 4000)
            else if Taxableincome <= 8000 then
               Incometax := 1110 + 0.24*(Taxableincome - 6000)
               .
               .
               .

            else if Taxableincome <= 100000 then
               Incometax := 46190 + 0.69*(Taxableincome - 90000)
            else Incometax := 53090 + 0.70*(Taxableincome - 100000)
```

When multiple conditions are tested by a cascaded conditional expression such as the one in the last example, the
computer will test for the occurrence of each condition in exactly

---

SCHEDULE X -- Single Taxpayers

If the amount on   Enter on
Form 1040,   Form 1040,
line 47 is: line 16a;

Not over $500   14% of the amount on line 47:

Over--	But not over --		of the amount over --
$ 500	$ 1,000	$ 70 + 15%	$ 500
$ 1,000	$ 1,500	$ 145 + 16%	$ 1,000
$ 1,500	$ 2,000	$ 225 + 17%	$ 1,500
$ 2,000	$ 4,000	$ 319 + 19%	$ 2,000
$ 4,000	$ 6,000	$ 690 + 21%	$ 4,000
$ 6,000	$ 8,000	$ 1,110 + 24%	$ 6,000
$ 8,000	$ 10.000	$ 1,500 + 25%	$ 8,000
$ 10,000	$ 12,000	$ 2,090 + 27%	$ 10,000
.	.	.	.
.	.	.	.
.	.	.	.
$ 90,000	$100,000	$46,190 + 69%	$ 90,000
$100,000		$53,090 + 70%	$100,000

Figure 3.2 -- Tax Rate Tables from the
            1975 Federal Income Tax Forms

the order given. Thus, in the example, if Taxableincome exceeds 100000, the computer will make all of the indicated comparisons with lesser amounts before discovering that fact. In this particular application, we have reason to believe that a taxable income in excess of $100,000 is much less likely than is one falling into a lower bracket, so that the relative inefficiency of the test for very high income does not worry us. In some other applications, however, we might wish to adopt a different strategy to avoid making more comparisons than necessary.

3.10 Making programs readable

Only rarely does one have occasion to write a computer program that will be read only by a computer, and never by another human being. Since a programming language is also a precise, formal language for the statement of algorithms, it seems natural that one should attempt to write algorithms so that they can be read and understood with a minimum of effort. As was pointed out previously, even if the reader is only yourself, you may not remember exactly what was in the back of your mind at the time that you first composed an algorithm, and it can be most useful to leave some hints for yourself in the form of a lucidly written program. We have already discussed the role of descriptive variable names and of strategically placed comments in making programs intelligible. There are some other rules to follow as well.

The control structure of an algorithm is organized into groups of statements that are executed in sequence. Such a group of statements can be written on successive lines of a page, and indented so that all statements of a group begin on a common left hand margin. If the group of statements happens to be bracketed by a begin...end pair, then the scope of the begin... end can be clearly indicated by writing each of these words on individual lines with the same indentation, and letting the group of statements they enclose be indented three spaces further than the begin and end. The program segment in the example of Section 3.7 illustrates this. In addition, one should indicate the scope of a conditional statement by indenting the statement or group of statements to be conditionally executed three spaces with respect to the left margin of the if...then clause. If multiple options are listed, then each else should begin on a common left margin. When a statement or group of statements is to be repeated, the scope of the repetition can similarly be indicated by indentation.

Although it may seem relatively unimportant to adhere to fixed rules of style in the physical appearance of programs (particularly if editing can only be done by retyping or keypunching), the effort spent in making programs readable so that a minimum of external documentation is required for their explanation is well worthwhile. When you have gained more experience in composing algorithms, you may wish to try an exercise, formulating an algorithm to have your programs automatically edited for indentation by the computer!

In this chapter, several of the examples have been chosen to illustrate business applications. This is because algorithms for business applications tend to involve a great deal of decision making, rather than a great deal of computation. In other chapters, we shall investigate many examples of applications from other fields.

Self-check question:

1) Can you rewrite the following segment of Pascal text, following the recommended indentation rules?

```
begin Balance := Balance + CurrentCharges;
    if Balance > MinimumPayment
then begin Payment := MinimumPayment; CarryingCharge :=
    0.15*Balance;
end else begin Payment := Balance; CarryingCharge :=
    0 end end
```

EXCERCISES FOR CHAPTER 3

3.1 Using a pencil and paper, follow the steps of the algorithm of Example 3.8.1 to determine whether or not there is an intersection of a pair of line segments whose endpoints coordinates are:

U1 = -2,	V1 = -3,	X1 = 4,	Y1 = 6,
U2 = 3,	V2 = 0,	X2 = 3,	Y2 = 8.

3.2 A computer dating service has solicited information sheets from potential customers of their service. The choice of a match is to be made on the basis of correlation of a list of personal interest preferences, but to guard themselves against suggesting unworkable matches, the dating service needs to screen potential pairs by physical, occupational, and social·characteristics before considering them as candidates. Each pair is to consist of one male and one female; if the age of the male is under 26, then the female should not be more then one year older; the male should not be more than two inches shorter nor more than 10 inches taller than the female; if both are employed, then they should work the same part of the day; if both indicate religious preferences, they should agree; their places of residence should not be more then 20 miles apart. Give an algorithm to screen a pair of information sheets to see if the persons submitting them are potential dating candidates.

3.3 The director of a zoo is preparing a new enclosure in which several animals of various species are to be housed. To achieve balance, he wishes to limit the number of individuals in the enclosure to 50, of which not more than 25 will be birds, not more than 25 mammals and not more than 15 reptiles. It is also necessary to ensure that the carnivores do not devour the herbivores, so the largest carnivore is not to be larger in body weight than the smallest herbivore. Give the director a program segment to determine whether or not a given animal can be added to the group he has already selected.

3.4 (moderately difficult) From plane trigonometry, you know that if given any of the following sets of data about a triangle, it is possible to find the remaining sides and angles not given as data:

all three sides,
two sides and the angle between them,
two sides and the angle one of them makes with the
        remaining side,
two angles and the side between them,
two angles and the side opposite one of them.

Give an algorithm as a Pascal program that will accept as
input six values to be interpreted as the lengths of sides
and the angles of a triangle given in the order side 1,
angle 12, side 2, angle 23, side 3, angle 31, with
all angles specified as interior angles. A zero value for
either a side or an angle will designate it as unknown. The
algorithm is to determine whether or not the data given
define a triangle, and if so, to determine the values of the
missing sides and angles.

3.5   A small manufacturing concern is converting its accounting
operations to a computer-based system. The firm has both
regular and part-time employees, all of whom are paid hourly
wages. Each week the personnel clerk submits a report of the
time each employee has worked, and of any vacation or sick
leave he may have taken. For the plant as a whole, he
reports the length of that particular work week, and the
maximum number of hours of overtime authorized for any
employee during that week.

    The task to be performed by the accounting system is to
verify that the weekly employment record of each employee
corresponds to the authorized figures (for instance, that an
employee does not claim more vacation leave than he is
entitled to), to prepare the paychecks after having calculated withholding tax and other deductions from gross pay,
and to update the personnel record of each employee to
reflect the week's transactions. The personnel record is to
contain the hourly pay rate, the number of days accrued
vacation leave, the number of days of vacation expended this
year, the number of days of accrued sick leave, days of sick
leave taken, total pay received during the current year,
total withholding tax, total social security tax withheld,
and total union dues deducted during the year. Assume that
withholding tax is deducted at a rate of 14% of total weekly
wages, but only on the first $9000 of wages earned during
the year, and that union dues amount to $3 per week. Also
assume that overtime is paid time-and-a-half, that ten days
paid vacation is authorized per year, and that sick leave

credit accumulates at a rate of one day for each twelve days actually worked.

List all of the program variables required to represent
(a) the weekly employment status of the plant as a whole,
(b) the weekly employment record of an individual employee,
(c) the cumulative yearly employment record of an individual employee.

Give an algorithm to compute the week's take-home pay for an individual employee, and to update his cumulative employment record each week.

3.6 The Albatross Boat Company manufactures a line of custom built pleasure craft. A buyer can choose his particular vessel by specifying a combination from the following list of characteristics:
(a) Length can be from 15 to 75 feet, in increments of one foot;
(b) Width can be from 5 to 25 feet, in increments of one foot;
(c) Number of sleeping accommodations can be from 0 to 14;
(d) Engine horsepower can be any one of (10, 20, 50, 100, 200, 300, 500, 1000).

The cost of an Albatross boat is $25 times the square of the length, plus $150 for each sleeping berth, plus $8 per unit of horsepower.

Some combinations of the specifications listed above would result in ludicrous boat designs, so certain constraints must be introduced. Specifically, the length of a boat must be at least three times, but not more that five times its width. The horsepower can be no greater than 0.6 times the product of length and width. And the number of sleeping berths cannot exceed 1/100 of the product of length and width. Should any of these constraints be violated, the customer is to receive one of the following notifications:
THE DESIGN REQUESTED IS TOO WIDE FOR ITS LENGTH,
THE DESIGN REQUESTED IS TOO NARROW FOR ITS LENGTH,
THE DESIGN REQUESTED IS OVERPOWERED,
TOO MANY SLEEPING ACCOMMODATIONS REQUESTED FOR A BOAT OF
        THIS SIZE.

Also, if a customer specifies a design parameter outside the range of values given by (a--d), he is to receive notification.

Compose and test a Pascal program that can be used by the Albatross Boat Company to check the acceptability of lists of design parameters submitted by its customers, and to compute the cost of each acceptable design. The program should accept, on successive input lines, the specifications submitted by several customers, terminating when it encounters a set of data for which the length is specified as zero.

4 REPEATING COMPUTATIONS

4.1 Computations that cannot be done in a single sequence of steps

Recalling the examples of Chapter 1, there were many algorithms calling for the repetition of a step or of a sequence of steps. In fact, there are many problems for which no algorithm can give an effective solution unless it provides some mechanism for repetition.

Repetition is a fundamental concept in controlling the execution of the steps of an algorithm, and there is a special notation for it in the language of iteration graphs. An iteration box contains a space with the shape of the letter 'L', or of an inverted letter 'L', enclosing a smaller rectangular box.

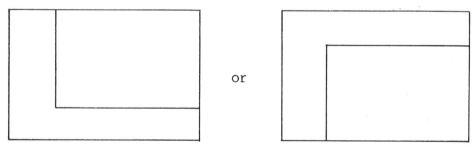

or

Within the 'L' is written a Boolean-valued expression that is used to control the iterated execution of the steps written within the smaller box. When the 'L' is drawn right side up it signifies that the Boolean expression is a condition for terminating the iteration; the expression is preceded by the word <u>until</u>, to remind us of its meaning. The terminating condition is evaluated after each execution of the controlled algorithm steps.

When the 'L' is inverted, the Boolean expression has the opposite interpretation. It then represents a condition under which the iteration is to be continued, and the condition is evaluated prior to each execution of the controlled steps. In fact, it is possible that the steps written in the smaller box will not be executed even once, in case the controlling test fails immediately. In the inverted 'L', the controlling expression is preceded by the word <u>while</u> to remind us of its significance.

To illustrate the notation and the concept, let us form an iteration box that will cause a step called 'operation' to be executed N times if N is a positive integer, and passed over in case N is zero or negative.

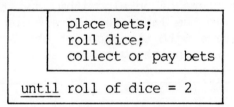

```
while N > 0
        operation;
        N := N - 1
```

The <u>until</u> form of iteration control is more appropriately used when the terminating condition does not depend on the initial data, but requires execution of the controlled steps for its determination. For example, the activity of gambling with dice might be governed by:

```
        place bets;
        roll dice;
        collect or pay bets
until roll of dice = 2
```

Pascal allows you to form an iterative statement controlled in either of these ways. The syntax of these statements is:

statement

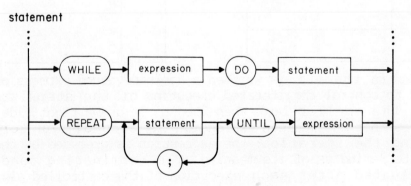

72

The first of these expresses the while form of iteration graph. Note that the while clause controls only a single statement; if several algorithm steps are to be controlled by a while clause they must be nested within a compound statement.

The second form directly translates the until form of iteration graph. Since the controlled steps are syntactically bracketed between the keywords repeat...until, one may write a list of one or more statements, without resorting to the compound statement form.

There will occur many circumstances in which a choice between these two forms of iteration control is arbitrary. However, one must be aware of the fact that the Boolean control expression that would be employed with the while has the opposite logical meaning to that used with the until form. We can give general guidelines as to how to construct the desired Boolean expression. Usually, the repeated steps perform some task intended to bring about a desired outcome. A Boolean expression will be written to test whether or not the desired condition is yet satisfied. Iteration will cease when either (a) the desired condition has been satisfied, or (b) the possibilities for bringing about the desired condition have been exhausted. In the while form we write

```
while <condition is not satisfied> and
      <possibilities are not exhausted> do
   <perform task>
```

but in the until form, we write

```
repeat
   <perform task>
until <condition is satisfied> or
      <possibilities are exhausted>
```

Example 4.1.1 -- Selecting a minimum value

Suppose that our task is to find the smallest positive integer such that its value squared is equal to or larger than the value of some number given as an input. Suppose further, that we wish to limit our search to the first 100 positive integers. Let N be a variable representing an integer value between 1 and 100, and let X represent the value input. Then the condition to be satisfied will be that $X <= Sqr(N)$, where Sqr( ) is the name of a Pascal function

that computes the square of a number. The condition that N
should be the least positive integer satisfying the condition can be met by searching through the positive integer
values in ascending order. The condition that the possibilities are exhausted is that N = 100.

A Pascal program segment to solve this problem using the
until form of control would be

```
Read (X); N := 0;
repeat
    N := N + 1;
until (X <= Sqr(N)) or (N = 100)
```

Alternatively, the while form of control can be used, but
in that case, the initial value of N should be set to 1, for
the condition is to be tested immediately, before the value
of N is incremented. Note that the relational conditions
that make up the Boolean expression are the opposite of
those used in the previous case.

```
Read (X);  N := 1;
while (X > Sqr(N)) and (N <> 100) do
    N := N + 1
```

The following is a simple example of a problem for which
some mechanism for repetition is required, and for which we shall
use iteration, but not simply counting.

Example 4.1.2 -- Finding the greatest common divisor of a pair
                 of positive integers

If we require an algorithm using as its primitive
operations only the elementary arithmetic operations
(addition, subtraction, multiplication, division) and
comparison of integers, a convincing argument can be made
that no algorithm which does not repeat any step can compute
the greatest common divisor of a pair of integers of
arbitrary size. On the other hand, Euclid's algorithm for
finding the greatest common divisor is particularly simple,
using only the operations of subtraction and comparison of
integers.

Euclid's algorithm is based on the observation that the
greatest common divisor of a pair of positive integers, M
and N, will also be a divisor of their difference, unless

the difference is zero. The difference of M and N will always be smaller than the larger member of the pair, and if the difference is in fact, zero, then the common integer value of M and N is also their greatest common divisor. Thus, an obvious step to iterate is the replacement of the larger member of the pair by the difference. This step is repeated until the difference becomes zero. The algorithm must be finite since the sum of the two members of the pair is reduced at each iteration, and neither number can be reduced to zero.

A first attempt at describing the algorithm by the use of an iteration graph might recognize the iteration control condition and the task of the step that is to be repeated.

```
while M <> N

      replace the larger
      of (M, N) by their
      difference
```

Recall that the operator symbol "<>" is to be read as "not equal to" in Pascal notation. In this description of the algorithm , the controlled step is not yet given in simple enough terms to permit direct translation to a Pascal program segment. Forgetting about the iteration control for the moment, let us concentrate on refinement of the controlled step. When it designates "the larger of (M, N)", we realize that a choice has to be made, depending on the relative values held by variables M and N. A different action is to be taken in each of the two alternate cases. We could describe the choice by a conditional box, and the actions to be taken in the two cases can be described by assignment statements. Thus the box

```
      replace the larger
      of (M, N) by their
      difference
```

can be refined to

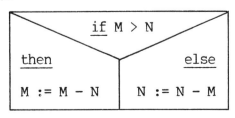

Substituting the conditional box for the controlled step in the original graph, we obtain an iteration graph describing the entire algorithm in elementary steps

GCD1:

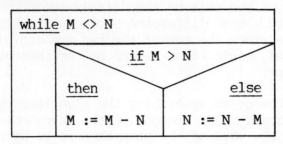

Translating the algorithm, to which we attach the label GCD1 as a means of naming it, into a Pascal program segment we obtain

```
GCD1:
    while M <> N do
        if M > N then
            M := M - N
    else
            N := N - M
```

The effect of the while clause is to cause repetition of the statement that follows it until the condition M <> N is no longer satisfied. The answer, the greatest common divisor of the original values of M and N, will appear as the final value of M (or N).

Self-check questions:

1. Carry out the steps of GCD1 by hand, entering the intermediate values in a table whose headings are:

number of iterations	M	N	M - N

using initial values of M = 63, N = 48.

2. Repeat the hand simulation of GCD1, but use initial values

    a) M = 12, N = 1;
    b) M = 1, N = -1;
    c) M = 0, N = 5;

76

can you estimate the number of steps required from the initial values of the data? For what values of data will the algorithm fail to give a result?

3. What special meaning is attached to the while clause in Pascal that is not implied by the common meaning of the word while in English? Hint: The usage of the word in the sentence, "While I'm cleaning out the garage, please wash the car" does not correspond to the meaning associated with the while clause as an iteration control.

4.2 Getting the initial values right

In the last example, we assumed that the variables M and N had received initial values by some means or other before execution of the program segment GCD1 was begun. We also assumed that the values given were both positive integers. (How would the computation proceed if one of the values were zero or a negative integer?) In formulating complete programs, it is always necessary to specify how the initial values of variables are to be acquired, and if there is any doubt as to whether the initial values lie within the range for which the algorithm is defined, then these values must be checked.

One way to initialize the values of M and N used in the GCD1 algorithm would be to have these values read from some device that supplies inputs to the computer, such as a punched card reader or a communications terminal. In such a case, out of range values might be submitted, so the initial data must be checked for validity. These tasks can be accomplished by appending the following Pascal test as a prefix to GCD1

```
Read (M, N);  Writeln (M, N);
if (M <= 0) or (N <= 0) then
    Writeln (' VALUE OUT OF RANGE')
else ...
```

In nearly every program segment whose execution is to be repeated a number of times, there are variables that must receive initial values before execution of the segment begins. It is easy to identify such a variable from the text of the repeated segment, for the first reference to it occurs in the evaluation of an expression, rather than as the left-hand side of an assignment or in an input statement. Such a variable is said to be, in the personified vernacular of computer science, live on entry into the iterated program segment. Failure to properly initialize a variable that is live on entry is the commonest cause of error in formulating algorithms as computer programs.

Failure to initialize a variable commonly occurs because, in inventing an algorithm, we tend to focus our attention first on the steps to be iterated and simply forget to fill in an intended initialization step later. Or, in an algorithm containing many conditionally executed statements, it may happen that we have not correctly analyzed all possibilities, and that a statement initializing a variable, which ought to have been executed before an iterated program segment was executed, was in fact passed by due to the occurrence of an unforeseen combination of conditions. What happens to the execution of an algorithm when an uninitialized variable is referenced? This depends on the particular computer and programming language you are using, but quite commonly the computer proceeds as though the uninitialized variable does have a value, perhaps one left over from a previous computation it has done for another user, and you get mysteriously wrong answers!

Self-check questions:

1. How are values of variables initialized in a program?

2. Which are the uninitialized variables in the following Pascal program segment?

```
begin
    J := J + 1;
    K := 5;
    while I > 0 do
        begin
            I := I - 1;
            L := I + J + K;
        end;
    Read (I, J, K, M, N);
    Writeln (I, L, N, P);
end
```

4.3 How do you know that an algorithm is correct?

This important question is one of the most difficult, yet obviously most important questions one can ask about computing. All that we can provide are partial answers; they will be sufficient to establish the correctness of simple algorithms and of some complicated ones, but they will not succeed in every case. On the other hand, in an attempt to verify that an algorithm is correct, one is very often led to exposure of its weak points, or the potential errors in it.

There are two principal methods for attempting verification of an algorithm: testing, and logical analysis. By correctness of an algorithm, we do not mean only that a program is free of syntax errors. Syntax errors are really errors in the statement of an algorithm, and are easily checked by submitting a program to the computer. What we mean by correctness is that an algorithm when executed on any values of data, either computes a correct result or else reports that the data values are unacceptable.

Testing of programs on a few "typical" sets of data is the most commonly used means of verifying correctness, but it suffers from an obvious flaw. Most algorithms are intended to work on such a large set of data values that it is impossible to test all combinations, and so testing is often confined to determining that a program works on the programmer's favorite example! Nevertheless, there are a few rules that can be followed in order to develop adequate sets of test data. The first rule is that every statement of the program should be tested. Not every set of test data will do this. For example, in the example of GCD1, given in the preceding sections, the data (24, 4) would never cause the assignment N := N - M to be executed. If this statement had been inadvertently omitted from the program segment, the correct result would still be computed on the data (24, 4). To fully exercise a program, it is often necessary to furnish it with several sets of test data. In order to be certain that a Pascal program has had all statements tested at least once, it will also be helpful to embed supplementary output statements in the program during testing.

Returning to the example of GCD1, a set of test data should include a pair of numbers relatively prime, a pair in which one divides the other, and a pair not relatively prime, but in which neither divides the other. Each set should be given in both orders, larger number first and larger number second. Thus a set of test data might be (5, 3), (3, 5), (4, 2), (2, 4), (6, 4), (4, 6) and (3, 3). These would test all normal states of the algorithm, that is, would test every instruction and test instructions in all relative orders of execution. But this amount of testing is still not sufficient. If there are other, abnormal sets of data that might be submitted to the algorithm, then it should be tested on such sets. In the case of GCD1, it is intended that it should get its input from a card reader, rather than some more benevolent device which checks data values before submitting them, and so the additional test data (1, 0), (0, 1), (1, 1), (1, -1), (-1, 1) should be added.

The other principal method for verification of algorithms is based on systematic mathematical reasoning about the computation that an algorithm describes. In mathematical reasoning we are not handicapped by the inability to describe all possible input values; we are used to making statements prefaced with phrases such as "for all positive integer values", or "there exists a pair of integers such that ...". Let's see how this technique works on GCD1.

The first thing to do is to rewrite the algorithm description, identifying points in the algorithm at which assertions can be placed about the values held by the program variables. In doing this, one is forced to realize that the execution of an algorithm is a dynamic process, and that the same algorithm steps may be repeated with several different sets of values of the program variables, as the evaluation progresses in time. In GCD1, we identify five points at which to make assertions:

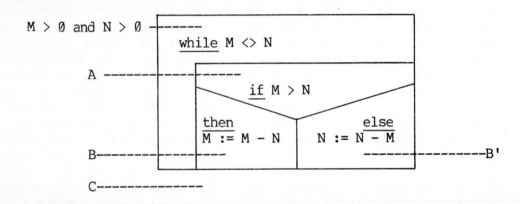

Since this algorithm performs iteration, we shall use a method of inductive assertions. This involves looking for a hypothesis that will be true of the values at point A no matter how many times the iterated statement is repeated. One way to form such a hypothesis is to look for a condition that will remain invariant from point A to either of points B or B', even though some change in the values of the variables occurs as a result of executing the intervening statements. For example, an invariant condition might be "M > 0 and N > 0". If this were true at point A, then in case M is the greater of M and N, the assignment M := M - N will be executed, replacing the value of M with a new value. The new value, however, is assuredly positive. The value of N remains unchanged, and so the assertion remains true. On the other hand, if the condition were false at A because N was negative, then it would remain false at B, with N still negative and M still positive (and larger). Thus the hypothesis "M > 0 and N > 0" is invariant from A to B. Since (M <> N) at point A is guaranteed by the while clause, the alternative to M > N at A is that M < N. In this case, the invariance of the hypothesis from point A to point B' can also be established by similar reasoning.

A more interesting hypothesis is that for any positive integer constant G, the condition that "G divides both M and N" will remain invariant from A to either of B or B'. If G divides both M and N, then there are positive integers P and Q such that M = G*P and N = G*Q. Thus, when M is replaced by M - N, the common factor G can be extracted, and the new value of M will be G*(P - Q). Thus G still divides both M and N at point B. Similar reasoning demonstrates the condition to be invariant from point A to point B' as well.

The utility of these invariant conditions lies in the application of the inductive method. There are just two ways by which values are obtained at point A. One is that M and N hold their initial values at point A and that these initial values are not equal. The other is that the values M and N held at point B or at point B' were not equal after some number of repetitions of the iterated statement, and that these values are inherited at point A. Thus any condition which is invariant from point A to both points B and B', and which can also be established to hold for the initial values, must always hold at point A. As an example of such a condition, let the constant G of the preceding paragraph be any member of the set of common divisors of the original values of M and N. Invariance of the condition "G divides both M and N" implies that the entire set of common divisors remains invariant throughout execution of the algorithm! In particular, when the algorithm terminates execution at point C, with M and N having equal final values, the set of common divisors will be the set of all factors of M, and the largest factor, the final value of M itself, will be the greatest common divisor of the pair of values given originally.

Lest it seem as if we are advertising logical analysis as a panacea for solving all problems of algorithm verification, two difficulties should be pointed out. First of all, there are some algorithms for which verification by mathematical reasoning is extremely difficult, perhaps even impossible, even though the algorithm may, in fact, have all the desired properties. Secondly, there is always a danger of acquiring a false sense of confidence by generating a logically invalid verification, just as one sometimes gives a false proof in mathematics, or composes an incorrect algorithm in the first place! However, the very act of going through a logical analysis of an algorithm will nearly always increase your understanding of it, even if it is an algorithm that you have composed yourself.

Self-check questions:

1.   Why are invariant conditions important in the verification of an iterated program segment? What is meant by an invariant condition anyway?

2.   Can you suggest how to introduce counting variables into the program segment GCD1 to determine how many times each statement is executed in a test of the program?

4.4   How many times should we repeat?

Frequently, when repetition of an algorithm step is called for, one can predict in advance exactly the number of repetitions required. For example, n! can be evaluated with exactly n multiplications. When an exactly predictable number of iterations is required, it is helpful to use an iteration control clause which counts the number of repetitions, instead of testing to see whether a specified condition is satisfied. Pascal (and most other, similarly conceived programming languages) has such an iteration control clause, the for clause. The syntax of the for statement is given by the chart on the following page, which is another possible form for ⌐statement⌐.

An elementary function that can be evaluated iteratively with the aid of a for clause is the factorial function, n! It can be computed as follows:

```
            Factorial := 1;
            for I := 1 to N do
                  Factorial := I * Factorial
```

Of course, not every iterated step can be controlled by a for clause, but for those which can, its use offers the advan-

statement

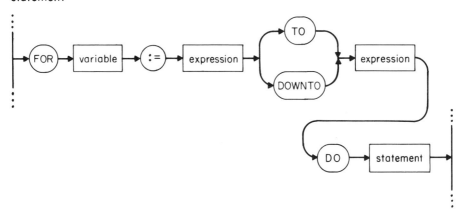

tage that the number of iterations is always bounded, whereas the execution of a while statement may loop forever in case its terminating condition is never satisfied. Also, there is much less chance that the controlling variable will be improperly initialized within the for clause, since its initialization is accomplished by a specific assignment. The controlling variable cannot be assigned a new value in the statement or compound group whose iteration is controlled by the for clause.

In order to get a more explicit understanding of the for clause, let us compare it with an equivalent while clause.

```
                              I := 1;  N' := N;
    for I := 1 to N do        while I <= N' do
        <statement>               begin
                                      <statement>;
                                      I := succ (I)
                                  end
```

In the program segment on the right, the variable N' is inaccessible to the programmer and never actually appears in his program. The program segment on the right can be taken to be a definition of the effect of the for statement on the left.

Notice that the for statement will always produce a finite number of iterations. The loop control variable cannot have its value changed by assignment, and the actual variable used to hold the upper bound is hidden. Thus, if the programmer attempted to increase the upper bound on the number of iterations by including

```
    N := N + 1;
```

83

within the controlled <statement>, it would have no effect on the number of iterations performed.

The _for_ clause in Pascal has another form, in which the iteration control variable is decremented upon each execution of the controlled statement, rather than incremented. This form uses the keyword _downto_ in place of the keyword _to_. For instance, the factorial function could be evaluated using the decrementing form of the _for_ clause by:

```
Factorial := 1;
for I := N downto 1 do
      Factorial := I * Factorial
```

In case the initial value assigned to the controlling variable is already out of the range of the count, as for instance, if N = 0 in the algorithm for the factorial function, then the statement under control of the _for_ clause is not executed at all.

In some algorithms the number of iterations required is obvious, but in others, we can often figure out a fixed number of iterations that will be sufficient.

Example 4.4.1 -- Computing the square root of a number

One of the oldest problems of real-valued arithmetic is that of computing the square root. There is a very simple algorithm for this computation, usually attributed to Sir Isaac Newton (1642-1727). Suppose N is any positive number whose square root is to be found, and suppose X is an estimate of the square root arrived at by some means, say initially by guessing. If X is actually greater than $\sqrt{N}$, then N/X will be smaller than $\sqrt{N}$, and conversely. The product of X with N/X is, of course N, so these two numbers serve as reciprocal estimates of $\sqrt{N}$. Newton's algorithm is to iteratively replace the estimate X with the mean of the reciprocal estimates, 1/2(X + N/X), until the difference of the reciprocal estimates, |X - N/X|, has been made as small as desired.

Since the algorithm itself is to be independent of the value of N whose square root is to be estimated, we are obliged to choose a constant value for the initial estimate, and one is as good a choice as any. The desired accuracy might be expressed as a constant multiple of the original number, or as a specified number of significant digits to be given correctly. In the first version of the algorithm, we shall ask for the difference of the reciprocal estimates to be made less than 10^{-7} times the value of the estimate.

```
(********************************************************
*  Newton1:                                            *
*      N is the number whose square root is to be found *
*      X is the current estimate of the root           *
********************************************************)

    X := 1;
    while Abs (X - N/X) > 1E-7 * X do
        X := 0.5*(X + N/X)
```

In the expression appearing within the while clause, Abs is a built-in Pascal function which takes the absolute value of a number.

There is one deficiency of the algorithm as given above. Although it will need only a few iterations to evaluate the root of a number not too far removed from 1, to take the root of a very large or a very small number will require a number of iterations that is approximately $1/2 \log_2 N$. When the reciprocal estimates are far apart, the new estimate which is found is just about half of the larger one.

The rate of convergence of the algorithm can be improved by selecting a better estimate than 1 before applying Newton's method. The initial value of the estimate can be preconditioned by multiplying it by some number chosen so that the estimate squared is still smaller than the large number whose root is desired. In fact, this preconditioning can be applied repetitively, until the square of the estimate is within some constant ratio of N.

An added benefit of preconditioning is that whenever it is known that the square of the initial estimate is within some given, fixed ratio of N, then we can also give a fixed bound on the number of iterations of Newton's procedure that will guarantee a specified number of significant digits in the result. Thus, it will no longer be necessary to control the iteration by testing the difference of the reciprocal estimates, but instead we can just iterate the procedure a fixed number of times. A modified form of the square root algorithm is

```
(**************************************************
*  Newton2:                                       *
*     N is the number whose root is to be found.  *
*     X is the estimate of the root of N.         *
**************************************************)

    X := 1;
    while N > 64*X*X do
        X := 8*X;
    while N < X*X/64 do
        X := X/8;
    for I := 1 to 6 do
        X := 0.5*(X + N/X)
```

Notice that at most one of the statements controlled by the while clauses will be executed, for any specific initial value of X.

When Newton's procedure is begun in the last line of the algorithm, it is known that X squared must be within a factor of 64 of N. When begun with an estimate this close to the square root, six iterations of Newton's procedure will suffice to give a result accurate to seven significant decimal digits. The factor of 64 was selected arbitrarily; however, on many computers, which use an internal representation of numbers with a radix of 2, 8, or 16, multiplications or divisions of integers by powers of 2 can be carried out very quickly. This is a use of machine-dependent knowledge, however, and the specific selection of 64 as the factor is in no way crucial to the algorithm.

It is instructive to compare the efficiency of Newton1 with Newton2, insofar as we are able. For very large (or very small) values of N, the number of iterations of the preconditioning step by Newton2 will be $1/2 \log_8 N$, which is 3 times smaller than the $\log_2 N$ estimate of the number of iterations that Newton1 will require. At first glance, it appears that Newton2 incurs some additional overhead when the value of N is within a factor of 64 of 1, for then the conditions of the two while clauses must be evaluated although no preconditioning is actually necessary. But because of the certain knowledge that X squared is within a factor of 64 of N when the last statement is begun, a simpler form of iteration control is used that requires less computation for its evaluations than does the while clause of Newton1. So Newton2 appears to be superior for any value of N (other than the very special case, N = 1).

Self-check questions:

1. Hand simulate the calculation of the square root by the
    program segment Newton1, recording the intermediate results
    in a table whose headings are:

number of repetitions	X	N/X	1/2(X + N/X)	|X - N/X|

    Use the following values of N
       a) N = 2;
       b) N = 0.5;
       c) N = 64

    (An electronic calculator will be helpful, although not
    essential.) Does the algorithm give an exact result for the
    square root of a perfect square? How many repetitions are
    necessary to obtain the prescribed accuracy for each of
    these cases?

2. What advantages are there to using a <u>for</u> clause to control
    repeated execution, instead of using a <u>while</u> or <u>until</u>
    clause? Are there circumstances under which a <u>while</u> or an
    <u>until</u> form of control is necessary?

4.5 Nested iterations

Since an iteration control clause can appear in a sequence
of algorithm steps just as a simple step might, there is an
opportunity to compose iterative statements, by including a
second iteration within the scope of control of a previous
iteration clause. When this happens, we say that the iterations
are <u>nested</u>. Nested iterations, when properly used, enable some
fairly complicated algorithms to be stated quite succinctly. The
following example is one in which trial and error will help us to
arrive at a solution. It involves computation with an iteration
of trials, using the result of each trial to improve the estimate
of the desired solution.

Example 4.5.1 -- Mortgage loans

The terms of a mortgage loan differ from those of simpler
consumer or business loans in that the amount of interest
paid in each monthly payment is calculated as a fixed per-

centage of the unpaid balance, rather than as a percentage of the total amount borrowed. In spite of the fact that the amount of interest paid declines from one month to the next, the amount of each monthly payment is to remain constant. Thus, in the first years of a mortgage, the payments are largely devoted to interest, while during the final year, the interest due is comparatively small and the payments are mostly applied to retirement of the principal.

A problem faced by a mortgage banker is the following. Given a rate of interest to be paid on the balance of the principal outstanding, and given a duration over which the mortagage is to be retired, how large should the monthly payments be, per $1000 borrowed?

We may not know how to solve this problem directly, but we can solve a somewhat different, although closely related problem. Given a fixed rate of interest and a fixed amount of each monthly payment, we can calculate the balance remaining after some specified number of monthly payments has been made. This can be done simply by calculating the actual amount to be paid in interest each month, subtracting this amount from the total monthly payment to determine the amount applied to reduce the balance, and thereby obtaining the new balance to be used in the calculation for the following month. If we let Balance represent the unpaid amount of the principal, Rate be the monthly rate of interest, Interest be the actual interest to be paid in a specific month, and Duration be the number of months in which the loan is to be repaid, the calculation of the final balance remaining would be:

```
for Month := 1 to Duration

    Interest := Rate*Balance;
    Balance := Balance - (Payment - Interest)
```

To gain a better understanding of the problem, one might carry out the above calculation, using initial values of Rate = .1, Balance = 1000, Payment = 150. This yields the following table, showing the accelerating rate at which the balance is retired.

Month	Interest	Balance	Payment − Interest
1	100.00	950.00	50.00
2	95.00	895.00	55.00
3	89.50	834.50	60.50
4	83.45	767.95	66.55
5	76.79	694.74	73.21
6	69.47	614.21	80.53
7	61.42	525.63	88.58
8	52.56	428.19	97.44
9	42.82	321.01	107.18
10	32.10	203.11	117.90
11	20.31	73.42	129.69
12	7.34	−69.24	142.66

If, after execution of the above program segment, the final value of Balance is not zero (or nearly zero), it means that the value guessed for the equal monthly payments was not correct. A positive final balance indicates that the payments have been too small, a negative value that they have been to large. What is needed is some way to systematically improve the guess of a value for the monthly payment. Then the calculation of the balance remaining after repayment can be iterated until the desired goal is achieved, that is, until a monthly payment is obtained that will enable the balance to be reduced to zero in the desired time.

Unfortunately, we may never be lucky enough to calculate a payment that will leave the balance exactly zero after the desired number of months. However, if the balance remaining was very small, say give or take 10 cents per 1000 dollars of the original loan, few people would quibble. So in the iteration control clause, we shall use this criterion to determine when to stop the trial-and-error process. Since it is immaterial whether the remaining balance is positive or negative so long as it is less than 10 cents, we shall use the condition of a negligibly small balance to control the iteration of a trial-and-error search for a solution.

At this point, a description of the partially formulated algorithm by means of an iteration graph will be helpful.

trial and error:

```
Guess a value for the monthly Payment

        calculate the final value of
            Balance after repayment;
        adjust the estimate of the
            monthly Payment

until Abs (Balance) < 0.10
```

Next, we must face the problem of how to refine an initial guess for the monthly payment. We have seen that the monthly payment consists of interest plus amortization. We have no direct control over the amount of interest that is due; it depends on the interest rate and the current balance to be repaid. However, the amount devoted to amortization, or retirement of the principal amount, is a parameter that can be adjusted. We should like to subject the adjustment of the amortization amount to an important constraint, that it should always be greater than zero. Since the amount of the payment available for amortization will increase as the balance (and therefore the interest owed) decreases, it is only the first month's amortization that must be constrained.

There are two obvious ways to adjust the value of InitialAmort, the variable whose value is the first month's amortization. One way is to add to it a positive or negative correction factor. In adding a correction, we run the risk that a large negative correction might leave the value of InitialAmort negative, in violation of our constraint. Multiplication by a positive factor, on the other hand, cannot change the sign of InitialAmort, although it can change its magnitude.

A suitable correction factor should turn out to have the value one in case the final value of the Balance is zero after repayment. If the final Balance is positive, the loan has been retired too slowly, and the correction factor to apply to InitialAmort should be larger than one, otherwise the correction factor should be a fraction less than one. We summarize these conditions in the following table:

90

When the final Balance is	the principal has been retired	and the correction factor of Initial-Amort should be:
positive zero negative	too slowly correctly too rapidly	greater than 1 equal to 1 less than 1

A suitable expression for the correction factor is

$$2000 \ / \ (2000 - \text{Balance})$$

This expression will take values between 0 and 2 as the final Balance varies between negative infinity and 1000. Since the intent of our constraint was that the value of Balance should never exceed the initial value of 1000, the expression given above appears to satisfy the requirements.

We can refine the iteration graph describing the trial-and-error process of approximating the correct value for the monthly Payment, taking notice of the fact that InitialAmort is the variable to which an adjustment is applied most directly. This iteration graph can also describe the calculation of the first month's interest and of an initial guess for the amortization in the first month. Since any positive value should do, we make a naive estimate that ignores the fact that the monthly value of Interest is expected to decline as the loan is repaid. This estimate is

$$\text{InitialAmort} := 1000 \ / \ \text{Duration}$$

The refined iteration graph becomes

trial and error:

```
InitialInterest := 1000 * Rate;
InitialAmort := 1000 / Duration;

    Balance := 1000;
    Payment := InitialInterest + InitialAmort;
    calculate the final value of Balance after
        repayment;
    InitialAmort := InitialAmort *
                2000 / (2000 - Balance)

until Abs(Balance) < 0.10
```

91

At this point, the iteration graph is sufficiently detailed that we can check it for completeness. The step called "calculate the final value of Balance after repayment" is to be replaced by the iteration graph previously composed.

Two variables require initial values before the computation can be carried out. These are Rate and Duration, whose values are to be furnished as input data. However, the units in which they would normally be given by a banker are not the same as the units used in the algorithm. The rate of interest charged for a mortgage is customarily given in percent per year. In the algorithm, Rate has been assumed to be a fraction of the Balance, yielding the interest per month. To convert from percent to a fraction, we divide by 100, and to convert from a yearly to a monthly rate, we must divide again by 12. Similarly, the Duration of a mortgage loan would be expressed in years, whereas we have assumed it to be in units of months. This is corrected by multiplying the input value by 12. The process of units correction is known as scaling. Our main iteration graph should be preceded by the operations of data input and scaling:

Input and scaling:

```
Read (Rate, Duration);
Rate := Rate / 1200;
Duration := Duration * 12
```

Both the Rate and Duration must have positive values; they should be checked when they are read. Also, the final value of Payment should be output. After putting together the component iteration graphs, we obtain the Pascal program given on the next page.

Self-check questions:

1. When iteration statements are nested, what determines the scope of control of each iteration clause?

2. Suppose that in a particular run of the program Mortgage-Payment, the body of the repeat ... until statement is executed six times. If the value of Duration is 120 (months) how many times will the following statement be executed?

   Interest := Rate * Balance

92

```pascal
program MortgagePayment (Input, Output);
  (***********************************************************
  *  Calculates the monthly payment needed to repay a mortgage *
  *     loan, given the interest rate and duration.          *
  *  Balance -- unpaid balance outstanding each month,       *
  *              initially 10000                             *
  *  Interest -- the amount of interest due each month       *
  *  Payment -- the amount of each monthly payment           *
  *  InitialInterest -- first month's interest              *
  *  InitialAmort -- amount of the first month's payment     *
  *                      available for amortization          *
  ***********************************************************)
var
  Month, Duration : Integer;
  Rate, Balance, Interest, Payment, InitialInterest,
    InitialAmort : Real;
begin
  Read (Rate, Duration);
  Writeln ('INTEREST RATE : ', Rate, '% PER YEAR. DURATION = ',
          Duration, ' YEARS.');
  Rate := Rate / 1200;  Duration := Duration * 12;
  if (Rate <= 0) or (Duration <= 0) then
    Writeln ('A NEGATIVE RATE OR DURATION IS NOT ALLOWED.')
  else
    begin
      InitialInterest := 1000 * Rate;
      InitialAmort := 1000 / Duration;
      repeat
        Balance := 1000;
        Payment := InitialInterest + InitialAmort;
        for Month := 1 to Duration do
            begin
              Interest := Rate * Balance;
              Balance := Balance - (Payment - Interest);
            end;
        InitialAmort := InitialAmort * 2000/(2000 - Balance);
      until Abs(Balance) < 0.10;
      Writeln ('THE REQUIRED MONTHLY PAYMENT IS ', Payment);
    end;
end.
```

EXERCISES FOR CHAPTER 4

4.1 Instead of repeated subtraction, one could make use of the integer division functions, <u>div</u> and <u>mod</u>, in an algorithm for the greatest common divisor of two numbers. Give such an algorithm as a Pascal program.

4.2 Compose an algorithm for the least common multiple of a pair of integers.

4.3 A well-known sequence in number theory is the Fibonacci sequence,

$$0, 1, 1, 2, 3, 5, 8, 13, 21, 34, 55, 89, 144, \ldots$$

This sequence is defined by a recurrence relation, after specifying the first two terms;

$F_0 = 0,$

$F_1 = 1,$

$F_{n+1} = F_n + F_{n-1}, \text{ for } n > 0.$

Compose an algorithm to compute and print the first 45 terms of the Fibonacci sequence.

4.4 Compose an algorithm to find all of the perfect squares that occur within a given interval of the positive integers.

4.5 What is the largest integer less than 100 whose square is the sum of the squares of two other integers? What is the second largest? Is there an integer less than 100 whose cube is the sum of the cubes of two other integers?

4.6 There are some sequences of values that can be generated in a regular manner and which tend to a limit. In some cases, the sequences are infinite, as is the sequence of reciprocal integers, 1/1, 1/2, 1/3, 1/4, 1/5, 1/6 ... which tends to the limit 0 as the integers tend towards infinity. If a sequence is generated by substitution of successive arguments of a function, its limit can sometimes be used to compute values of the function that could not be calculated by conventional means. From each of the following functions, generate a finite sequence that approaches a limiting value. From the sequence, estimate the value of each function at the limit point specified.

a) $\dfrac{\sin x}{x}$ as x -> 0;

b) x ln(x) as x -> 0;

c) $\dfrac{\ln(x)}{x-1}$ as x -> 1;

d) $\dfrac{e^{-x^2/2} - 1}{x^2}$ as x -> 0.

In each case, display the results in the form of a table of values of the argument and values of the function. Then give your estimate of the limiting value of each sequence.

4.7 Compound interest means that a bank will reinvest the interest payments it makes to depositors at regular intervals, and by crediting the interest payment to the depositor's account, that sum in turn is used as part of the balance on which interest is computed during the next interval. Compute the accumulation of funds in a savings account with an initial balance of $1000, drawing interest at the rate of 6% per year, over 20 years if the interest is compounded

   a) yearly;
   b) quarterly;
   c) monthly;
   d) weekly;
   e) daily.

Give the accumulation in the form of tables, showing the balance in the account initially and at the end of each year. If interest is compounded quarterly, what is the effect of reducing interest to 3% per year? Of doubling it to 12% per year? Is the balance after 20 years altered in direct proportion to the rate of interest paid?

Recently, some banks have advertised that they offer continuous compounding of interest. This does not mean that they run their computers continuously, at least not on interest calculations. There is a mathematical function, the exponential function e^x, that has the property that upon increasing x by a small amount, δ, the value of

95

$e^{x+\delta}$ exceeds the value of e^x by an amount δe^x. Thus, if x is allowed to represent the rate of interest multiplied by the time in years since the original deposit, the value of $e^{rate*time}$ gives the factor of expansion of the principal using continuous compounding. (Pascal has a built-in function, Exp ( ), which evaluates the exponential function.) The calculation is not made continuously, but only for those discrete time values at which one wants to know the balance. Calculate the accumulation of a 1000 dollar savings account over 20 years, at 6% interest compounded continuously. If interest was compounded yearly, what equivalent rate of interest would produce the same growth of the balance as does 6% interest compounded continuously?

4.8 An infinite sum has a value if the sequence formed by the finite partial sums of the first n terms (n = 1, 2, 3, ...) approaches a limiting value as n tends to infinity. Write a program to investigate the sequence formed by the finite partial sum of each of the following infinite sums:

a) $\displaystyle\sum_{n=0} \frac{1}{n!}$

b) $\displaystyle\sum_{n=1} \frac{1}{n}$

c) $\displaystyle\sum_{n=1} (-)^{n-1}\frac{1}{n}$

4.9 An infinite power series provides a means of specifying a function, since for each value of the argument, it defines an infinite sum. If the infinite sum has a value, then the value of the function is given by the sum for that particular value of the argument. If the sum does not have a value, then it may be that the function is undefined for that particular value of its argument, or it may simply be that the power series does not correspond to the function for the argument. Evaluate the infinite sums given by the following power series at values of the arguments of 0, 1/2, 1, and 2, and try to guess the function to which each series corresponds.

a) $\sum_{n = 0} \dfrac{x^n}{n!}$

b) $\sum_{\text{odd } n = 1} \dfrac{(-)^{(n-1)/2} x^n}{n!}$

c) $\sum_{n = 1} \dfrac{(1 - x)^n}{n}$

4.10 Newton's method can be extended to find integral roots other than square roots. The reciprocal estimates of the nth root of N become X, and N/X^{n-1}. Compose an algorithm to evaluate integral roots by Newton's method. Does it require more or fewer iterations to achieve comparable accuracy in evaluating the 5th root of two as it does to evaluate the square root of two? Compare the rates of convergence for other powers and other arguments.

4.11 Use mathematical reasoning to verify that in any single evaluation by Newton2 of Example 4.4.1, at most one of the statements X := 8*X and X := X/8 that are controlled by the <u>while</u> clauses will be executed, although whichever statement is executed may be repeated.

4.12 Compose an alogrithm which will read a sequence of N integers (where N is to be read first, and must be positive) and will select and print the largest of the values read (not including N).

5 TELLING THE COMPUTER ABOUT THE DATA

Up to this point, we have described computations involving individual variables taking values that are integers, real numbers, or Boolean truth values. Any particular variable is only used to represent values from one of these types, however. We can associate with each variable a property, or attribute describing the set of possible values that variable is allowed to take. This attribute is called the data type of the variable, and its use is to guide us (and the computer) in making proper interpretations of operations on the program variables. In Pascal, there are a number of mechanisms that can be used to define data types, including explicitly listing a set of values, specifying a range of values from a type previously defined, and the use of type composition to build compound data types out of previously defined types. It will require some investment of time and effort to learn how to utilize the data types of Pascal to good advantage, but this investment will pay off handsomely by increasing your knowledge and skill in designing algorithms.

5.1 Simple types

We can divide the Pascal data types immediately into two categories, simple or compound, according to whether a variable of the type takes a single value or is composed of an ensemble of values. The simple types start from those that we regard as elementary. These are called scalar types, and consist of the predeclared types Integer, Real, Boolean, and Char, plus the class of user-defined scalar types. Type Integer consists of the machine-representable integer numbers, both positive and negative, and type Real consists of a finite set of floating-point numbers that provide us with an approximation to the continuum

type

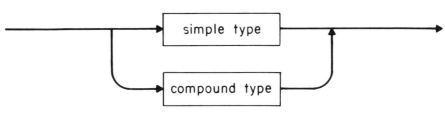

simple type

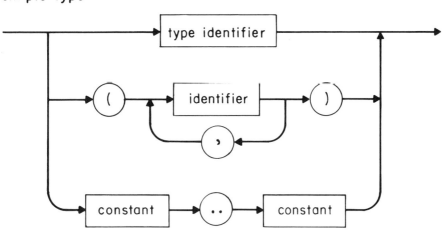

of real numbers of mathematics. You have already gained some experience with the use of these arithmetic data types, as well as with the scalar type Boolean. The values of type Char are just the individual characters that comprise the character set accepted by the computer. Because of a failure to standardize character sets in the earliest days of computers, there persist today a number of different character sets in use, but the commonest of these are called by the acronyms ASCII and EBCDIC. It is likely that the type Char implemented on the computer that you will use agrees with one of these.

A user-defined scalar type consists of a set of identifiers that are declared to be its members. These identifiers have the status of constants of the declared scalar type, whenever they appear subsequently in the program. An example of a scalar type definition is

        type ShirtSizetype = (Small, Medium, Large, XLarge);

99

The predeclared scalar types differ from the user-defined scalar types only in that certain operations are defined upon some predeclared types. In particular, the elementary arithmetic operations are defined on values of types Integer and Real, and logical operations are defined upon Boolean values. All the scalar types have in common the properties that each is finite, and each is ordered. Values of arithmetic types are ordered numerically. In type Boolean, the ordering is False < True, which is consistent with the axioms of Boolean algebra. The ordering of type Char is more nearly arbitrary; it is imposed by the computer's internal representation of the character set. However, any of the character sets in use preserves the relative ordering among alphabetic characters, and among decimal numerals. The ordering of values in a user-defined scalar type is completely arbitrary. It is the order in which the constants of the type are listed in the type definition.

5.1.1 Subrange types

From any simple type other than Real, a range of values may be specified by giving the least- and largest-ordered values of the range. Such a designation may be used as a type, called a subrange type. Designating a subrange informs the reader of a program that only certain values from a scalar type are intended to be used in a particular context, or by a particular variable. In addition, the Pascal compiler will check that values assigned to a variable of a subrange type do indeed lie within the specified range. These checks catch a great many programming errors that might otherwise be much more difficult to find. Some examples of subrange types are

```
type  OneToTen = 1..10;   (* a subrange of Integer *)
      Alphabet = 'A'..'Z';   (* a subrange of Char *)
```

5.2 The functions Pred( ) and Succ( )

Each of the simple types (except the Pointer types) has the property that its values are ordered, yet only the arithmetic and Boolean types have associated operations that act on values to produce new values. To make it easier to utilize the ordering of values of non-arithmetic scalar types, Pascal provides a pair of predefined functions, called Pred( ) and Succ( ). These functions give the values of the elements preceding or following the argument value in the ordered set of values of a scalar type. They apply also to type Integer (but not to type Real) where they are defined to be

$$Pred(K) = K - 1, \text{ and } Succ(K) = K + 1.$$

100

On other scalar types, Pred( ) and Succ( ) are defined by the order of enumeration of values. For instance, in type Char, we have

$$Pred('B') = 'A', \text{ and } Succ('B') = 'C'.$$

When the argument given to Pred( ) is the first value of the scalar type, the result of applying the function is undefined; similarly, Succ( ) applied to the last value yields an undefined result. Pred( ) and Succ( ) can also be applied to variables of subrange types, but in case the argument value is the initial or the final value of the range, the result may be outside of the subrange. These functions are useful primarily in conjunction with iteration over the values of a scalar type or a subrange.

Self-check questions

1. What is the value of Pred(10)? of Pred(0)?

2. What is the value of Succ(False)? of Succ(True)?

3. If X is a value from a scalar type, what is the value of Pred(Succ(X))? What if X is the highest-ordered value of the type?

5.3 Compound data types

As the name implies, compound data types are formed by composition of simpler components into a composite structure. A compound data type is employed in a program when a sequence of values is to be subjected to a common set of manipulations, or when several values are related to one another as attributes of a common object. In Pascal there are four classes of compound types: arrays, files, records, and sets.

5.3.1 Array types

An array is an indexed sequence of elements, each belonging to a common component type. The syntax of an array type definition is given by the following syntax chart, in which the last box denotes the component type, and the simple type defines the set of index values. The number of array elements is the cardinality of the simple type by which the array is indexed.

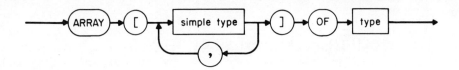

A component of an array can be used as an individual
variable of the component type, but it must be referred to by
applying a value from the index type to the name of the array.
Thus, for instance, if Realarray is the name of a variable whose
type is

    <u>array</u> [1..10] <u>of</u> Real

then we would refer to the fifth element by the notation
Realarray[5]. The index value could also be given by a variable
or expression belonging to the same scalar type as the index
type. Then if K were a variable of type Integer (or of type
1..10) and held the value 5, the reference Realarray[K] would
denote the same component variable as does Realarray[5].

    The component type of an array may be any Pascal data type,
and in particular, may be another compound type, even another
array type. Also, as the syntax chart indicates, there may be
more than one index type given in an array type definition. When
two or more index types are given, the set of index values is
formed by taking the cartesian product of the separate index
types. This means that an index value may be an ordered pair, or
a triple, or a quadruple, ... of individual scalar values, with
one value taken from each of the index types. In analogy to the
way that the cartesian product of scalar number spaces forms a
higher-dimensional space, we refer to arrays with more than one
index type as multi-dimensional arrays. By way of illustration,
suppose that the variable IntMatrix is of type

    array [1..10, Char] of Integer

Then a component of Intmatrix must be specified by an index that
consists of a value from 1 .. 10, paired with a value from type
Char. For instance, Intmatrix[5, 'C'] would be a valid component
reference.

    When an array is defined with a component type that is
itself an array, the effect is exactly identical to the definition of a multi-dimensional array. For instance, the array
variable Intmatrix could have been given the type

```
array [1..10] of
    array [Char] of Integer
```

and the effect would have been the same as that of the
two-dimensional type definition given previously. This similarity
carries over to the form of the array references as well. No
matter which of the two forms above was used to define the type
of IntMatrix, both of the reference forms IntMatrix[5, 'C'], and
IntMatrix[5]['C'] would be valid, and equivalent to one another.
Also, the reference IntMatrix[5], in which only the first index
component is given, refers to a component variable whose type is

```
array [Char] of Integer
```

Self-check questions:

1.   Give a type definition for an array of 80 characters.

2.   What is meant by a three-dimensional array type?

3.   (a) How many integer values can be held by a variable of
     the type
         `array [1..10, -2..2] of Integer` ?

     (b) If V is a variable of this type, what is the type of the
     component variable referred to by V[5] ?

     (c) How would you refer to the individual integer component
     indexed by the pair of values 5, 2 ?

5.3.2 Record types

When data that describe real-world objects are entered into
a computer, the commonest means of representation of an object is
by a list of attribute values that are to be associated with the
object. For example, some of the physical characteristics of a
person that might be useful in a description would be height,
weight, color of hair, eyes and skin, the person's age and sex.
If appropriate values of these attributes were associated with an
abstract identification of the person, such as his or her name,
the aggregate collection of data would constitute a record
describing the person. In Pascal, you can also define a compound
type that gives the template of a data record. Each of the components that will hold an individual attribute value is called a
field. The fields of a record need not all be of the same type,
as are the components of an array, but instead are given indivi-

dual identifiers, as are variables, and their types are individually declared. A list of field declarations, bracketed between the keywords <u>record</u> and <u>end</u> constitutes a record type definition.

compound type

For example, a record type suitable for holding the values of physical attributes of a person might be:

<u>record</u>
    Name : <u>array</u> [1..24] <u>of</u> Char;
    Height, Weight : 0..300;
    Haircolor, Eyecolor, Skincolor :
        (Black, Blond, Blue, Brown, Green, Grey, Hazel,
        Red, White);
    Age : 0..100;
    Sex : (Female, Male);
<u>end</u>

The fields of a variable of this type would be used just as are ordinary variables, but they can only be referred to by using the name of the record variable. This name is qualified with the field name, separated by a dot, in order to designate which field is to be referred to. For instance, if there were declared a variable, Sportstar, of the record type given above, then the field references

    Sportstar.Name, Sportstar.Haircolor, Sportstar.Age

would all be valid, and each of these references could be used as an individual variable in an assignment statement or an expression.

Self-check questions:

1.   How do record types differ from array types?

2.   What is meant by a field of a record type? How many fields appear in the record type definition of the preceding example?

3. Referring to the example, give an assignment statement to set the value Female into the appropriate field of the record variable Sportstar.

5.3.3 File types

In data processing applications, it is often necessary to store a sequence of data items for subsequent reference, frequently for reference by another program. The variety of schemes employed in storage of data and their retrieval represent one of the more complicated technological aspects of computing. However, in Pascal, a simple and commonly used technique for data storage has been standardized in the form of a compound data type. The Pascal <u>file</u> types can be used to define sequential files of component values, all belonging to the same component type.

The adjective "sequential" implies that the storage of data items must be done in sequence, from the first to the last, and that values retrieved from the file can only be taken in the same order in which they were originally stored. This is one respect in which a file type differs from an array type, for elements of an array can be accessed in any order, merely by specifying the desired index values. Another way in which a file type differs from an array is that its length is not bounded. Any number of components can be put into a file; it simply grows in length to accomodate new entries. The third aspect of a file that is unlike any other compound type is that a file variable may be declared to be external to the program, and if so, its values may be preserved indefinitely, with the aid of one or another of the mass storage media available on a computer system.

The syntax of a file type definition is given by

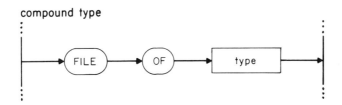

compound type

where the component type may be any Pascal type except another file type, or a type containing a file as a component. Variables of a file type maybe declared, just as is the case with other compound types, but a file variable cannot be directly referenced in an expression, or assigned a value. Instead, for each file variable, there is an associated variable of the component type called the file buffer, which can be referred to or assigned directly. The file buffer is denoted by the name of the file variable with the symbol ↑ appended onto it. For instance, if F is the name of a file variable, then F↑ is the associated file buffer.

Pascal provides a pair of predefined procedures, Put( ) and Get( ), to perform transactions between the file buffer and the file itself. These functions take the name of a file as their argument. The effect of Put(F) is to transfer the value held in the file buffer to the file, appending that value at the end of the file. Get(F) does the opposite, taking the next component from file F and copying its value into the file buffer. Put(F) obviously alters the state of the file variable by appending a new component; Get(F) does not alter the file, however.

We can illustrate the use of the buffer variable by giving a program segment to read a sequence of positive integers and write them to a file. Suppose that F has been declared to be

        var F : file of Integer

and that K is an integer variable. Then the segment

```
        Read (K);
        while K > 0 do
            begin
                F↑ := K; Put(F);
                Read (K);
            end
```

will continue to read integer values from the input and store them into file F until either a zero or a negative value is encountered in the input sequence. To reverse the process, the file must be readied for input, and then a similar iteration of Get(F) operations can be executed.

Notice that in the program segment given above, there is no index or other identification used to distinguish one file component from another. How does the computer keep track of which component in a file is to be selected for input or output? The logical behavior of file operations can be understood in terms of a hidden variable that can refer to the relative position of a component in the sequence. This variable, which we shall call the file pointer, marks the position in the file of the component available in the file buffer variable. The file pointer itself is not directly accessible by a Pascal program; it is only utilized

106

by the standard procedures Put( ) and Get( ). Whenever a new component is to be appended to the file by a Put( ) operation, the file pointer should refer to the end of the file. When a Put( ) is executed, the new component is appended at the place indicated by the file pointer, and the file pointer is updated so that it indicates the end of the extended file.

At the conclusion of output to a file, the file pointer will always point to the end of the file. Therefore, before component values can be read by a program from the file, the file pointer must be reset to indicate the beginning of the file. Pascal furnishes a status function, and two additional procedures that operate on file variables, and whose action can be understood in terms of the file pointer.

It is important to be able to determine when the file pointer refers to the end of a file, for although one can count on this fact after performing a Put( ), it is also necessary to know when the end of a file has been reached as a consequence of a sequence of Get( ) operations. A Boolean-valued function, Eof( ), will return a value of True or False according to whether or not the current position of the file pointer is at the end of a file.

Regardless of where the file pointer is positioned, it can be repositioned to indicate the beginning of the file by executing the operation Reset( ). This is performed to ready a file for input. Analogously, there is an operator which readies a file to receive new contents. This operation, Rewrite( ), positions the file pointer at the beginning of an empty file, with the end-of-file condition true. If the file had previously contained values, these would be lost when the Rewrite operation is performed.

Assuming that the file F had been filled with values by the program segment of the preceding example, we can now give a program segment that will recover the sequence of values and cause them to be printed.

```
Reset (F);  (* prepares the file to supply input *)
while not Eof(F) do
    begin
        K := F↑; Write (K);
        Get (F);
    end
```

107

Actually, the use of the program variable K is these examples was superfluous. The file buffer variable F↑ could have appeared directly in the argument lists of the Read and Write procedures.

Self-check questions:

1. How many component values can be contained by a file variable?

2. What are the four operators defined as predeclared procedures for file types?

3. What is the significance of the Boolean function Eof( )?

4. What is meant by the file buffer? By the file pointer?

5. Give a Pascal program segment that will cause the file pointer to be positioned at the end of a file (assuming that it is not so positioned initially) and store the value of a variable X as a new file component.

5.3.4 Set types

In certain applications, it is useful to characterize an individual object by means of yes-or-no answers to a set of questions. This technique is widely employed in market research, for instance. A brief set of questions about individuals might be:

a) Over 30 years of age?
b) Male?
c) Personal income in excess of $15,000 per annum?
d) Homeowner?
e) Automobile owner?
f) Attended college?
g) Union member?

Such simple questions are not used to obtain a detailed description of a particular individual, but rather to enable quick identification of those individuals whose characteristics are believed to correlate favorably with the ability and inclination to purchase particular products. To record the answers to these questions about an individual, one could resort to a data representation in the form of an array of Boolean components, or to a record containing fields that take Boolean values. Since all of the values to be recorded are Boolean, however, an even simpler representation is possible.

Recalling that the mathematical notion of a set is simply a collection of abstract objects, we might let the questions of the example be the abstract objects of our representation, and include in a set that describes the properties of an individual, all of those questions to which his or her answer was affirmative. This type of representation is particularly compact in the computer, since the only thing that must be retained is a single binary unit of information (a <u>bit</u>) to denote each of the possible abstract objects.

Before continuing the illustration, let us investigate the compound type of Pascal that is used to represent finite sets of abstract objects. The syntax of this type definition is:

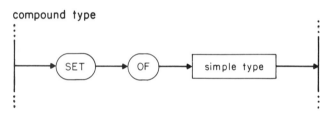

where the simple type serves to provide names for the abstract objects that are to be represented.

For the example given above, in which the abstract objects are questions indexed by letters of the alphabet, a suitable type definition would be

        set of 'A'..'G'

in which the letters A to G serve as the names of the objects. The set constant given by ['B', 'C', 'E', 'F'] would represent a set of answers from an individual not over 30, male, earning more than 15,000 dollars per year, who does not own a house, does own an automobile, has attended college and does not belong to a union.

The operators +, -, and * are defined on variables and expressions of set types to mean set union, set subtraction, and set intersection respectively. The operator <u>in</u> relates a value of the element type to a value of a set type and yields a Boolean value, True if the element is a member of the set, and False otherwise.

Set types are potentially very useful tools of data representation, and are a feature of Pascal not found in most other
programming languages. They are not difficult to use, and can be
employed to advantage in the solution of several of the programming exercises. However, since many more programming concepts
remain to be introduced in this book, the author has reluctantly
decided not to develop the use of set types further.

Self-check questions:

1.   How many distinct values of the type

            set of 1..10

      are possible?

2.   Which of the following expressions are valid in Pascal? What
      are their values?
      a) 'G' in [2, 3, 5, 7]
      b) 'G' in ['A', 'B', 'D', 'G']
      c) 'G' in [ ]
      d) 'G' + ['A', 'B', 'D']
      e) ['G'] + ['A', 'B', 'D']
      f) ['G', 'A', 'B', 'D']
      g) [ ] + ['G']

3. What is the value of the set expression

        [1, 5, 7] * [3] ?

5.4 Declarations

The "sentences" of Pascal have distinct kinds of meanings,
also found in sentences of natural languages. In Pascal, a
statement is an imperative sentence; it directs the computer to
carry out a specific computational action, and the Pascal compiler will translate it into primitive instructions intelligible to
the computer. There are also declarative sentences whose sole
purpose is to provide information about the environment in which
statements are to be interpreted. These sentences are called
declarations; they define the names given to constants, to data
types and to variables, and also associate the names with the
definitions of data types. Later in the book, we shall also
encounter declarations that associate names with user-defined
procedures and functions. Each named object (constant, type, or
variable) must have its attributes defined before it can be used
in a program statement. Pascal will not attempt to infer the

attributes of a name from the context of its use, for although such an inference might be helpful in case you have forgotten to declare a variable, it could also be incorrect.

Declarations of names all appear in a $\boxed{\text{block}}$ following the program heading. The syntax of a $\boxed{\text{block}}$, expanded to include declarations of constants and types, as well as variables, is given below.

block

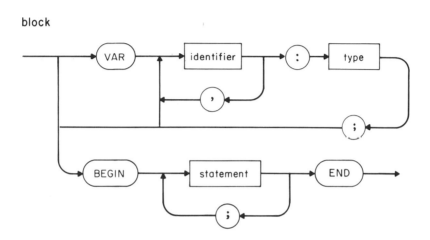

As you can see from the syntax, the declaration part of a $\boxed{\text{block}}$ is very orderly. Since constants may appear in the definition of a type, the declarations of named constants appear first in the $\boxed{\text{block}}$. Since a named type can be used in the declaration of a variable, the type declarations come next after the constants. Then follow the declarations of variables, in order that they can be used in the final section, the statement part. Each of these sections, or program paragraphs, is headed by a reserved keyword that acts as a subtitle to avoid possible confusion.

The use of named constants is optional. Literal constants (explicit numerals or character strings) will do as well, for many purposes. But the use of a named constant, in which an identifier is used as a pseudonym for a literal constant, is often advantageous for two reasons. If a constant value has some meaning in an application, that meaning can often be reflected in a mnemonic name given to the constant, and this can make a program easier to read and understand than would be the case if it

111

were filled with "magic" numbers.

If a constant is actually a parameter of the application, such as a bound on the size of some quantity, and the program is to be used and maintained over some period of time, then the value of the parameter may eventually have to be changed. In order to alter a parameter that has been expressed as a literal constant, one must locate all uses of that constant throughout the text of a program, and alter each instance. If one instance is missed, the program may be made incorrect in the course of being modified. However, if a named constant is used to represent the parameter value, then the only modification needed will be to change the literal value associated with the name in the declaration of the constant. Since the designer of a program will seldom be able to anticipate all modifications ultimately required of it, he will be on the safe side if he makes use of named constants freely.

A type definition can also be given a name, to allow it to be used in more than one declaration of variables. In order to provide syntactic distinction betweem the declaration of a type name and the declaration of a variable belonging to the type, notice that the equals sign is used to separate the name declared for a type from its definition, while a colon is used to separate a list of variable names from their associated type. Experience with large Pascal programs has shown that the use of identifiers both for types and for value-holding variables or constants sometimes makes a program more difficult to read. To avoid the possibility of confusion in a reader's mind, we suggest that names given to types should contain the letters "type" as a suffix of the name.

We have encountered the declarations of variables belonging to the predeclared types of Pascal in the example programs of previous sections. Declarations of variables belonging to user-defined types are no different. Either a type definition, or the name of a previously defined type may be used on the right-hand side of a variable declaration. Types that have the same definition are taken to be equivalent types, even if their names differ.

You may find it helpful to look at a simple example illustrating a sequence of declarations that builds upon previously defined types:

```
const
   Maxhours = 12;
type
   Daytype = (Mon, Tues, Wed, Thurs, Fri, Sat, Sun);
   Weekdaytype = Mon .. Fri;
var
   Day : Daytype;
   Hoursworked : array [Weekdaytype] of 0 .. Maxhours;
```

Self-check questions:

1. What is the difference between a named constant and a literal constant? Why are named constants used in a program?

2. Must every type definition be named in a type declaration?

3. Must every variable used in a Pascal program be declared?

5.5 Using the computer for record-keeping

Although the original motivation for the development of digital computers was to perform scientific calculations rapidly and accurately, the application of computers to tasks involving a large component of record-keeping did not lag far behind. Record-keeping is the principal activity in the immense field of computer usage known as automatic data-processing. We shall investigate the facilities provided by Pascal for such applications. In the process we may learn about some of the standard techniques employed in data-processing, as well as encountering some of the potential sources of difficulty in employing such techniques.

Traditionally, the basic concept in record-keeping is that a record is a description of a real world object. The object to be described may have a manifest reality, as does a person, a building, or a ship, or it may be an abstract object whose reality exists in the minds of men, such as a bank account, a corporation, or the academic record of a college student. The record of an object will usually contain only partial information; it must include those attributes of interest for the intended data-processing applications, and it must include attributes needed to identify the particular object that it describes. These attributes are the individual items of information within a record, and are called fields. A subset of the attributes that enable unique identification of the object is called a key to the record. A collection of records of similar

113

objects is called a file. These are the entities that we shall deal with.

Before we can understand how records may be kept by a computer, it may be helpful to understand how they are usually kept by hand. If you were given the assignment of establishing a set of records, you would probably first try to determine what information would be needed in each record. This would include some means of identification of each object (a key), and a variety of information fields that would be used in the applications anticipated for your record-keeping system. Next, you would decide upon a uniform layout of the desired information fields on a sheet of paper. Planning the layout of a form to be used in record-keeping is important, because a well-designed form will help to prevent errors when data are entered into or retrieved from a record. After designing a suitable form, you might provide for building a file of these records, by designating a drawer in a filing cabinet that is to receive the forms as they are filled in. Exactly analogous steps are followed in setting up a computer-based record-keeping system. Let's consider an example.

Example 5.5.1 -- Designing a file of sports records

Suppose that you have been assigned by the sports editor of your local newspaper to set up a file of information about professional boxing champions, present and past. In consultation with the editor, you decide that the important information about a boxing champion should include some personal data about him, a statistical summary of his boxing record, and some data about each title that he has held.

The personal data are to include his name, year of birth, year deceased (in case he is no longer living), his nationality, and his height and weight. The year of birth has been selected in preference to giving his age, for two reasons. If he is deceased, the age is not meaningful, and in any case, the age that is recorded will be dependent on when the record was created, rather than on the current age of the person. Other values (the weight in particular) may be inaccurate, or may vary over the life span of a boxer. They are included, nevertheless, as items of interest to your editor. Other possible items of information, such as the sex of the person, are omitted (in this case because ladies' boxing has not yet caught on widely as a professional sport).

The boxing record is separated from the personal data as a subfield, since it constitutes a distinct conceptual unit of information. It will contain four values: the number of professional fights, the number of these that were won, that were lost, and that were won by knockouts.

Finally, the record of each championship that the boxer has held is listed as a distinct subfield. It contains the weight class in which the title was won, the year in which it was won, the year in which it was surrendered, and the name of the fighter defeated in gaining the title. It may seem as if the weight class is redundant information that could be inferred from the weight given for the boxer. It is, in fact, not redundant, for some of the most outstanding boxers have held titles in successively heavier weight classes as they matured, and a few have held multiple titles simultaneously. Since a fighter may have held more than one title during his career, there may be multiple instances of the championship subfield in his record.

Given these specifications, you might design the format of a paper record as shown in Figure 5.1. The decision to allow for up to three Championship subfields is made as a matter of convenience, as three happen to fit conveniently onto a single sheet of paper. If fewer than three are required in most cases, there will have been no waste, for a record would have required a sheet of paper in any case. In those few cases of a boxer who has held more than three championships in his career, it will be necessary to append a second sheet to his record. In order to designate these cases, the small box marked "Extension follows" has been inserted at the bottom of the record template. This information field has no direct relationship to the object that is being described; it is merely an artifact of the record-keeping system.

After securing approval of the form from the sports editor, the remaining steps in creating a manually maintained file are to designate a storage drawer, to reproduce blank copies of the form, and to begin searching for data to be entered into the records. As each record is completed, it is placed into the file drawer to become a part of the permanent file.

Let's see how the same process of file design and creation would be done with the computer, using the data types afforded by Pascal. We can use the template of the paper record as a guide to the design of a record template for the computer. The template itself will be given as the definition of a Pascal record type. Whereas in laying out the paper record, we were concerned with the placement of information fields on the page, for the computer record we need only give the data type of each field, from which the Pascal compiler will determine the amount of storage that it is to be allocated in the internal memory of the computer.

As we inspect the list of individual attributes to be recorded, we see that there are just three classes of values. A name, which must be represented by a sequence of characters, is one; another is a number between zero and some maximum value, and the third is a year, ranging between a time in the 19th century when formal rules were adopted for boxing matches, and some time in the future when our file will no longer be actively maintained. We begin our task by identifying some important constants:

```
const Maxnumber = 300;
      Firstyear = 1850;
      Eternity = 2000;
```

The value 300 was selected because it is believed to be large enough to bound the number of professional fights of any boxer, as well as his height and weight (whether given in English or metric units). In terms of these values, we can declare some named types:

```
type  Nametype = array [1..24] of Char;
      Numbertype = 0 .. Maxnumber;
      Yeartype = Firstyear .. Eternity;
```

Although the restriction of names to 24 characters is somewhat arbitrary, the value 24 has not been made a named constant because it will not be used as a computational value. Nevertheless, once a file is created, the decision to restrict names to 24 characters may become extraordinarily difficult to change, for to change it will require modification of every record in the file, as well as modification of every program that utilizes these records.

The subfields of a boxer's record can themselves be declared to be of record types. However, since these types are only to appear as subordinate records of the principal

116

Name: _____

Nationality: _____

Height: _____   Weight: _____

Date of birth: ____   Date deceased: ____

Fight record

    Number   Number   Number   Number
    fought:____ won: ____ lost: ____ kayoed:____

Championship

    Weight class: _____

    Year won: ____   Year lost: ____

    Fighter defeated for title: _____

Championship

    Weight class: _____

    Year won: ____   Year lost: ____

    Fighter defeated for title: _____

Championship

    Weight class: _____

    Year won: ____   Year lost: ____

    Fighter defeated for title: _____

Extension follows: __

Figure 5.1 -- Layout of a paper record of a boxing champion

117

record type, they need not be declared separately. Notice that the subrecord Championship is declared to be an array of instances of a record type, to allow for multiple instances of this field.

```
Boxertype =
    record
        Name, Nationality : Nametype;
        Height, Weight : Numbertype;
        YearOfBirth, YearDeceased : Yeartype;
        FightRecord :
            record
                NumberFought, NumberWon,
                NumberLost, NumberKayoed : Numbertype
            end;
        Championship : array [1..3] of
            record
                WeightClass : (Bantam, Fly, Light, Welter,
                                Middle, LightHeavy, Heavy);
                YearWon, YearLost : Yeartype;
                FighterDefeated : Nametype
            end;
        ExtensionFollows : Boolean
    end
```

This type declaration is the template for the computer managed record, analogous to the template for the paper record illustrated in Figure 5.1. It is more difficult to read, for it is less explicit in giving the visual appearance of a record, but it is more precise in that the data type of each field and subfield is given. The boxer's weight class is specified, for instance, as a user-defined scalar type.

There are still some questions to be resolved in the interpretation of computer-based records. For instance, if there is no information present in one of the fields of a paper record, that field is ordinarily left blank. In the computer-based record we do not have the option of "leaving the field blank", for we are not starting with a blank sheet of paper. If the contents of a field are to be given a value to indicate that no meaningful information is present, then this value must be explicitly designated as such. For the fields whose type is an array of characters, an appropriate value is a string of blank characters. For numeric fields, the decision requires a little more thought. In this

118

example, zero is an unreasonable value for most of the numeric fields (with the possible exception of NumberLost and NumberKayoed in the fight record). Therefore we can use zero to represent missing numeric information in fields of Numbertype. For the fields that represent years, the constant Eternity, a pseudonym for a year far in the future, will be a suitable choice for an invalid entry. No provision has been made for a special value to be used as an invalid entry in the WeightClass field. Instead, a user of the record will have to surmise that if the field called YearWon contains an invalid entry, then the WeightClass field within the same Championship subfield is of no consequence. These are some of the problems accompanying the use of computer-based records that do not occur when paper records are used.

After securing the approval of the sports editor for the suggested record template, our next task is to allocate a file for storing these records. This is a two-step process. The easier step is to declare the existence of such a file in our Pascal programs. This involves a declaration

var BoxerFile : file of Boxertype;

and if the file is to be stored permanently by the computer system, the name BoxerFile must also be mentioned in the list of identifiers in the program heading. The second step is to inform the computer system of our intention to create this file. Unfortunately, the method used to carry out this step is particular to each computer system, and therefore, we cannot illustrate it here.

Pascal has made the declaration of record formats very convenient for us. However, the use of files of applications-tailored data types, while convenient for student programs and for small or short-lived applications, offers some disadvantages in commercial practice. The reasons are that files of data in large, commercial applications may have to be processed by many different programs, over a period of years of useful lifetime, and may even have to be interpreted by a number of different computer systems.

The need for interpretation of files by various programs running on different systems argues strongly in favor of standardization of file formats, to whatever degree can be agreed upon, rather than specialization of formats to each application. Therefore, in commercial practice, the design of records contain-

119

ing fields of numerical data types, or of user-defined scalar types, is avoided. Instead, a more common practice is to translate all data into character string formats, and to restrict data fields to be character strings of appropriate fixed lengths. Character strings can be interpreted by any computer system, even though different computers may use different conventions for the internal representation of data.

Even this degree of standardization does not avoid all sources of difficulty, for the lengths and formats of character strings must still be made known to every program that is to interpret a given record type. A modern trend, as yet not standardized, is to include within each file itself a special record of information that describes the formats of all succeeding records in the file. The obstacle not yet overcome is to agree on a universally acceptable standard for these special format-describing records.

Self-check questions:

1. a) What is the relationship between a file, a record and a field?

    b) How can a record be extended in a manual filing system?

2. Declare a Pascal type whose values describe a course for which you have registered. The data should include the course identifier (an identification code), the course name, the number of credits, the term in which it is offered, and its time and place of meeting.

3. What difficulties can occur in reading computer files that have been created by another program?

5.6 Defining special cases

There are some computing applications that do not seem to admit solution by any concise and elegant algorithm, but instead require the analysis of a number of special cases. If these cases do indeed require distinct actions to be taken (as opposed to performing a common activity on distinct items of data) then a program must contain a decision-making clause to determine which action is to apply. Pascal provides a control statement specifically designed to allow the selection of one action from among several. It is the case statement, and its syntax is given by the following diagram:

120

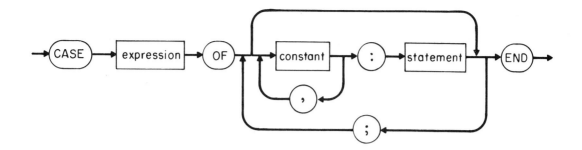

The ⏐expression⏐ appearing after the keyword case in the selection clause is required to be of the same type as are the constants that label the statements in the case list. These labels serve as names for the various special cases. Although the labels may be chosen from a range of integer values, integers do not provide very suggestive names. Alternatively, the labels may be chosen from a scalar type. The imaginative programmer may wish to define his own set of names for special cases, in order to enhance the readability of his program. For this purpose, Pascal allows you to define a scalar type by enumerating the identifiers that are its constants (recall Section 5.1).

For instance, a chess-playing program may contain a segment that suggests possible moves of the pieces. The form of move that can be made depends on the kind of piece to be moved, however. To make this distinction, in a chess program one might define a scalar type enumerating the kinds of pieces,

type Piecetype = (Pawn, Knight, Bishop, Rook, Queen, King);

and a variable to represent the kind of piece to be moved,

var Piece : Piecetype;

The move generator will have to proceed by considering the allowed move of each kind of piece as a special case. It may be governed by a case statement, such as

```
case Piece of
    Pawn :    ...;
    Knight :  ...;
    Bishop :  ...;
    Rook :    ...;
    Queen :   ...;
    King :    ...
end
```

121

in which a simple or compound statement following each label gives the action to be performed in case the value of Piece matches the value of that label.

The case statement can be thought of as a generalization of the conditional statement. In fact, the effect of any conditional statement

```
if <Boolean expression> then
    <statement 1>
else
    <statement 2>
```

can be exactly duplicated by an equivalent case statement, since Boolean is a scalar type. The equivalent statement is:

```
case <Boolean expression> of
    True : <statement 1>;
    False: <statement 2>
end
```

Since constants of the scalar types you may define have no universal meaning, Pascal makes no special provision for their conversion to character sequences for input or output. What this means is that you cannot furnish values of scalar types as arguments to the standard procedures Read or Writeln. Since that sometimes seems as if it would be desirable, let us investigate a generally applicable programming technique that can be used to allow input or output of special case names.

Although the identifiers that name constants of a user-defined scalar type will not automatically be recognized in the input stream, a correspondence can be established between these names and a set of single letters that can be read directly. From our previous illustration, in which constants were named to identify kinds of chessmen, such a correspondence might be:

```
King      -- 'K'
Queen     -- 'Q'
Rook      -- 'R'
Bishop    -- 'B'
Knight    -- 'C'
Pawn      -- 'P'
```

in which we have used 'C' (abbreviating Chevalier) to stand for the knight, since the letter 'K' has already been taken by the King.

When any of these letters is read by our program, we wish it to be translated immediately to furnish a corresponding value of Piecetype. For this purpose, we employ a <u>translation table</u>, which is an array, indexed by a range of values from type Char, and holding the values of Piecetype corresponding to each of the designated index values. This array can be declared as

<u>var</u> TranslationTable : <u>array</u> ['B'..'R'] <u>of</u> Piecetype;

and initialized by a sequence of specific assignments, such as

TranslationTable['K'] := King

Subsequently, when a character obtained from the input is to be converted, a statement such as

Piece := TranslationTable[Ch]

will accomplish the translation. The following example illustrates the use of one translation table for input and another for output

Example 5.6.1 -- Using translation tables

```
program Translate (Input, Output);
    type
        Piecetype = (Pawn, Knight, Bishop, Rook, Queen, King);
    var
        Ch : Char;
        Piece : Piecetype;
        TransTable : array ['B'..'R'] of Piecetype;
        NameTable : array [Piecetype] of
                        packed array [1..6] of Char;
    begin  (**** initialize the tables ****)
        TransTable['K'] := King;    NameTable[King] := 'KING  ';
        TransTable['Q'] := Queen;   NameTable[Queen] := 'QUEEN ';
        TransTable['R'] := Rook;    NameTable[Rook] := 'ROOK  ';
        TransTable['B'] := Bishop;  NameTable[Bishop] := 'BISHOP';
        TransTable['C'] := Knight;  NameTable[Knight] := 'KNIGHT';
        TransTable['P'] := Pawn;    NameTable[Pawn] := 'PAWN  ';
        repeat
            Read (Ch);
            if Ch in ['P', 'C', 'B', 'R', 'Q', 'K'] then
            begin
                Piece := TransTable[Ch];
                Write (NameTable[Piece], ' ');
            end;
        until Eof;
    end.
```

123

In this program, the conditional clause verifies that each character is one of the six letters that can be translated, or else translation is not attempted. When presented with the input stream

    K B R

the program will print

    KING   BISHOP ROOK

In the next example, we shall see how the names of a scalar type are used as special case designators.

Example 5.6.2 -- Calculating the areas of geometric figures

Just as a handbook may contain formulas for evaluating the areas of a variety of geometric figures, we can also program the computer to perform the evaluations, upon demand. The shapes that we consider will be kept to a few simple ones, that need only one or two parameters to characterize their dimensions. For a circle or a square, only the diameter or the length of a side must be given; for an ellipse or a rectangle, a pair of values is necessary.

As input, the program should receive a letter which represents the kind of figure. This is to be followed by one or two real numbers representing the dimensions. If there is any inconsistency in the specification, the program will be permitted to regard the figure as a blob, whose area cannot be computed. Otherwise, the area is to be evaluated and printed. We shall make use of a case statement, since the area of each kind of figure is computed by a different formula.

```
program Areas (Input, Output);
    const
        Pi = 3.1415926;
        Blank = ' ';
    type
        Figuretype = (Blob, Circle, Square, Ellipse, Rectangle);
    var
        Ch : Char;
        D1, D2, Area : Real;
        Shape : Figuretype;
        Translate : array ['A'..'Z'] of Figuretype;
```

```
          begin
              (**** initialize the translation table ****)
              for Ch := 'A' to 'Z' do
                  Translate[Ch] := Blob;
              Translate['C'] := Circle;  Translate['S'] := Square;
              Translate['E'] := Ellipse; Translate['R'] := Rectangle;

              Write ('DIMENSIONS ARE:');
              repeat
                  Read (Ch);
              until Ch <> Blank;
              Shape := Translate[Ch];
              Read (Dl);  Write (Dl);
              if Shape in [Rectangle, Ellipse] then
                  begin Read (D2); Write (D2) end
              Writeln;

              Write ('THE AREA OF A ');
              case Shape of
Circle:           begin Area := Pi*Sqr(Dl)/4; Write ('CIRCLE') end;
Square:           begin Area := Sqr(Dl); Write ('SQUARE') end;
Ellipse:          begin Area := Pi*Dl*D2/4; Write ('ELLIPSE') end;
Rectangle:        begin Area := Dl*D2; Write ('RECTANGLE') end;
Blob:             begin Area := 0.0; Write ('BLOB') end;
              end; (* case *)
              Write (' OF THESE DIMENSIONS IS');
              if Area > 0.0 then
                  Writeln (Area)
              else
                  Writeln (' UNKNOWN');
          end.
```

Self-check questions:

1. When is the use of a case statement justified?

2. What is meant by a translation table?

EXERCISES FOR CHAPTER 5

5.1 From the file of boxer's records defined in Example 5.5.1, several interesting statistics can be gathered. Assuming that such a file has been created on your computer system, design a Pascal program to extract the answer to one of the following questions, by examining the data in the file:

a) have any heavyweight boxing champions retired undefeated? Who, and in what years?

b) what boxer held the heavyweight title for the greatest number of years?

c) which boxers have held titles in more than one weight class simultaneously? Which titles, and when?

d) who were the tallest and the shortest heavyweight champions?

e) who defeated John L. Sullivan for the heavyweight title? In what year?

f) which boxers held the best lifetime records? (You can define what you mean by "best").

g) what boxer has fought the greatest number of fights?

h) in what years was Floyd Patterson the heavyweight champion? Who defeated him to take the title?

5.2 A deck of playing cards consists of 52 cards, each marked with one of four suits (called Clubs, Diamonds, Hearts and Spades) and one of thirteen ranks (called Ace, Two, Three, ... Ten, Jack, Queen, King). In order to represent a playing card for input from a Text file, a possible format is to give the rank by one or two numerals, or a letter, followed by the suit given by a single letter. For instance, the ten of Diamonds, the Ace of Hearts, and the Queen of Spades would be represented on the input file by the sequence

    10D AH QS

Design a Pascal program to read a sequence of these terse representations, and to verify that each is a valid playing card, and that no two cards in the sequence are identical. Print the description of each card by giving its full name,

    TEN DIAMONDS
    ACE HEARTS
    QUEEN SPADES

5.3 In the game of bridge, the first phase involves "bidding", a complex pattern of token betting based on evaluation of a hand of thirteen playing cards that a player is dealt. One simple scheme for evaluation awards points to each card according to its rank, as follows:

rank	points
2..10	0
Jack	1
Queen	2
King	3
Ace	4

In addition, one point is added if there is a suit for which the hand contains only a single card (not a facecard), and two points are added if there is a suit in which the hand is void (contains no card of that suit).

Design a Pascal program to accept as input a description of a bridge hand, in the format specified for Exercise 5.2, and to evaluate the point count of the hand by applying the rules given above.

5.4 Declare a Pascal record type, that can contain all of the information pertaining to the academic record of a college student. Include identification, place of residence, personal data, the college attended, courses taken, credits and grades received.

5.5 When freight is transported by a common carrier, the rate basis depends strongly on the mode of transportation. Air freight is priced by weight, but shipboard freight is commonly priced only by volume. Rail transport charges for both weight and volume. Given the following point-to-point freight rates,

a) design a Pascal program to compute the cost of sending a shipment of freight, given its weight, volume, and the mode of transportation as input.

by air: -- $2.40 per kilogram

by sea: -- $18.00 per cubic meter

by land: -- $85.00 per cubic meter, plus
             $0.05 per kilogram

b) Between any given pair of points, one or more of the modes of transport may be unavailable. Extend the program of part (a) so that it can find the least costly means of transport, given the size and weight of an item of freight, for shipment between each of the following pairs of points:

  i) New York and London (air and sea only)

 ii) Atlanta and Chicago (air and land only)

iii) New York and Los Angeles (air, land, and sea)

For the sake of simplicity, assume that the point-to-point rates are as given in part (a) for any of these routes, in spite of the fact that the distances covered are not the same.

6 REPRESENTING DATA WITH ARRAYS

Arrays are the most commonly employed of the structured data types. The data of many diverse problems can be represented as indexed sets, and an array type is exactly the analog of an indexed set of values. Frequently, however, the problems that we face do not dictate any unique choice of representation of data; the choice is one of the decisions to be made in the course of composing an algorithm. This choice can have a profound effect on the ease with which the remaining steps can be conceived, and upon the efficiency of execution of the final product. In this chapter we shall investigate some examples for which an array representation of data is appropriate.

6.1 Indexed sets of values

What do we mean by an indexed set of values? We actually mean a set of ordered pairs, (i, x), in which the first element of each pair comes from an ordered set, such as the integers, or one of the enumerated scalar types of Pascal. The second element of each ordered pair is a value from some designated type, let's call it type T for the time being. In addition, the value of the first element, called the indexing value or simply the index, is required to be unique among the pairs that make up the indexed set. That is, there are not to be two distinct pairs both having the same indexing value. The standard interpretation made of an indexed set is that it defines a sequence of values from the type T. The ordering of the sequence is not determined by the values of the type T elements themselves, but by the progression of indexing values. In addition, each index also provides a name by which to refer to an element in the sequence. The ability to name values is obviously a very powerful aid to computation.

In order that an indexed set can be easily represented in the computer, we usually impose another constraint upon it, namely that it should be finite. Thus the data type Real is excluded from consideration as an indexing type, and if integers are to be used as indices, a finite subrange must be specified. Notice that the enumerated scalar types of Pascal, such as type Char and the user-definable scalar types, also meet the criteria for use as index types. In the following example, we shall see how the use of an array allows a sequence of values to be accumulated and the desired values to be recovered.

Example 6.1.1 -- Finding the nth prime number

The prime numbers are of central importance in number theory, and one of the earliest computational problems for which an algorithm was developed was the computation of primes. We shall first propose an algorithm for this problem that appears to be correct, and yields answers for a few primes, but will be seen to fail because of an unfortunate choice of data representation. A second algorithm, using a more appropriate representation, will then be constructed.

The prime factorization theorem of number theory tells us that any positive integer can be represented as a product of prime factors, and that the factorization of a number into its prime factors is unique. We can use this fact to advantage in proposing a seemingly simple test of whether or not a number is prime. Since we know how to find the greatest common divisor of a pair of numbers (Example 4.1.1) and we know that a given integer is prime if and only if its greatest common divisor with each smaller prime is unity, we can accomplish the test for primeness in a single application of the g.c.d. algorithm. The trick is this; keep a test integer which is the product of all previously found primes. Then a given number will be relatively prime with respect to all previously found primes if its g.c.d. with this test integer is one. In fact, we need not even test all integers for primeness, because since the first prime number is 2, we know that all other primes must be odd numbers. An algorithm to search through odd integers, counting primes found until the nth one is reached can be informally described by the following iteration graph:

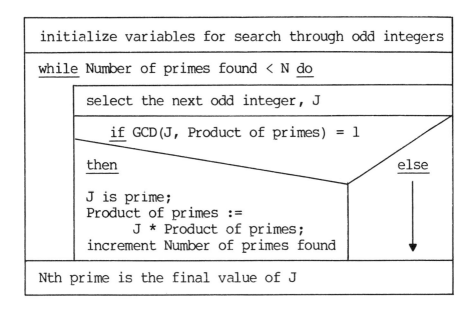

In this algorithm the variables needed will be integers and can be declared in Pascal by

var N, PrimesFound, J, Product : Integer;

In translating the iteration graph to a Pascal program, if we decide to initialize the value of the index, N, by a Read statement, then the value received must be checked to ensure that it is positive. We should also make provision for the case that N = 1, which is not covered by the iteration graph above, but which is valid as the index of a prime. The graph can be translated to the program given on the following page. In this algorithm, the program segment to compute the function GCD has not been specified. However, it can be filled in later if we are satisfied with the rest of the algorithm. This will be a technique often used as it enables us to concentrate our attention first on the fundamental questions.

131

```
program Primesl (Input, Output);
    (***********************************************
    * N is the index of the prime being sought,    *
    * J is an integer being tested for primeness,   *
    * PrimesFound records how many have been found, *
    * Product records the product of all odd primes *
    *     found previously.                         *
    ***********************************************)

    var
        N, PrimesFound, J, Product : Integer;
    begin
        Read (N); if N <= 0 then Halt;
        if N = 1 then
            J := 2
        else
            begin
                J := 1; Product := 1; PrimesFound := 1;
                while PrimesFound < N do
                    begin
                        J := J + 2;
                        if GCD (J, Product) = 1 then
                            begin (* J is prime *)
                                PrimesFound := PrimesFound + 1;
                                Product := Product * J;
                            end;
                    end;
            end;
        Writeln ('PRIME', N:3, ' IS ', J);
    end.
```

As it stands, it appears that the algorithm will be effective, but if we were to submit it to the computer and ask for the evaluation of several primes, we might discover that it can only determine values for the first ten of them! What has gone wrong? The difficulty is with the representation of the values of all previously found primes in the form of a product. The product of the first ten primes is

3*5*7*11*13*17*19*23*29 = 3,534,515,985

which is already greater than the largest value that a Pascal variable of type integer can have on a computer with a 32-bit word size.† The specific limitation on the largest representable integer is due to the particular computer on which the computation is done, but the limitation of the

132

algorithm is not. Using the largest computer in existence would only enable a few more primes to be evaluated by this algorithm. In trying to put all of the information about previously calculated primes into a single number, we have accumulated an amount of information that requires a very large number for its representation. The use of a product for this purpose is a form of information encoding. Encoding can be a useful strategy, but must not be overdone.

Let us start over again to compose an algorithm to find the Nth prime. Perhaps a more suitable way to record the primes previously found will be to treat them as an indexed set of integers, and to define an array to represent this set. We shall also need a variable to count the number of primes that have been found so far.

    var Prime : <u>array</u> [1..1000] of Integer;
        PrimesFound : 1..1000;

The size of the array limits our algorithm to the first thousand primes, but if this limit is too small, it can easily be increased.

Next in the algorithm should come some steps that initialize PrimesFound and if necessary, the first few elements of the table of primes. These initialization steps will be filled in later when we know what values are to be assigned. Right now, suppose that the table contains some primes already known, and that the Nth prime is desired. It might be that it is already in the table.

    <u>if</u> PrimesFound < N <u>then</u>
        <u>compute more primes</u>
    <u>else</u>
        the Nth prime is Prime[N]

To compute the additional primes will be an iterative procedure. It should be continued until the number of primes in the table includes the Nth:

----

†   The maximum representable integer value is related to the number of bits, w, in a word of the computer's registers, by the formula
       $Maxint = 2^{w-1} - 1$

while PrimesFound < N do . . .

Since only the odd integers need to be considered as candidates, there is no point in testing any candidate to see whether it is divisible by two. The testing can begin with the second prime, which is 3. Also, a little thought will tell us that if a candidate passes the test of having no prime divisors up to a certain point in the table, then none of the remaining primes in the table can be a divisor either. It should not be hard to convince yourself that for any positive integer which is not a prime, at least one of its prime factors is less than or equal to its square root. If no prime less than or equal to its square root is found, then the smallest prime factor must be the number itself.

At this point in the evolution of the algorithm, it is useful to summarize the structure we have designed so far by giving an iteration graph.

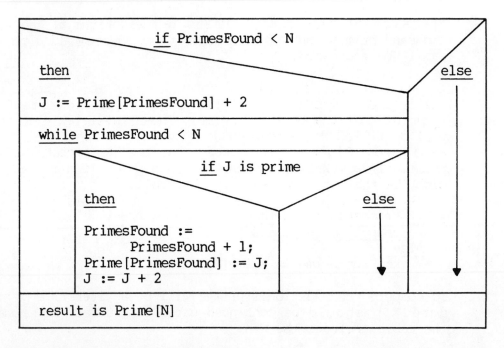

Since it appears that the test "J is prime" cannot be done by a single expression evaluation, we should elaborate on this clause in the iteration graph, replacing

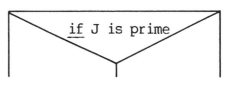

by

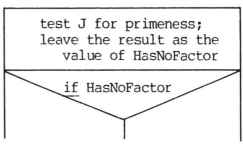

Turning our attention to the operation "test J for primeness", we know from the preceding discussion that this test can be carried out by the determining whether J can be divided by any of the primes starting from 3, and which are less than or equal to the square root of J. If any such prime divides J, the test can be terminated, with the outcome that J is not prime. Otherwise, the test will be completed when the designated list of primes has been exhausted, and it has been found that none is a factor of J. Informally, this test can be represented as

test J for primeness:

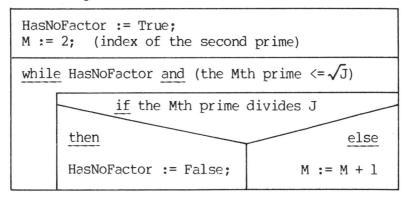

In translating this iteration graph into a Pascal program segment a few changes of form can be made. First of all, an easy way to tell whether the Mth prime is less than or equal to the square root of J, without actually evaluating the square root function, is to compare the square of the Mth prime with J itself. The iteration control clause can be written as

while HasNoFactor and (Sqr(Prime[M]) <= J) do

where Sqr is a predeclared function of Pascal, which takes the square of any number.

Secondly, Pascal contains an integer division function, mod, which evaluates the remainder in a division. A test of whether or not one integer divides another is that the remainder is zero. Thus the phrase "the Mth prime divides J" can be translated to

J mod Prime[M] = 0

Upon incorporating these modifications, to take advantage of the programming language capabilities, the operation "test J for primeness" becomes the program segment

```
HasNoFactor := True; M := 2;
while HasNoFactor and (Sqr(Prime[M]) <= J) do
   if J mod Prime[M] = 0 then
      HasNoFactor := False
   else
      M := M + 1
```

It is now straightforward to translate the iteration graph that describes the entire algorithm. Of course, in completing the translation, a program prefix must be added in which variables are declared, some variables are initialized by assignment of constant values, data are read and tested for validity, and comments are inserted. This necessary but somewhat verbose portion of the program text may be as lengthy as the portion which directly translates the iteration graph.

In this example program, we have used a subrange type to distinguish between variables used to index the primes and the integer variables used to represent primes themselves. Not only does this aid the reader of the program to discern our intent, but it often enables the Pascal compiler to catch some of our programming errors, and to validate input data without requiring extra programming on our part.

136

```pascal
program Prime2 (Input, Output);
  (***********************************************************
   * Given a positive number N, this program is to locate the *
   *     Nth prime number.                                    *
   * J is an odd integer, a candidate for a prime.            *
   * Prime is an array of the primes already found.           *
   * M is an index into the array of primes.                  *
   * PrimesFound is the number of primes already located.     *
   * HasNoFactor is a Boolean flag, used to record the out-   *
   *     come of testing J for primeness.                     *
   ***********************************************************)
  const
     Maxindex = 1000;
  type
     Indextype = 1..Maxindex;
  var
     N, M, PrimesFound : Indextype;
     J : Integer;
     Prime : array [Indextype] of Integer;
     HasNoFactor : Boolean;
  begin
     (************************************************
      *   initialize the table of primes to contain 2   *
      *   and the first odd prime.                       *
      ************************************************)
     Prime[1] := 2;  Prime[2] := 3;
     PrimesFound := 2;
     Read (N); (* if N is out of range, a Read error will occur *)
     J := Prime[PrimesFound] + 2;
     while PrimesFound < N do
        begin
           HasNoFactor := True;  M := 2;
           while HasNoFactor and (Sqr(Prime[M] <= J) do
              if J mod Prime[M] = 0 then
                 HasNoFactor := False
              else
                 M := succ(M);
           if HasNoFactor then
              begin (*** J is prime ***)
                 PrimesFound := PrimesFound + 1;
                 Prime[PrimesFound] := J;
              end;
           J := J + 2;
        end;
     Writeln ('PRIME[', N:3, '] =', Prime[N]);
  end.
```

6.2 Some applications from linear algebra

If one can think of a satisfactory data representation, then it is often possible to devise computational algorithms for tasks that are not obvious applications of computing. For instance, in doing algebraic operations on polynomials in one variable, we are accustomed to spreading out the calculations over a piece of paper in order to keep separate the terms of different powers in the variable. But another representation might use indices to keep track of powers. In manipulating polynomials in a single variable, the name of the variable is of no importance whatever, and need not be represented. The individual arithmetic operations are all performed on coefficients of the various powers of the variable, and these coefficients are just numbers. So it seems that operations on polynomials should be able to be performed by algorithms in which the only primitive operations required are arithmetic operations on numbers.

Example 6.2.1 -- Multiplication of polynomials

In representing a polynomial in a single variable, the name of the variable is unimportant; only the coefficients of the powers of the variable that appear in the various terms need to be remembered. An easy way to represent a polynomial is by an indexed set of its coefficients. If the indices start from zero, then the index of each element corresponds to the power of the variable in a term of the polynomial, and the value of each element is the coefficient of that term. Since negative coefficients can be represented let us adopt the convention that the polynomial is the algebraic sum of products of coefficients with powers of the variable. Then we won't have to worry about some terms being added and others subtracted. Various representations of an abstract polynomial in one variable are

$$a_n x^n + a_{n-1} x^{n-1} + \ldots + a_1 x + a_0$$
    (an expanded pencil-and-paper representation)

$$\sum_{i=0}^{3} a_i x^i$$ (pencil-and-paper representation in summation form)

var A : array [0..N] of Integer; (Pascal representation
                                    as an array of coefficients)

To make these representations fit a concrete example, we can give values to the coefficients;

$$x^3 + 12x^2 - 9x + 22 \qquad \text{(expanded representation)}$$

$$\sum_{i=0}^{3} a_i x^i, \text{ where } a_0 = 22, \ a_1 = -9, \ a_2 = 12, \text{ and } a_3 = 1$$
(summation representation)

A[0] := 22; A[1] := -9; A[2] := 12; A[3] := 11
(Pascal representation)

Now let us think about the operation of multiplying two polynomials in the same variable. When this operation is carried out with pencil on paper, we write down in succession a list of polynomials, each obtained by multiplying the entire first polynomial by a single term of the second. These intermediate polynomials are then summed, using the rule that coefficients of terms of like power in the variable are added. As an aid in keeping terms of dissimilar powers separated, the whole computation is spread out over the paper like this:

$$
\begin{array}{r}
x^3 + 12x^2 - 9x + 22 \\
3x^2 \qquad\quad - 2 \\
\hline
- 2x^3 - 24x^2 + 18x - 44 \\
3x^5 + 36x^4 - 27x^3 + 66x^2 \\
\hline
3x^5 + 36x^4 - 29x^3 + 42x^2 + 18x - 44
\end{array}
$$

The calculation looks very much like the way we would do a long multiplication of integers on paper, but in fact, it is easier than multiplying integers because there is no carry from one column to the next in adding polynomials. Thus, it is not really necessary to follow any fixed order in deciding which column to total first. Also, notice that as soon as any coefficient of one of the intermediate polynomials has been included in the summation of the column to which it belongs, that coefficient is no longer needed. This suggests that in an algorithm for the computer, we might as well incorporate each intermediate coefficient into the final sum as soon as it has been found, avoiding the effort of saving its value. This idea can be expressed concisely in the mathematical summation notation as

$$c_k = \sum_j a_{k-j} b_j$$

where polynomials being multiplied are represented by coefficients a_{k-j} and b_j, and c_k is the coefficient of the term of kth power in the product. In the informal summation notation, it is to be understood that the sum is carried out over all indices j for which it makes sense. In a computational algorithm we must be more specific.

Let us study polynomial multiplication in the pencil-and-paper representation, and attempt to identify the indices of terms in the summation of intermediate products.

$$x^3 + 12x^2 - 9x + 22 \quad \text{polynomial A}$$
$$3x^2 \qquad\qquad - 2 \quad \text{polynomial B}$$

j = k - degree A

$$-2x^3 \quad -24x^2 \quad +18x \quad -44 \qquad j = 0$$
$$0x^4 \qquad 0x^3 \qquad 0x^2 \qquad 0x \qquad\qquad 1$$
$$3x^5 \quad +36x^4 \quad -27x^3 \quad +66x^2 \qquad\qquad\quad 2$$

j = k

$$k = 5 \qquad 4 \qquad 3 \qquad 2 \qquad 1 \qquad 0$$

Here the rows to be summed are indicated by the index j, corresponding to powers from 0 to the degree of polynomial B. Powers of the product polynomial are indicated by the column index, k. The summation would be carried out exactly over the row indices from 0 to degree B if it were not for the fact that the trapezoidal array of coefficients has diagonal sides. The equations of these diagonal lines specify relations between values of j and k which limit the summation over rows, j = k on the right diagonal, and j = k - degree A on the left. Therefore, the limits for the summation indices are

$$c_k = \sum_{\max(0,\, k - \text{degree A})}^{\min(k,\, \text{degree B})} a_{k-j} b_j$$

140

A Pascal program segment to carry out the multiplication is:

```
program PolynomialMultiplication (Input, Output);
   (***************************************************
    * multiplies a pair of polynomials whose integer     *
    * coefficients are represented by vectors "A" and    *
    * "B". The result is represented by the vector "C".  *
    * The degrees of the polynomials are given by values*
    * of the variables DegreeA, DegreeB, DegreeC.        *
    ***************************************************)
   const
      MaxDegree = 50;
   var
      DegreeA, DegreeB, DegreeC, J, K : 0..MaxDegree;
      A, B, C : array [0..MaxDegree] of Integer;
   begin
      initialize A, B, DegreeA and DegreeB;
      DegreeC := DegreeA + DegreeB;
      for K := 0 to DegreeC do
         begin
            C[K] := 0;
            for J := max(0, K - DegreeA) to min(K, DegreeB) do
               C[K] := C[K] + A[K-J]*B[J];
         end;
      (*** output the results here ***)
   end.
```

In the last example, we saw that the form of an algorithm for the computer could differ appreciably from a familiar pencil-and-paper algorithm for the same task, but that arraying interme- diate results on paper can sometimes suggest an algorithm that we might not easily have discovered otherwise. The following example provides another illustration of this aid to discovery.

Example 6.2.2 -- Evaluation of binomial coefficients

From high school algebra, you are familiar with the binomial expansion, and probably remember that a formula for the coefficient of the rth power of x in the expansion of

$(x + 1)^n$ is

$$\binom{n}{r} = \frac{n!}{r!\,(n-r)!}$$

where n!, read as "n factorial", stands for the product

141

1*2*3*...*n. An obvious algorithm for the evaluation of the binomial coefficient is

```
var N, R, Binomial, J : Integer;
begin
    Read (N, R);
    Binomial := 1;
    for J := N downto N - R + 1 do
        Binomial := J * Binomial;
    for J := 1 to R do
        Binomial := Binomial div J;
    Writeln (Binomial);
end
```

This computes the product n*(n-1)*(n-2)* . . . *(n-r+1) first, then divides it by r!

But this algorithm is not much good except for small values of n. It cannot even evaluate $\binom{13}{13}$, because it must first compute 13!, which is larger than the maximum integer representable in a 32-bit register. Of course, we have not taken advantage of all we know about the binomial coefficients. In particular, we know there is a symmetry, that

$$\binom{n}{r} = \binom{n}{n-r}$$

and so the algorithm could be improved by inserting after the Read step, the conditional statement

if R > N then R := N - R

Then the number accumulated in the first iterated step will have the fewest possible factors. However, even this improvement does not help much, for $\binom{17}{8}$ cannot be computed on a computer with 32-bit registers by the improved algorithm, although its value is only 31310 which is much smaller than the maximum representable integer value. It seems that the algorithm fails for large n by computing a numerator much larger than will be the final result, then dividing it by a succession of factors to reduce its size. Is there a different way to compute binomial coefficients?

Suppose we consider a pencil-and-paper algorithm for expansion of a binomial by successive multiplications. If the expansion of

142

$(x + 1)^{n-1}$ has been obtained, then to get the expansion of $(x + 1)^{n}$, one more multiplication by $x + 1$ is performed. Writing out this multiplication on paper, it looks like:

$$\binom{n-1}{0}x^{n-1} + \ldots + \binom{n-1}{r-1}x^{n-r} + \binom{n-1}{r}x^{n-1-r} + \ldots + \binom{n-1}{n-2}x + \binom{n-1}{n-1}$$

$$x + 1$$

$$\rule{10cm}{0.4pt}$$

$$\binom{n-1}{0}x^{n-1} + \ldots + \binom{n-1}{r-1}x^{n-r} + \ldots \ldots \ldots + \binom{n-1}{n-2}x + \binom{n-1}{n-1}$$

$$\binom{n-1}{0}x^{n} + \binom{n-1}{1}x^{n-1} + \ldots + \binom{n-1}{r}x^{n-r} + \ldots \ldots \ldots + \binom{n-1}{n-1}x$$

$$\rule{10cm}{0.4pt}$$

$$\binom{n-1}{0}x^{n} + \ldots + \left[\binom{n-1}{r-1}+\binom{n-1}{r}\right]x^{n-r} + \ldots \ldots \ldots + \binom{n-1}{n-1}$$

Recalling that $\binom{n}{r}$ is equal to the coefficient of x^{n-r} in the expansion of $(x+1)^{n}$, we can see from the above display a recurrence relation that is satisfied by the binomial coefficients:

$$\binom{n}{r} = \binom{n-1}{r} + \binom{n-1}{r-1}$$

The extremal coefficients, $\binom{n}{0}$ and $\binom{n}{n}$ are 1 for any n.

The formula for the binomial coefficients in terms of factorial functions gives a concise representation, but it does not provide the only means for their evaluation. The recurrence relation suggests a different form of iterative calculation. When the iterative calculation of the binomial coefficients is carried out by hand, the results can be displayed in an attractive array that we know as Pascal's triangle.

143

```
                        1
                    1       1
                1       2       1
            1       3       3       1
        1       4       6       4       1
      1     5      10      10      5       1
    1     6      15      20      15      6       1
  1     7      21      35      35      21      7       1
1       8      28      56      70      56      28      8       1
1       7      36      84     126     126  .  .  .  .  .
```

However, if our purpose is to evaluate a single binomial coefficient, we should not try to duplicate Pascal's triangle, for that will require a large number of coefficients to be remembered when we are ultimately interested in only one. By displaying Pascal's triangle in a somewhat less elegant form, it is easy to see which terms contribute to the calculation of a given coefficient.

```
n=0  | 1
  1  | 1   1
  2  | 1   2   1
  3  | 1   3   3   1
  4  | 1   4   6   4   1
  5  | 1   5  10  10   5   1
  6  | 1   6  15  20  15   6   1
  7  | 1   7  21  35   .   .   .   .
     |_____

       r = 0   1   2   3   4   5   6   7
```

The diagram above illustrates the succession of terms needed in the evaluation of $\binom{7}{3}$.

A logical way to compute the terms of Pascal's triangle is row by row. Within each row, the terms might be computed from left to right,

```
  1       6      15      20      15       6       1
  1       7      21      35
```

or from right to left,

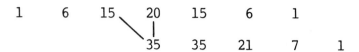

$$\begin{array}{ccccccc} 1 & 6 & 15 & 20 & 15 & 6 & 1 \\ & & & 35 & 35 & 21 & 7 & 1 \end{array}$$

If the evaluation is done right to left, then the values of the preceding row which lie to the right of the element being computed need not be remembered, for they will not be used again. The "old" values of elements of the preceding row could be crossed out and replaced by newly calculated elements, allowing the entire computation to use only a single row for remembering values,

$$\underline{1} \quad \underline{6} \quad \underline{15} \quad 35 \quad 35 \quad 21 \quad 7 \quad 1$$

The array shown above represents a partial computation of the seventh row of Pascal's triangle. The elements underlined are elements of row six which have not yet been replaced. The next element of row seven that will be calculated is the third. Its values will depend on elements two and three from row six, whose values still remain available in the array.

The conservation of space needed to remember intermediate values of the computation is unimportant in a pencil-and-paper calculation, for the amount of paper that could be saved is not worth the effort of erasing. But in programming a computer to do the same computation, no effort is required to erase old results, and the amount of memory space saved might be significant in a large computation.

The algorithm just developed by considering examples can now be given as a Pascal program. In this case, we shall omit the step of giving an iteration graph, because the iteration control required is just to sequence through the rows and columns of Pascal's triangle. Care must be taken that the unit values that occupy the borders of the triangle are properly set.

The notation pred(J) is read as "the predecessor of J", and since J is an integer, is equivalent to J - 1. Pred( ) is a predeclared, built-in function of Pascal, and is defined on any scalar or subrange type, as well as on type Integer.

```
program BinomialCoefficient (Input, Output);
   (****************************************************
    * evaluates Binomial[N, R] by calculation of the   *
    * Nth row of Pascal's triangle. As each succeeding  *
    * row is computed, its values replace those of the  *
    * previously computed row in the vector "Pascal".   *
    ****************************************************)
const
    Maxindex = 50;
var
    N, R, Row, J : 0..Maxindex;
    Pascal : array [0..Maxindex] of Integer;
begin
    Read (N, R);
    Pascal[0] := 1;
    for Row := 1 to N do
        begin
            Pascal[Row] := 1;
            for J := Row - 1 downto 1 do
                Pascal[J] := Pascal[J] + Pascal[pred(J)];
        end;
    Writeln ('BINOMIAL COEFFICIENT (', N, R,
            ' EQUALS', Pascal[R]);
end.
```

6.3 Analyzing character strings

There are a great many computing applications which either
do not involve numbers at all, or in which numerical computation
comprises only a relatively small part of the overall task. Most
such applications involve analysis, storage, and transformation
of data represented by character strings. To some extent, a
computer can also be programmed to interpret the data represented
by strings, although more frequently, the final interpretation of
such data is left to a human reader.

It is at first surprising that computations on character
strings are of much practical importance, because the algebra of
operations that can be performed on strings is so much less
powerful than is the algebra of numbers. The basic operations on
strings are selection of a substring of one or more characters,
and catenation, whereby two strings are laid end-to-end to form
a longer string. Indeed, in the early days of computing, not much
attention was paid to string processing. However, the importance
of character strings as data representations is exactly due to

146

the fact that humans most often choose this representation for the data they use in their own transactions, most of which are not intrinsically numerical.

Pascal does not directly support the operations that can be defined on character strings, but by the use of array indexing, in conjunction with iterative program control, any definable string operation can be accomplished. Pascal does allow entire arrays to be compared with one another, or copied by assignment, provided that their data types are compatible. The following example will illustrate some of the basic operations on character string data.

Example 6.3.1 -- Picking words out of a line of text

A line of text is merely a string of characters, in which the blank character plays the role of a separator. A word consists of any unbroken sequence of non-blank characters. By this definition, we include a lot of "words" that would not be well-formed in any known natural language, let alone be meaningful, but it would be asking too much of the computer to make a judgement about which words were meaningful in the English language, unless we were prepared to provide it with a complete dictionary. To keep the problem simple, we will not even require that punctuation marks or invalid characters be distinguished. It is not hard to describe in informal terms an iterative algorithm for extracting words. An iteration graph for such an algorithm is:

```
while not at the end of the line

    scan across any blanks;
    copy a sequence of non-blanks,
        calling it a Word;
    print the Word
```

Each of these informally described operations can be translated using array operations, although some of these operations will translate into program segments longer than a single statement. In this example, the character string data could just as well have been obtained directly from a file of type Text, as we intend to examine the characters in a strict sequence. However, it is our purpose here to show you how to utilize arrays.

147

Suppose that the length of a line of text is bounded by some constant value, MaxLength, and that a variable called LineLength describes the actual length of a particular line. This allows us to treat a line of arbitrary length, up to a maximum, by specifying that only an initial segment of the array representing the line is to be used. We require that

    0 <= LineLength <= MaxLength

Declarations of these variables are:

    var TextLine, Word : array [1..MaxLength] of Char;
        LineLength, WordLength : 0..MaxLength;

In addition to these variables, we shall need a marker for each character array, to record the position of a particular character within a string. The names given to these variables are abbreviations for the names Text Pointer and Word Pointer.

    var TP, WP : 1..MaxLength;

Using these variables, the condition "not at the end of the line" refers to the position of the Text Pointer, and can be expressed by the condition

    TP <= LineLength

The operation "scan across any blanks" cannot be realized by the execution of a single Pascal statement, but can be expressed by iteration. The operation of scanning refers to positioning the Text Pointer. The iteration control tests the condition that the character indexed by the Text Pointer is a blank. Since one cannot be certain that a non-blank character will be encountered before reaching the end of the line of text, a test for the end of line is also included in the iteration control clause.

    while (TP <= LineLength) and (Textline[TP] = Blank) do
        TP := succ(TP)

After executing the while statement that scans over blanks, the Text Pointer will either be positioned at a non-blank character or at the end of the line. If the end of the line has not been reached, then a copy is to be made of the word whose first letter is marked by the Text Pointer. Otherwise, the search for words is to be terminated. Copying the word is another task calling for an iteration statement.

148

In this case, there are two position pointers to be advanced. Prior to actually copying the word, the Word Pointer must be set to indicate the initial character position in the array that will hold the word.

```
WP := 1;
while ·(TP <= LineLength) and (TextLine[TP] <> Blank) do
    begin
        Word[WP] := TextLine[TP];
        WP := succ(WP);   TP := succ(TP);
    end;
WordLength := WP - 1;
```

In the program segment above, the final value of WP is one greater than the number of characters copied, since it was incremented after copying each letter, including the last one. Therefore, WordLength is set to one less than the final value of WP. An easy way to check this calculation is to consider the case that no characters are copied; then Word remains empty, and WordLength should be set to zero. Is it?

The operation of printing the contents of the array Word is easily accomplished by means of a for loop

```
for WP := 1 to WordLength do
    Write (Word[WP]);
if WordLength > 0 then
    Writeln;
```

Following the for loop, we have terminated the print line by calling the Writeln procedure, but only after checking that some characters were actually written.

We have now given program segments for all of the operations described informally in the iteration graph. The task of writing a complete program is only to assemble these program segments, preface them with the declarations of variables, and in this case, to add some means of obtaining lines of text from the input stream so that the program can be tested.

149

```pascal
program PrintWords (Input, Output);
    const
        Blank = ' ';
        MaxLength = 240;
    var
        TextLine, Word : array [1..MaxLength] of Char;
        LineLength, WordLength : Integer;
        TP, WP : 1..MaxLength;
    begin
        while not Eof do
            begin
                (*** get a line of text ***)
                TP := 1;
                while not Eoln do
                    begin
                        Read (TextLine[TP]);
                        TP := succ(TP);
                    end;
                LineLength := TP - 1;
                (*** analyze the line into words ***)
                TP := 1;
                while TP <= LineLength do
                    begin
                        (*** skip over blanks ***)
                        while (TP <= LineLength) and
                              (TextLine[TP] = Blank) do
                            TP := succ(TP);
                        (*** copy a word ***)
                        WP := 1;
                        while (TP <= LineLength) and
                              (TextLine[TP] <> Blank) do
                            begin
                                Word[WP] := TextLine[TP];
                                WP := succ(WP);   TP := succ(TP);
                            end
                        WordLength := WP - 1;
                        (*** print the word just found ***)
                        for WP := 1 to WordLength do
                            Write (Word[WP]);
                        if WordLength > 0 then
                            Writeln;
                    end;   (* of TextLine *)
                (*** reposition the Input file pointer ***)
                Readln;
            end;   (* of Input file *)
    end.
```

6.4 Sorting

The simplest kind of ordering relation is a total order, defined between every pair of values in a set. For example, the integers are totally ordered by the relation "less than"; for every pair of distinct integer values, one of the values will be less than the other. The letters of the alphabet are totally ordered, by their definition as a sequence.

When a set of values is put into a list, the order of their appearance in the list also defines an ordering relation. When this order of appearance is consistent with the natural order defined on values of the listed elements, we say that the list is properly ordered, or sorted. Depending upon the use to be made of a list of items, it may be of some importance that it is sorted. For instance, it is the property of being sorted (by the alphabetical order defined upon words) that enables us to make practical use of a dictionary by allowing binary search in locating a word (recall Example 1.2.3).

Sorting of a list is one of the commonest operations performed in computing, although it is by no means as simple as appending or deleting a single element of a list. There have been numerous algorithms developed for sorting, volumes written on the subject, and thousands of years worth of accumulated human effort devoted to developing and analyzing sorting algorithms. We shall consider the topic very briefly. The only representation of a list of items that we consider in this chapter is the contents of an array. Obviously, other representations are possible.

In sorting a small set of fixed size, such as a bridge hand of 13 cards, it may be possible for the human observer to scan the entire set at a single glance, and to improve the sequencing by making judicious removals and reinsertions of elements without following any fixed algorithm. For the computer, whose powers of observation are much more limited than our own, or even for ourselves if the set of objects is too large to scan all at once, we need to employ a more systematic approach. We shall assume that the scope of a comparison of values is limited to two objects at one time, thus decisions on changing the sequence of listing must be based on binary comparisons, made one at a time.

The method of sorting that we are about to describe is called an insertion sort; it is based on the idea that a sorted list can be constructed out of an initially unordered set by inserting each new element in the list in its proper position.

Thus, the partially-built list is properly ordered at all times. To begin the construction of an ordered list, some arbitrarily chosen element is put in at the head of the list, forming a list of length one. A list of unit length is always properly ordered. From that point onward, insertion of each new element requires comparison with other values, in order to determine where to place it.

The criterion for placing a new item into a sorted list is that the element just preceding the new item should not be greater in value, and the element just following it should not be less. To locate such a spot in the list, we could begin searching in the list from its tail (the element whose position index is largest), progressively comparing the value of the item to be inserted with the value of each element already in the list, stopping when we come to an element whose value is less or equal to that of the item being inserted. For instance, if the list already assembled is:

scarf, shirt, socks, sweater

and the item to be inserted is "shorts", then we would first compare "shorts" to "sweater", then to "socks", and then to "shirt". Upon finding that "shirt", an item from the list, has a value less than that of "shorts", the search stops. The proper position at which to insert "shorts" is immediately following "shirt".

A first try at an iteration graph describing the insertion of an item into a sorted list might be

```
┌─────────────────────────────────────────────────────────┐
│ select the element at the end of the list                │
├─────────────────────────────────────────────────────────┤
│ while item-to-be-inserted < selected list element        │
│  ┌──────────────────────────────────────────────────────┐│
│  │ select the preceding element in the list             ││
│  └──────────────────────────────────────────────────────┘│
├─────────────────────────────────────────────────────────┤
│ insert the new item following the last element           │
│    selected in the list                                  │
└─────────────────────────────────────────────────────────┘
```

Before attempting to translate this iteration graph into a program segment, however, we should take note of a possible difficulty. If the item to be inserted in our previous example of a list of clothing to wear to a picnic had been "sandals",

152

instead of "shorts", then the sequence of comparisons would have failed at the step of selecting the preceding element, after making comparisons with each of the elements already in the list. In that case, the proper location for the item to be inserted is at the head of the list, and some provision must be made to terminate the sequence of iterated comparisons when the head of the list is reached.

A particularly easy and foolproof way to ensure that the sequence of comparisons will terminate properly is to prefix the list with a dummy element that is not actually a part of the set to be sorted, and to give this dummy element a value that will assuredly precede the values of all items in the actual set. For example, we could prefix our picnic clothing list with the word "aardvark", which would not be desirable to wear on an outing, but certainly precedes the names of items of clothing in alphabetic order. This dummy item prefixed to a list for the purpose of terminating a sequential search is called a sentinel value.

The next problem we must face in refinement of an algorithm for insertion sorting has to do with the representation of a list by an array. Assuming the existence of a sentinel value, the iteration graph can be refined directly, giving

```
J := LastIndex

while Item < List[J] do

      J := pred(J)

insert Item following List[J]
```

In general, however, the array element following List[J] will already contain the value of another item, which must be displaced. In fact, all of the items for which the comparison in the while clause was satisfied must be displaced.

Instead of trying to correct this situation after having completed the search for an insertion location, we could move each list element by the required displacement, one index value, during the sequence of comparisons. If this strategy is followed, you can think of the array location indexed by succ(J) as corresponding to a vacancy. At each comparison, if the item at List[J] is to be displaced, it can be moved into the vacancy at

List[succ(J)]. By moving the element, the vacancy is also moved up by one index value. When the sequence of comparisons terminates, the position of the vacancy will still correspond to List[succ(J)], and that will be the location in which to insert the new item.

Rewriting the iteration graph one more time to reflect the provision of a moving vacancy, we get

insert Item:

J := LastIndex
while Item < List[J] do
List[succ(J)] := List(J);   J := pred(J)
List[succ(J)] := Item;

Up to this point, we have not specified how the item to be inserted is to be selected. The actual means of its selection does not matter, since any item selected will be put into the sorted list in the proper position. In such a case, we may as well select an item to suit our convenience. In fact, the items to be inserted are not chosen from some unspecified heap of available data; they are the elements of the initially unsorted array itself. A natural way to select these items is according to the sequence of their indices in the array as it is initially presented to us. In fact, the variable that we have called LastIndex in the iteration graphs above does not correspond to the maximum index value for the array, but to the index value separating the initial segment of the array, known to be sorted, from a terminal segment whose elements are still in the sequence originally given.

154

To transform the initially unsorted array into a sorted array containing the same set of elements, we merely have to choose each element of the initial array as the item to be inserted, and execute Insert Item.

insertion sort

```
prefix a sentinel value to List;
for LastIndex := First to pred (Last)

        insert Item
        {where Item = List [succ (LastIndex)]}
```

A complete Pascal program is obtained by translation of the iteration graphs and introduction of suitable declarations for the variables involved. Input and output have also been added to allow the algorithm to be tested.

```
program InsertionSort (Input, Output);
        (**** an array sorting algorithm ****)
        const
            N = 25;
        type
            Indextype = 0..N;
        var
            List : array [Indextype] of Integer;
            J, LastIndex : Indextype;
            Item : Integer;
        begin
            (*** initialize the array from input ***)
            for J := 1 to N do
                Read (List[J]);
            Writeln ('THE UNSORTED ARRAY IS:');
            for J := 1 to N do
                begin
                    Write (List[J]); (*** five values per line ***)
                    if J mod 5 = 0 then
                        Writeln;
                end;
```

```
(*** sort the array ***)
List[0] := -Maxint;   (*** post a sentinel ***)
for LastIndex := 1 to pred(N) do
    begin
        J := LastIndex;  Item := List[succ(LastIndex)];
        while Item < List[J] do
            begin
                List[succ(J)] := List[J];
                J := pred(J);
            end;
        List[succ(J)] := Item;
    end;

(*** print the array ***)
Writeln ('THE SORTED ARRAY IS:');
for J := 1 to N do
    begin
        Write (List[J]);
        if J mod 5 = 0 then
            Writeln;
    end;
end.
```

Before leaving this example, let us attempt to verify that the algorithm we have formalized in the program InsertionSort is correct. There is no need to verify that the list is input correctly or printed as desired; simply testing the program will confirm that. The central part of the program, the one that actually sorts the list, deserves some attention. While testing it may increase our confidence that it is correct, unsystematic testing can really establish only that the sorting algorithm works for the few examples on which we happen to try it.

At the point in the program where the sorting begins, the list to be sorted is represented as the sequence of elements in the array List[1..N]. We need to confirm that executing the sorting algorithm will satisfy three requirements:
a) the sorted array is to contain exactly the same elements as before, altered only in the sequence in which they occur;
b) in the sorted array, the inequality
    List[j] <= List[succ(j)]
is to be satisfied, for j in 1..N - 1;
c) execution of the algorithm always terminates in a finite number of steps.

156

Each of these properties can be established independently, by analyzing the program segment that performs sorting. To confirm (a), we need to consider the assignments made to elements of List. In the body of the while loop, we find the assignment

    List[succ(J)] := List[J]

This ensures that a duplicate of the value of List[J] is made at the succeeding index position, but it also overwrites the value that previously occupied that position. However, the next statement in the body of the same loop,

    J := pred(J)

causes the index J to be decremented through the index values. Therefore, the value overwritten by the first assignment will have been copied to a higher indexed position during the previous execution of the loop. All that remains is to analyze the first and the last executions of the loop.

When the while loop is initially entered, the value of J is equal to the value of LastIndex, and the value of succ(J) has been duplicated as the value of the variable, Item. Therefore, the value overwritten during the first execution of the loop has been saved. After the final iteration of the loop, the only value that was originally in the array, and which may no longer be present, is the value copied into Item. Also, the value in List[succ(J)] duplicates the value of List[J] (or of Item, if the body of the while loop is not executed even once). Thus the final assignment

    List[succ(J)] := Item

leaves the array with the same set of values that it had prior to executing the while loop.

The properties (b) and (c) are easier to verify, for this algorithm. To confirm (b), we hypothesize that before the while loop is executed, the elements of List[0..LastIndex] satisfy (b). Immediately after the while loop terminates execution, we know that Item < List[J], and that for all indices k in the range succ(J)..succ(LastIndex), Item >= List[k]. Also, the relative order of elements in the ranges 0..J and succ(J)..succ(LastIndex) has been left unchanged by executing the while statement. Therefore, property (b) is preserved when Item is inserted at index position succ(J).

The other piece of information required to assure that property (b) holds for the entire array is that every element of

157

the original array has been subjected to this re-insertion procedure. The <u>for</u> statement indexing over LastIndex assures this. The hypothesis assumed to hold at the beginning of the compound statement controlled by the <u>for</u> clause is that property (b) holds for the array segment List[0..Lastindex], and the result of executing the compound statement is to establish property (b) for the extended segment List[0..succ(LastIndex)]. After the final iteration, LastIndex equals pred(N), and succ(LastIndex) equals N, hence (b) holds for List[0..N].

Termination of the algorithm could only fail if the <u>while</u> loop failed to terminate. But the body of the <u>while</u> loop decrements the index J once in each execution, so the <u>while</u> loop cannot fail to terminate if there is any value in List[0..LastIndex] that is less than or equal to Item. The sentinel value at List[0] is such a value; it was placed there for exactly this purpose. Thus property (c) is assured.

Another question of some interest concerning sorting algorithms is their relative efficiency. The algorithm we have given is not particularly efficient, but on the other hand it is particularly simple. The degree of one's concern about efficiency depends on the magnitude of the task he sets out to perform. To sort an array of a few tens, or a few hundreds of elements, the insertion sort is perfectly adequate. To sort an array of thousands, or hundreds of thousands of elements, the cost of executing the simple insertion sort might be intolerable, and it would be worthwhile to search for more efficient algorithms, even though they are also more complex †.

Self-check questions:

1. In the program InsertionSort, what is the largest number of times the comparison Item < List[J] will be performed in the <u>while</u> clause? What is the least number of times?

2. What is meant by a sentinel value, and why is it used?

---

† For a comprehensive survey of sorting algorithms, see Wirth, N., <u>Algorithms + Data = Programs</u>, Prentice-Hall, Englewood Cliffs, N.J. 1975, Chapter 2.

6.1 The fundamental theorem of arithmetic tells us that every positive integer can be written as a product of primes, and that the factorization of a number into prime factors is unique. Compose an algorithm to find the prime factors of a positive integer, and use it to obtain the prime factorization of 204; 13,915; 22,019; and 27,648.

6.2 Every integer can be expressed as the product of a pair of integers, and for integers greater than 1, the pair is only unique if the number is a prime. Devise an algorithm that will give all pairs of factors of any positive integer, and try it on the integers 204; 13,915; 22,019; and 27,648.

6.3 Given a sequence of n elements, it is easy to generate permutations of the sequence by interchanging elements. It is not quite so easy to generate all of the n! possible permutations of the sequence. Compose an algorithm that will generate and print all permutations of a sequence represented as a vector of length n. Try it out by generating the 120 permutations of the sequence 1, 2, 3, 4, 5.

6.4 The binomial coefficients are important in combinatorial theory because the number of distinct ways of choosing a subset of r objects from a set of n is the value of $\binom{n}{r}$. Several interesting problems are of this type.

    a) A political banquet is being held for 100 loyal supporters of the party. The head table will seat only 10. How many ways are there to compose the group that will be seated at the head table?

    b) The same political banquet is being held in a hall that has 10 tables, each seating 10 persons. If the tables are all alike, how many ways are there to compose the groups of persons assigned to various tables?

    c) The aforementioned banquet is being held for 100 people, to be seated at 10 tables of 10 persons each. All tables are alike but one, that one being distinguished as the head table. How many ways are there to distribute the party regulars at tables? (Do you see how difficult it is to be a politician?)

6.5 For some combinatorial problems, it is difficult to give solutions in terms of simple formulas, but it is possible to compose an iterative algorithm to generate solutions.

a) A hostess is holding a dinner for an important group of guests, all of whom are arriving as couples. She has a long, rectangular table and wishes to seat her husband at the head of it, herself at the foot, and the guests along each side in equal numbers. An additional constraint is that men and women are to be seated alternately around the table, and no woman is to be seated next to her escort. How many seating arrangements are there if the number of diners (counting the host couple) is 6? How many for 8, 10, 12, 14, 16, 18 or 22 diners?

b) The hostess, having discovered a source of difficulty when the number of diners is divisible by four, has purchased a round table. No place is distinguished, but she still wishes men and women to be seated alternately, with no woman seated next to her escort. How many seating arrangements are possible for parties of the sizes given in (a)?

6.6 Compose an algorithm to divide one polynomial by another, giving as results a quotient and a remainder polynomial.

6.7 a) Devise an algorithm which, when presented with two lists of names, each sorted in alphabetical order, will merge them into a single list that is sorted in alphabetical order. (This is a commonly performed operation on pairs of lists, known as merging.

b) Modify your algorithm of part (a) so that any name appearing on both of the original lists will appear only once on the merged list. This corresponds to taking the union of two sets. It is an operation that should be used, for instance, in merging lists for direct mail advertising in order to avoid duplicate mailings.

6.8 Compose a Pascal program to:

a) Read a list of names in the format

first name { middle name / or / middle initial } last name

where middle name is optional, middle initial is optional, and if middle initial is present, the period that may follow it is optional. Names are to be separated from one another by one or more blank characters.

b) Sort the list into alphabetical order by last name, or if last names are the same, by first name and middle name (or initial).

c) Print the sorted list in the format:

last name, first name, middle name or initial

d) Include in the test data the names:
Jack S. Phogbound
Jubilation T Cornpone
John Q.Public (no space after the period; must be rejected)
Abner Yokum
Daisy Mae Yokum
U. R. Stuck   (invalid format for first name; must be rejected)

Hint: if the acceptable names are transformed into the desired output format prior to sorting, the comparison operation required for sorting will be easier to program.

6.9 Compose a Pascal program that will:

a) Read a sequence of data records, each record in the form of a name, given as a string of up to 36 characters, and followed by a real number representing the height in centimeters of the named individual. Reading should terminate when a data record containing a zero value for height is encountered.

b) Compute the average height from the sequence read in (a).

c) Compute and print a distribution function of the number of heights falling into each 10-centimeter interval from 100 to 220 centimeters.

d) Compute and print the median value of height, and list the names of those individuals (there may be more than one) having the median height.

6.10 Given a list of names of persons, and a binary symmetric relation of friendship (if A is a friend of B, then B is a friend of A), find two names that have the greatest number of friends in common.

6.11 Use mathematical reasoning to prove that the algorithm of Example 6.3.1 always terminates normally.

7 GETTING INFORMATION IN AND OUT OF A COMPUTER

Since a computer has neither eyes, ears, fingers, nor tongue, we must put forth more effort to communicate with it than we are used to in conversing with our fellow human beings. When we input information to ourselves from the printed page, an enormous amount of information processing is done by our eyes and by a large portion of our brain that is specialized for vision, and does no 'thinking' in the usual sense. This magnificient structure of nerve cells enables us to perceive letters of the alphabet from a physical stimulus that consists of tiny patterns of light focused on the retinas of our eyes. Even though the images of a few words of text constitute only a very small part of the total visual stimulus, our visual information processing system is so effective that we are able to perceive whole groups of letters without conscious effort, and in a time so short that to us it seems immediate. This marvelous visual perceptual system is the end product of evolution since life began, and is not available on the latest models of electronic computers designed by man.

Instead of supplying the computer with a printed page, one must resort to cruder and less flexible media for passing information. First of all, we must agree on a standard, finite set of characters that we will have our computer recognize. Then, these characters can be encoded in some form acceptable to the computer. Depending on the conceptual level on which you are examining the computer, you may think of the encoded equivalent of a character as being an integer number, a sequence of binary bits, or as a sequence of electrical signals. By means of the encoding, it is possible to transmit sequences of characters to the computer from a terminal resembling an electric typewriter or from a punched-card reader. Encoded sequences can be transmitted over telephone lines or by radio, from the next room, or halfway around the world. But these are technical matters, and the point to remember now is that the entire perceptual ability of a computer is limited to accepting input sequences formed from a prescribed set of characters. Our communication with the computer is always subject to this limitation, although it can be partially overcome by devising algorithms to enable the computer to interpret the input sequences in a way we desire.

Another obligation we incur if we wish to communicate with the computer is that of putting our inputs - character strings - into machine readable forms. This means that we must enter all the information through a keyboard, either for direct transmission to a computer, or in order to punch rectangular holes in paper cards, later to be read by a card reader attached to the computer. It is the laborious task of retyping huge stores of information to get it into machine readable form that is one of the greatest obstacles to the formation of large computer-managed data bases, such as the card catalog of a labrary, or an index to the collections of a museum.

7.1 Character-stream input

For most computing applications, one wishes to have the computer analyze and interpret a string of input characters, using agreed-upon conventions of meaning. When this is done, one need not worry about all of the details of how the interpretation is done; conversion is automatic. The agreed-upon conventions used in Pascal are quite simple. In an input statement, (Read or Readln) there is a list of variables whose values are to be set by reading and interpreting an input string. The particular conversion algorithm to be used on each successive non-blank substring of input is determined by the declared data type of the variable whose value is being set. For integers, an input string is to consist of numerals, possibly preceded by a plus or a minus sign. For real variables, an input string is to be an integer or a decimal number, possibly preceded by a sign and followed by an exponent in scientific notation. The exponent is set off from the modulus by the letter "E", so that $3.5*10^{-4}$ would appear as 3.5E-4. Boolean values are represented by the words TRUE and FALSE. Variables of type Char receive the values of individual characters as they appear in the input. Standard conventions used for the conversion of Pascal input are among the simplest in general use.

At times, however, it is important to have some knowledge of the mechanism underlying the input translation mechanism. Writing a program to solicit input from a client at a computer terminal is one such instance. As we have mentioned previously, the data available to a Pascal program from the standard file Input consists of a stream of characters. Input is a predefined file of a standard type, Text, whose definition is equivalent to:

```
type
    Text = file of Char;
var
    Input : Text;
```

As you learned in Chapter 5, this implies that there also exists a special variable of type Char called the Input file buffer, which can be referred to by the name Input↑.

The action of the standard procedure Read on an argument of type Char can be quite simply described in terms of file operations. If Ch is the name of a Char variable, then Read (Ch) is equivalent to:

```
begin
    Ch := Input↑;
    Get (Input);
end
```

Text files are extraordinarily useful, and Text files other than Input and Output may be declared in a Pascal program. The standard procedure Read may be applied to any Text file, by giving the file name as the first argument to the procedure, i.e.

Read (Filename, Ch)

The Read procedure, unlike a user-defined procedure, may have any number of parameters, subject to the restrictions that

a) only the first parameter may be a Text file variable,
b) each parameter must be a variable or a field name,
c) the type of each parameter (other than the file designator) must be Boolean, Char, Integer, Real, or Alfa.

Text files also provide a line structure for the convenience of the user. A line is a sequence of characters terminated by a special, end-of-line character. Since the internal representation of an end-of-line character will vary from one computer

165

system to another[†], Pascal does not provide a standard end-of-line character, but only a means by which to test its occurrence. A Boolean function, called Eoln, returns the value True if the character obtained in the last Get was the end-of-line, and returns False otherwise. In order that a user will not be troubled by the appearance of an unrecognizable character in his input stream, the file buffer is automatically assigned a blank character whenever the end-of-line occurs. When the function Eoln indicates that an end-of-line has been reached, a subsequent execution of Get will produce the first character of the following line (if any) in the file buffer.

Frequently, one will wish to align the buffer pointer at the beginning of a new line of a Text file. This can be done by the following sequence of statements:

```
while not Eoln (Input) do
    Get (Input);
Get (Input);
```

The while statement causes Get to be repeated until the Eoln function returns a True value. One more Get is then performed in order to obtain the first character of the following line in the input buffer.

This action is combined with he Read procedure in another Pascal procedure called Readln. The effect of

```
Readln (A, B, C);
```

is equivalent to the sequence

```
Read (A); Read (B); Read (C);
while not Eoln do
    Get;
Get;
```

The procedure Readln is often invoked with an empty argument list, just in order to reposition the input buffer pointer at the beginning of a new line.

[†]   In fact, some computer systems don't even employ such a convention. Instead, a line may be preceded by an integer value giving its length in characters.

In fact, if you are writing a program whose function is to exchange messages with a user at a computer terminal, then Readln is exactly the procedure which solicits input from the terminal. An exchange with the terminal might be programmed as follows:

```
Writeln ('HOW'S THE WEATHER TODAY?');
Readln; (*Solicits Input from the user*)
CP := 0;
while not Eoln do
    begin
        CP := succ (CP);
        Read (Message [CP]);
    end;
Write ('OH IT'S ANOTHER ');
for I := 1 to CP do
    Write (Message[I]);
Writeln (' DAY.');
```

For this program segment to work properly, however, the initial state of the end-of-line condition must be True. Otherwise, the situation is that the computer will expect the first character of a user's response to be furnished before it has had an opportunity to print a message on his terminal to request it!

In Pascal implementations designed to be used primarily with input taken from punched cards or stored files, an initial test of the end-of-line condition will return False. An implementation designed for a live input environment will make the end-of-line condition initially True. You will have to consult the documentation for your local Pascal compiler to determine which condition applies on the computer you are using.

Self-check questions:

1. Give a sequence of Pascal file manipulation and assignment statements equivalent to Read (Ch), where Ch is a variable of type Char.

2. When a test of the function Eoln (F) returns True, what value is held by the file buffer F↑?

3. Is there any logical relation between the functions Eoln and Eof?

4. Of what use is the procedure Readln?

167

5. Given the following three lines of text in an Input file,
      ABCDEF
      GHIJKLMN
      OPQRST
and variables C1, C2, C3, of type Char, what values would be produced by each of the following statement sequences? Assume the end-of-line condition is initially False in each case.

a) Read (C1); Read (C2); Read (C3);

b) Readln (C1); Readln (C2); Readln (C3);

c) Readln (C1, C2, C3); C1 := Input↑;

7.2 Interpreting the input

If all input to the computer must be in the form of character strings, how does one input numbers in order to do numerical computations? Quite obviously, by representing numbers as strings of numerals, just as is done on a printed page. We have learned in the primary grades of elementary school how to interpret these strings of numerals as numbers. In order for the computer to interpret them, someone must provide a computational algorithm for this task. Ordinarily, in composing computer programs, one does not worry about providing such an algorithm; the programming language provides standard functions already implemented as computer programs to interpret several forms of numeral strings as numbers. However, just so that we can gain an appreciation for what is involved, let us go through the development of such an algorithm from the ground up.

Although for some scientific applications in which the computer is used in data collection, one will find it convenient to invent a special set of characters to be used as input to the computer, for the vast majority of general purpose computing, people use one of two standard sets of characters and encodings for computer input. The characters consist of the twenty-six letters of the Roman alphabet, in upper and lower case, the ten decimal numerals, between 20 and 30 special symbols and punctuation marks, and the blank space which is also an encoded character.

What we really mean by "interpreting the input" is a change of representation within the computer. So long as a number is represented as a string of numerals, one can only do operations with it that are defined on characters; these operations have nothing to do with arithmetic. In order to make use of the computer's arithmetic operations, a number must be represented within the computer in a standard form designated by its designer. Pascal provides a pair of standard functions that can be used to translate between these representations for individual characters. If Numeral is a variable of type Char, then the numerical representation of this character can be obtained by means of the expression

        Ord (Numeral)

This function translates each character into the ordinal number that describes its position in the character set, starting from ordinal 0 for the initial character. All we know for certain about the internal representation of the numerals '0'..'9' in the character set is that they form an ascending sequence, without "gaps". It is necessary to translate this sequence of ordinals,

        Ord ('0') .. Ord ('9')

into the sequence 0..9. To do this, it will suffice to subtract Ord ('0') from the internal representation of each numeral. Thus the interpreted value of Numeral is

        Ord (Numeral) - Ord ('0')

Once it is known how to translate an individual numeral to its equivalent numerical representation, the arithmetic capability of the computer can be applied to calculate numerical values equivalent to strings of numerals. The idea is simple. If you scan a character string from left to right, proceeding one character at a time and decoding each numeral as it is found, then you can accumulate the value of the number built up so far. Each time another digit is found, the previously accumulated number should be multiplied by 10 and the newly found digit added to the result. When no new digit is found, the accumulated result will be the desired interpretation of the string of numerals. Initially, when no digits have been found, the accumulated result should be zero. An iteration graph describing this portion of the algorithm is

```
┌─────────────────────────────────────────────────────────┐
│ Accumulator := 0;  Digit := Input↑                       │
├─────────────────────────────────────────────────────────┤
│ while not end-of-number                                  │
│   ┌─────────────────────────────────────────────────────┤
│   │ Accumulator := 10*Accumulator +                      │
│   │         Ord (Digit) - Ord ('0');                     │
│   │ Get (Input);  Digit := Input↑                        │
└───┴─────────────────────────────────────────────────────┘
```

169

Although the iteration graph given above could be translated into a Pascal program segment, and would yield correct results for many numeral strings, it fails to check for numeral strings that cannot be translated to a directly representable integer. If translation of a number that exceeds that maximum representable integer is attempted, the computer will balk at the attempt, issuing a message that there has occurred integer overflow. If we wish to check for this condition as the input string is interpreted, then the magnitude of the accumulated value must be checked before it is increased, each time another digit is about to be appended. Upon including this test, the algorithm becomes

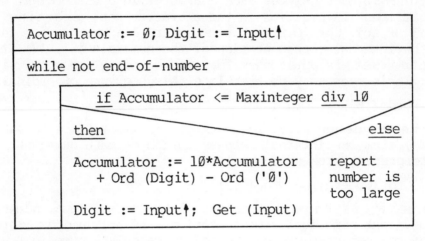

To complete the translation of the algorithm into a Pascal program, some declarations must be given,

    var Accumulator : Integer;
        Digit : Char;

The iteration control clause "while not end-of-number" should include both a test that the end of the input string has not been reached and that the next character to be analyzed is in fact a numeral. Since the numerals are encoded in ascending order as characters, this clause can be given by

    while not Eoln and (Digit >= '0') and (Digit <= '9') do

In testing the magnitude of the accumulated result, there is a predeclared and preinitialized Pascal constant called Maxint, whose value is that of the maximum representable integer. Thus the expression to be tested could be written as

    Accumulator <= Maxint div 10

170

A final step in the Pascal program will be to print the result.

```
program InterpretNumerals (Input, Output);
   var
      Digit : Char;
      Accumulator : Integer;
   begin
      Accumulator := 0;  Digit := Input↑;
      while not Eoln and (Digit >= '0') and (Digit <= '9') do
         begin
            if Accumulator <= Maxint div 10 then
               Accumulator := 10*Accumulator +
                     (Ord (Digit) - Ord ('0'))
            else
               Writeln
               ('NUMERAL STRING IS TOO LARGE TO BE REPRESENTED');
            Get (Input);  Digit := Input↑;
         end;
      Writeln (Accumulator);
   end.
```

The careful reader will note that the scheme used here to test for integer overflow is not foolproof! Although it will catch almost all numeral strings that would produce an integer too large to be represented, one could, knowing the value of Maxint, devise an input that would produce overflow of Accumulator, but that would not be detected as too large by the above algorithm. It is left to the reader to determine how, by trying to devise such an input.

The algorithm has been left in this state, almost but not quite perfect, to make a point. The point is this. Almost perfect algorithms may be fully satisfactory for your own personal use since you have no reason to sabotage a computation by malicious intent, and since you are in complete control of the inputs to be furnished to the algorithm. But as soon as you begin to advertise an algorithm as suitable for public use, or to incorporate it into a large group of programs that interact with one another in a manner not always predictable, the flaw in the almost perfect algorithm is very likely to be found out. The best programming proctice is to proceed as though you will not have control over the inputs to be furnished, and not to be satisfied with almost perfect algorithms. As an exercise, try to correct the flaw in this algorithm.

Self-check questions:

1. Why must the representation of numerical input be altered by the computer?

2. When a digit is read, why is Ord ('0') subtracted from Ord (Digit) to obtain its numerical value?

7.3 Output

Now that we know something about how information is input to the computer, it will be easier to describe the output system as well. Output is pretty much the reverse of input. Data exist in the computer in internal forms that depend on the data type of each item. For output, these internal forms must all be converted to representations of the data items by character strings. The characters to be output are assembled in an output buffer, that you may think of as an array of characters of sufficient length to hold one output line. When the end-of-line character occurs in the output stream, the buffer array is transmitted to an output device. If this device is a typewriter terminal or a line printer, the line is printed for the benefit of a human observer. The output device might also be one that provides storage for future reference of the data by a computer, in which case the data may be represented by patterns of magnetism in metallic oxides on the surface of a plastic tape, a disc or a drum, or by holes in a card or a paper tape. We shall only consider printed output.

Just as with input, the conversion from internal representation to character representation for output is done automatically, using an algorithm appropriate to the data type of each output expression. The output procedures are Write and Writeln. One of these procedure names is followed by a parenthesized list of expressions that may, of course, include the names of variables or constants as special cases of expressions. When Write is used, characters are added to a line of output, but the line is not terminated. Writeln adds an end-of-line character after the characters to be output. Writeln can be called with no arguments to cause subsesquent printing to begin a new line, or to skip a line.

Initially, when you compose and run your own computer programs, you may be quite satisfied merely to print the value of a variable that represents the result when the execution of the algorithm is completed. An instruction such as

172

```
Writeln (X)
```

will cause the value of the variable X to be printed by itself in a line of output. As you gain more experience in running programs on the computer, you will either encounter the problem of printing several values and forgetting in which order you had called for them to be output, or else you may feel that a single lonely number appearing on a large and otherwise blank sheet of paper does not do justice to the effort expended in producing it. In either case, you will wish to produce output containing some annotation. This is easily done.

One of the ways to have a comment printed is just to include the desired message, enclosed in quotation marks, in the list of expressions to be output. Thus, to dress up a naked number, one might ask to have an introductory message printed, such as

```
Writeln ('THE ANSWER IS', X)
```

If the value of the variable X is 24, for instance, then this instruction will cause the following line to be printed:

```
THE ANSWER IS          24
```

Or, if the purpose of the annotation is to identify which variables the printed values belonged to, the appropriate output instruction might look like:

```
Writeln ('A =', A, 'B =', B, 'C =', C)
```

Other uses of messages in the output are to identify unexpected or erroneous values of data that are encountered in the course of the computation as the algorithm tests data for validity. You may also wish to have printed on the output a title, a brief description of the problem for which you have composed your algorithm, the initial values of data used for the computation, your own name and the date, or other information relevent to the computing application.

As you gain more experience in planning the layout of computer-generated output, you will soon become aware of the fact that the width allocated by Pascal for printing of numerical values is sometimes excessive. Numerical output is allocated sufficient space in which to print the largest value that might be generated. For Real values, as many as 13 characters may be printed: a minus sign, seven decimal digits, a point, an apostrophe to indicate an exponent of ten, the sign of the exponent, and two decimal digits for the value of the exponent. A print field width of fourteen spaces is allowed. For integers, a print field width of twelve characters is specified as the default option, but in recognition of the fact that in many cases, fewer characters will actually be printed, Pascal allows the width of the print field for integers to be controlled. Following any expression in an output list, one may put : <integer> where <integer> designates the number of characters to be included in the print field of that item. For instance,

        Writeln ('THE ANSWER IS', 24 :4)

will produce the output line

        THE ANSWER IS   24

in contrast to the wider spacing obtained by default.

Self-check questions:

1.   What will be printed by the following Writeln statements?

      a) Writeln ('P', 'ASC', 'AL');

      b) N := 50;   Writeln ('(', N, ')');

      c) N := 50;   Writeln ('(', N :2, ')');

      d) N := 50;   Writeln ('(', N :1, ')').

7.4 Constructing tables

There are many computing applications in which the result is not expressed as a single number or even a few numbers, but as a whole table of values giving results applicable to a variety of cases. When humans prepare tables by hand, they usually use special forms, or lacking a suitable form, prepare one for themselves by ruling lines on a piece of paper. The form indicates the alignment of entries in the table. If a table is to be prepared with a typewriter, the problem is complicated slightly. Unless the typewriter is being used to fill in spaces on a prepared form, tab stops can be used to obtain alignment of entries into columns. Constructing tables with a computer is similar to using a typewriter for the task, in that one must decide in advance on the spacings needed for alignment, and incorporate these spacings into the output instructions that will direct the printing of lines of the table. The process is best illustrated by an example.

You have seen from a previous example (4.3.1) that a computational algorithm can be devised to work out the monthly payments required to pay off a mortgage at a given rate of interest and extending over a given number of years. Now suppose the banker, as a service to his customers, wants to show them how much interest will be paid on a mortgage each year, and how rapidly the balance of the principal amount is being reduced. We shall not review the computation required to obtain the values, but shall concentrate on providing a tabular output that can be shown to a customer.

Example 7.4.1 -- Mortgage repayment tables

The body of the tables indicating the yearly progress of mortgage repayment is to consist of lines listing the year, the amount of interest paid in that year, and the balance remaining at the year's end. The display is to be approximately centered on a page 60 columns wide. An equally important part of preparing tables is to provide appropriate titles and column headings. A logical way to proceed will be to write out a page in the way it is intended to appear, and to use this sample page as a guide to the composition of output instructions. In preparing the sample page, we have allowed each numeric variable sixteen columns. Within the sixteen columns allocated for each number, the actual number will be printed as far to the right as possible.

Most of the lines of the title and introductory text can be generated just by duplicating them in Writeln statements, allowing for indentation where required. For example, the principal title would be generated by

```
Writeln
('*****  M O R T G A G E   P A Y M E N T   T A B L E S  *****')
```

Lines in which a number is printed must allow for printing the value of a variable between sequences of text. Thus, the fifth through eighth non-blank lines could be generated by the instructions

```
                    (Sample page)

***** M O R T G A G E   P A Y M E N T   T A B L E S  *****

LISTING THE INTEREST PAID AND THE BALANCE REMAINING
AT THE END OF EACH YEAR OF THE DURATION OF A MORTGAGE

PREPARED BY THE DIME SAVINGS BANK FOR MR. OWEN PLENTY

TERMS: PRINCIPAL AMOUNT:   30000 DOLLARS
       RATE OF INTEREST:       7 PER CENT
       DURATION:              25 YEARS
       MONTHLY PAYMENT:   208.70 DOLLARS

NOTE: THE MONTHLY PAYMENT DOES NOT INCLUDE LOCAL TAXES

       YEAR    INTEREST PAID     BALANCE
       1973        2089          29581
       1974        2076          29153
        .            .              .
        .            .              .
        .            .              .
       1988          88           2416
```

Writeln ('TERMS: PRINCIPAL AMOUNT:', Principal:8, ' DOLLARS');
Writeln ('   RATE OF INTEREST:', Rate :8, ' PER CENT');
Writeln ('   DURATION: ', Duration :8, ' YEARS');
Writeln
('   MONTHLY PAYMENT: ', MonthlyPayment :8:2, ' DOLLARS');

Notice that the subtitles must be padded on the right with
blanks so that each string is of the same length, in order
that the units descriptors in the right column of the
printed page will be aligned. Since each variable has its
value printed in a field of fixed width, no misalignment can
occur in printing these values.

    The column titles of the table are printed in similar
fashion,

Writeln ('   YEAR   INTEREST PAID   BALANCE');

but some care must be taken to ensure that the spacing of
column titles agrees with the spacing of the columns of

numbers. We first decide upon the spacings of the columns, in order to allow sufficient room for the longest number anticipated in each column to be printed, and to obtain the desired visual appearance of the table. Here, for instance, we have allowed sixteen columns in which to print each dollar amount, four columns to print the year, and have chosen to indent the first column by eight spaces for the sake of appearance. Subsequently, we count the characters to be printed in the column headings, so as to secure alignment.

The output instruction to enter numbers in the table would be embedded in an iteration loop, such as

```
for Year := Firstyear to Lastyear do
    begin
        .
        .
        Writeln (Year :12, Interest :16, Balance :16);
    end
```

For those parts of the table in which a blank line is called for to improve the appearance, we invoke the procedure Writeln, giving no arguments.

There is one more potential problem in creating a program for the banker to use. The fourth non-blank line contains the name of the bank and the name of the customer. If our program is to be designed for use by more that one bank, then the name of the bank will not appear explicitly in the program but will consist of a sequence of characters whose exact length cannot be predicted by the programmer. To accomodate names of various lengths, the character strings may be kept in arrays,

```
const
    Maxlength = 44;
var
    Bankname, Customername: array [1...Maxlength] of Char;
```

Integer variables Lengthbank and Lengthcustomer may be used to record the actual number of characters representing each name.

When initial data are supplied to the program, the names and their lengths may be read from an input file by a statement sequence such as:

```
Readln (Lengthbank);
for Index := 1 to Lengthbank do
   Read (Bankname [Index]);
Readln;
Readln (Lengthcustomer);
for Index := 1 to Lengthcustomer do
   Read (Customername [Index]);
Readln;
```

where the lines of input contain:

```
17
DIME SAVINGS BANK
15
MR. OWEN PLENTY
```

To print strings whose lengths depend on the data, a for statement can also be used. Thus, a line of output containing the names could be generated by:

```
Write ('PREPARED BY THE');
for Index := 1 to Lengthbank do
   Write (Bankname [Index]);
Write (' FOR ');
for Index := 1 to Lengthcustomer do
   Write (Customername [Index]);
Writeln;
```

At this point it should be clear that we have not yet solved the problem. For part of the specification was that the table was to be printed on paper 60 columns wide, and if one happens to encounter a bank and a customer both having long names, they won't fit into such a line. For example, a report prepared by Manufacturer's Hanover Trust for Mr. Alexander Graham Bell will appear as:

PREPARED BY THE MANUFACTURER'S HANOVER TRUST FOR MR. ALEXAND

Something must be done, or the public relations department of the bank will arrange to have its computer programmer replaced. The problem can be solved with a little compu-tation. An equally attractive display would be

             PREPARED BY THE MANUFACTURER'S HANOVER TRUST
                 FOR MR. ALEXANDER GRAHAM BELL

In order to have these lines printed with the indentation required to center them, we need to do a little arithmetic. The string 'PREPARED BY THE ' contains sixteen characters, and so the sum of 16 plus the value of Lengthbank plus twice the length of the indentation should total the length of a line, 60 characters. We can use an integer variable Indent, and compute its value by

Indent := (60 - 16 - Lengthbank) div 2

The first of the two lines containing names is printed by the following sequence of instructions,

```
for Index := 1 to Indent do
    Write (' ');
Write ('PREPARED BY THE ');
for Index:= 1 to Lengthbank do
    Write (Bankname [Index]);
```

In the execution of these instructions, the indentation and the name of the bank will be assembled into the output buffer one character at a time. A similar sequence of instructions can be used to write the line containing the customer's name. This scheme should secure the computer programmer's reputation with the public relations department of the bank for yet another fortnight.

7.5 Using the computer to generate reports and catalogs

As you are no doubt aware, computers are routinely used to prepare reports and catalogs. Either the computer output itself is the finished product, or is reproduced by a photocopy process. In more sophisticated applications, the computer may control a typesetting machine. The direct use of computer printout for reports has many limitations from the point of view of the printer's art, but it has one great advantage to recommend it: it is cheap, when only a small number of copies is required. Because of the limitation of only a single type font and size, often restricted to upper-case letters, the appearance of computer printout is monotonous. Special care must be taken to organize the display of information so that it will be intelligible to a human reader. Unfortately, most computer programmers are not experienced in the graphic arts, and have themselves grown so used to reading computer printout that they tend to overlook its deficiencies as a medium for visual display of information. The standard for appearance of computer-generated reports is not high.

Nevertheless, computer printout has found widespread acceptance. Typical of the types of reports prepared by computer are monthly financial statements, inventory reports, library catalogs, work schedules, and bibliographies. We can learn some principles of organizing information on a printed page that will help us to prepare readable reports.

The basic rules accepted by people who read one of the Indo-European languages are that clues as to what data are contained on a page are to be found in some sort of heading at the top of the page, and if a page consists of several separate items appearing in a column from top to bottom, then clues as to the content of each item are to be found by scanning down the left side of the column. These rules are implemented in our practice of displaying titles at the tops of pages, of putting page numbers in an upper corner, of heading dictionary pages with the initial and final words that appear on each page, of indenting from the left margin in a column, and of aligning paragraph numbers and subtitles on the left column boundary.

There is one other important rule, and it is the hardest to implement successfully in computer printout. Titles and headings are to be made strikingly different in appearance from the body of text that they head. This last rule is of particular importance in newspapers in which an enormous amount of information is competing for the limited attention of the reader. There are some other general guidelines as well, all having to do with the physical appearance of the text. The ratio of the length to the height of a printed line should not be greater than about 36:1, or else the reader tends to lose track of which line he is on as hhs eye scans back from the right end of one line to the left end of the following one. If the line is interrupted by large spaces, this ratio should be lowered.

A few ways that people have found to make titles and headings stand out in printouts are to use extended spacings, to bracket titles in patterns of special symbols, usually asterisks, to enclose them in boxes constructed from asterisks, plus signs, or vertical and horizontal bars, to underline them, and to create large font letters by pictorial representation. Here are some illustrations.

Underlining: (This requires a printing device capable of overstriking)

THIS IS A TITLE

Extended spacing:

T H I S   I S   A   T I T L E

Bracketing with asterisks:

***** THIS IS A TITLE *****

Enclosing in a box:

```
++++++++++++++++++++++++++++++++++++++
+                                    +
+          THIS IS A TITLE           +
+                                    +
++++++++++++++++++++++++++++++++++++++
```

Using large font, pictorial letters:

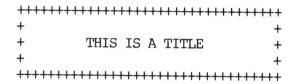

The techniques used to manage the display of titles constructed by any of these means (except underlining) are similar. In a later section, we shall investigate printing with pictorial letters. For now, however, we shall continue to be less concerned with the details of how to program the printing of a page of a report than with how to lay it out for ease of reading.

Example 7.5.1 -- Printing the semester time schedule

An example of a report that is usefully generated by computer is the time schedule of courses offered each semester at a university. The time schedule must be produced quickly, at low cost, for use by students and advisors in advance registration for the next semester. The information it is to contain is already under the management of a computer-based accounting system. An example of a page of a time schedule formerly in use by one university, and printed from computer output, is shown in Figure 7.1. This report relies for its success on a high degree of motivation by the reader to ferret out the information he requires, for it was not designed with much consideration for the human reader. We can improve it.

CALL#	DPT	CRS	TITLE		CRD

15630 HBW 111 INTRO HEBREW I 3.0

	SEC	TYP	DAYS	TIME	BUILDING	ROOM	INSTRUCTOR
15631	1	REC	MWF	11:00-11:50	RM TO BE ARR		STAFF
15632	2	REC	MWF	12:00-12:50	RM TO BE ARR		STAFF
15633	3	REC	MWF	2:00- 2:50	RM TO BE ARR		STAFF

15660 HBW 151 INTERMED HEBREW I 3.0

PREREQ: HBW 112 OR EQUIV

	SEC	TYP	DAYS	TIME	BUILDING	ROOM	INSTRUCTOR
15661	1	REC	MWF	10:00-10:50	RM TO BE ARR		BEIZER

15690 HBW 221 ADVANCED HEBREW I 3.0

PREREQ: HBW 152 OR EQUIV

	SEC	TYP	DAYS	TIME	BUILDING	ROOM	INSTRUCTOR
15691	1	REC	MWF	9:00- 9:50	RM TO BE ARR		BEIZER

15720 HBW 285 CLASSICAL HEBREW 3.0

PREREQ: HBW 222 OR PERMIS OF INSTR

	SEC	TYP	DAYS	TIME	BUILDING	ROOM	INSTRUCTOR
15721	1	LEC	MWF	1:00- 1:50	RM TO BE ARR		LICHTENSTEIN

****************************** HIS COURSES ******************************

CALL#	DPT	CRS	TITLE		CRD

15750 HIS 101 EUR HIS: PRE-INDUSTR 3.0

	SEC	TYP	DAYS	TIME	BUILDING	ROOM	INSTRUCTOR
15751	1	LEC	MW	11:00-11:50	RM TO BE ARR		WELTSCH
		REC	F	11:00-11:50	RM TO BE ARR		
15752	2	LEC	MW	11:00-11:50	RM TO BE ARR		WELTSCH
		REC	F	11:00-11:50	RM TO BE ARR		
15753	3	LEC	MW	11:00-11:50	RM TO BE ARR		WELTSCH
		REC	F	12:00-12:50	RM TO BE ARR		

15780 HIS 103 INTRO-STUDY AMER HIS 3.0

	SEC	TYP	DAYS	TIME	BUILDING	ROOM	INSTRUCTOR
15781	1	LEC	TU	10:00-10:50	RM TO BE ARR		KAVENAGH
		REC	TH	10:00-11:50	RM TO BE ARR		
15782	2	LEC	TU	10:00-10:50	RM TO BE ARR		KAVENAGH
		REC	TU	12:00- 1:50	RM TO BE ARR		
15783	3	LEC	TU	10:00-10:50	RM TO BE ARR		KAVENAGH
		REC	TH	12:00- 1:50	RM TO BE ARR		
15784	4	LEC	TU	10:00-10:50	RM TO BE ARR		KAVENAGH
		REC	TU	12:00- 1:50	RM TO BE ARR		
15785	5	LEC	TU	10:00-10:50	RM TO BE ARR		KAVENAGH
		REC	TH	10:00-11:50	RM TO BE ARR		
15786	6	LEC	TU	10:00-10:50	RM TO BE ARR		KAVENAGH
		REC	TH	12:00- 1:50	RM TO BE ARR		

15810 HIS 140 PERSPECT WORLD HIS 3.0

PREREQ: FRESHMAN STANDING

	SEC	TYP	DAYS	TIME	BUILDING	ROOM	INSTRUCTOR
15811	1	LEC	TUTH	9:30-10:45	RM TO BE ARR		WEINSTEIN

Figure 7.1

As it stands, the page of Figure 7.1 does not make proper use of a tabular display of data, for its column headings are repeated so often that they get in the way of the information. Also, there is no visual means of distinguishing the column headings from items of information in the columns. One must read and interpret the headings, in order to determine that they are indeed headings.

On each page, information is grouped by academic course and by sections of that course. However, upon scanning down the left margin where one has been taught by experience to look for markings distinguishing the individual items of a table, the indices encountered first are the call numbers. These call numbers are used for internal bookkeeping purposes by the accounting system, and are of very little interest to the student who is looking up an entry for a particular course. They should not be given such a high priority in their placement on the page.

In Figure 7.2 an alternate format is suggested for displaying exactly the same information. Since the courses are grouped in the time schedule according to their general academic subject area, this designation is the one that a reader would use as a coarse index in seeking a particular course. Therefore, the subject area of the first course appearing on the page is displayed at he top of the page, just as is done in dictionaries or telephone directories to indicate the range of content of a page.

The information display on the page is not strictly tabular, since successive lines may have differing information content, and since some lines will be used for prose comments. Nevertheless, the organization is sufficiently regular that a template of the information fields of each entry can appear just once under the subject area heading and the reader will not be confused.

The entries corresponding to individual courses now contain only information, uncontaminated by intermixing column headings as was done previously. In order to locate an individual course, the reader can scan down the left margin, where he finds listed only the course designation codes that are in common use throughout the university. If the entry for a course must be broken, listing some sections on a following page, then the course designation is repeated there. Since the subject area defines the major groupings of

```
+++++++++++++++++++++++++++++++++++++++++++
+                                         +
+              H E B R E W                +
+                                         +
+++++++++++++++++++++++++++++++++++++++++++
COURSE   CREDITS     TITLE
  SECTION TYPE DAYS    TIME         CALL#   INSTRUCTOR    BLDG   ROOM


HBW 111   3          INTRODUCTORY HEBREW I
     1    REC   MWF     11:00-11:50  15631   STAFF
     2    REC   MWF     12:00-12:50  15632   STAFF
     3    REC   MWF      2:00- 2:50  15633   STAFF


HBW 151   3          INTERMEDIATE HEBREW I
  PREREQ:  HBW 112 OR EQUIV
     1    REC   MWF     10:00-10:50  15661   BEIZER


HBW 221   3          ADVANCED HEBREW I
  PREREQ:  HBW 152 OR EQUIV
     1    REC   MWF      9:00- 9:50  15691   BEIZER


HBW 285   3          CLASSICAL HEBREW
     1    LEC   MWF      1:00- 1:50  15721   LICHTENSTEIN


          +++++++++++++++++++++++++++++++++++++++++++
          +                                         +
          +              H I S T O R Y              +
          +                                         +
          +++++++++++++++++++++++++++++++++++++++++++
COURSE   CREDITS     TITLE
  SECTION TYPE DAYS    TIME         CALL#   INSTRUCTOR


HIS 101   3          EUROPEAN HISTORY: PRE-INDUSTRIAL
     1-3  LEC   MW     11:00-11:50           WELTSCH
     1    REC   F      11:00-11:50  15751
     2    REC   F      11:00-11:50  15752
     3    REC   F      12:00-12:50  15753


HIS 103   3          INTRODUCTION TO THE STUDY OF AMERICAN HISTORY
     1-6  LEC   TU     10:00-10:50           KAVENAGH
     1    REC   TH     10:00-11:50  15781
     2    REC   TH     12:00- 1:50  15782
     3    REC   TH     12:00- 1:50  15783
     4    REC   TU     12:00- 1:50  15784
     5    REC   TH     10:00-11:50  15785
     6    REC   TH     12:00- 1:50  15786


HIS 140   3          PERSPECTIVES ON WORLD HISTORY
  PREREQ:  FRESHMAN STANDING
     1    LEC   TUTH    9:30-10:45  15811   WEINSTEIN


HIS 150   3          CIVILIZATION OF ISRAEL I
  REMARK:  CROSSLISTED WITH INT 150
     1    LEC   HBTA               15841


                     Figure 7.2
```

courses, a boxed title identifies the beginning of each new subject area group.

Surprisingly, when the format of the report has been modified for improved readability, the amount of information that can be put on a single page is also increased, instead of decreased, although this was not part of our consideration in redesigning the format. In order to design a program to print pages of this report, none of the individual programming steps is more difficult than those studied in the example of the last section; there are just more of them. Specifying a program in detail is left as an exercise for the reader.

Self-check question:

1. What principles of page format layout are violated by the example of Figure 7.1?

7.6 Teaching the computer to draw

With a little effort, we can have the computer print pictures for us. There are many types of graphical display devices that can accept output from a computer, and draw graphs, pictures and charts as desired. However, we shall assume that the only output device available to us is a line printer, and shall start from there. The main thing to remember when you are trying to generate graphical output on a line printer is that the image to be printed must be dissected into horizontal slices, and each slice or line will have to be assembled for output in order of its appearance from top to bottom on the page. Since this line-by-line assembly is not the way we ordinarily go about generating a pencil drawing, it will cause us a certain amount of trouble. However, it is exactly the way that a television camera scans an image to generate a video signal representing a frame of a TV picture, and thinking about the formation of a picture by scanning successive lines may help us to visualize the procedure that the computer must follow.

There are several ways that images may be represented in a in a computer. The computer may hold in an array, a line-by-line replica of the image in which light and dark spots along each line are represented by binary values, 0 or 1. Alternatively, a scale of light values from black through shades of gray to white may be represented by a range of integer values. Each such value represents the shade of a single point of the image. The location of a point in the image is indicated by the indices of the element in the array. For instance, an image consisting of 200,000 points might be represented by an integer array,

var Image : array [1..500, 1..400] of Integer;

In this representation, the value of the point lying in the 40th row from the top, and 135th column from the left margin would be represented by the element Image [40, 135]. Many of the pictures generated on a line printer and that you see hung around the halls of every computing center are represented in the computer in this way.

Another way in which images can be represented in the computer is by parameters of mathematical formulas. We have already seen (in Example 3.8.2) how straight lines can be represented. More complicated geometric figures can also be represented using formulas of analytic geometry, or as solutions to systems of equations whose parameters are stored as values of computational variables. In these cases, the images are actually generated by computation. Most of the so-called "computer generated art", consisting of abstract patterns of geometrical figures and printed on computer-controlled plotting devices, is of this type. We shall study simple examples of each type of image representation in order to discover how to have the images printed on a line printer.

Example 7.6.1 -- Printing with large-font pictorial letters

In the last section, we saw that large-font, pictorial letters are often useful in forming titles that are visually distinguishable from the surrounding text in a page of computer output. Since a line printer allows the use of only a single type font, any large letters we intend to use must be constructed as a pattern of standard, printable symbols upon a blank background. This affords us a good example of the technique of forming pictures by printing patterns of small symbols. A single line of the large font letters must extend over several actual print lines.

First of all, suppose that images of the letters we intend to use have already been stored in the computer, presumably by reading punched cards or by input from a typewriter terminal. As a standard format for the alphabet, assume that each letter is five print lines in height, and may be three, four, or five print columns in width. Since we will need spaces between letters, let each letter be preceded by a single print column of blank characters. Thus, the images we are to represent look like:

```
 XX    XXX    XXX    XXX    XXXX   XXXX    XXX
X  X   X X    X      X X    X      X       X
X  X   XXX    X      X X    XXX    XXX     X XX
XXXX   X X    X      X X    X      X       X  X
X  X   XXX    XXX    XXX    XXXX   X        XXX
```

each letter will be represented by an array consisting of five strings of six characters each. Thus the letter 'A' is represented by

' XX ', ' X X ', ' X X ', ' XXXX ', ' X X ',

and these strings are read from an input device to initially store the image of an 'A' in the computer. The twenty-six letters of the alphabet, plus a blank symbol five print lines high, are stored in a two dimensional array of six-character strings, declared by

> var Alphabet : array [0..26] of
> array [1..5] of
> packed array [1..6] of Char;

In the array reference Alphabet [1,3], the first index picks out letter number 1, which is 'A', and the second index tells that the third row of the letter is to be selected. The strings of Alphabet whose first index is zero are all blank, and will be used to obtain spaces between words in the large print.

The elements of the array representing the 'A' are:

```
Alphabet [1, 1] = '  XX  '
Alphabet [1, 2] = ' X  X '
Alphabet [1, 3] = ' X  X '
Alphabet [1, 4] = ' XXXX '
Alphabet [1, 5] = ' X  X '
```

To print an 'A' in large font pictorial type, we could execute the iterated instruction

> for Line := 1 to 5 do
> Writeln (Alphabet [1, Line])

187

Since we have provided for letters of variable width, so that an 'I' requires fewer print columns than an 'M', the printing of a word will not look well if six print columns are allowed for each letter. In that case, the spacings between letters within the word may not be uniform. In order to overcome this difficulty, we can define a second array to keep track of the number of print columns actually required to print each letter, including an initial column of blanks to achieve separation between successive letters. This array is defined by

var Letterwidth : array [0..26] of 0..6;

The value of Letterwidth[1] will be initialized to 5, allowing one column of spacing and four columns of printed symbols to form an 'A'. Letterwidth[9] will be 4, to print an 'I', and Letterwidth[13] will be 6, to print an 'M'. Now we are ready to give an algorithm to print a whole title in large font pictorial type as we have defined it.

Suppose that the title we wish to have printed is the message 'THIS IS A TITLE'. In order to encode the message for printing, the input representing this message should give the index of each letter of the message, that is, should give in place of each letter the integer representing the order of that letter in the alphabet. An input line would look like:

20 8 9 19 0 9 19 0 1 0 29 9 20 12 5

in which each zero stands for a blank to separate successive words.

At this point, we have created an assemblage of inter-related data objects, called a data structure, and it may be well to pause to describe the structure by means of a diagram.

In Figure 7.3, the bracket indicates that the length of the significant portions of the array Message is given by the value of the variable Numberletters. The arrows drawn from elements of Message to the boxes that enclose letters of Alphabet indicate that Message encodes a sequence of elements of the array, Alphabet. At the Ith position in the sequence, the value of Message[I] tells which letter

188

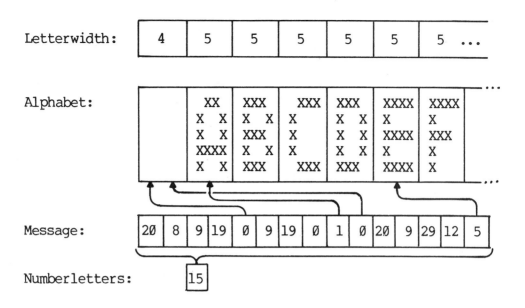

Figure 7.3 -- A data structure diagram

is to occupy that position. This means that a particular letter of the message to be printed would be referred to indirectly. For instance, the third line of the tenth letter of the message would be referred to by

Alphabet [Message [1Ø], 3]

Frequently, by taking the time to draw a data structure diagram, one can save considerable time and effort in the formulation of an algorithm to operate on the data structure. In fact, the chance of getting the algorithm correctly designed without referring to a data structure diagram is relatively slight.

The first task of the algorithm is relatively easy; it must read data describing the indices of the letters to be printed. Then it must check that the number of columns required to print the message is not greater than the width of the paper, and finally, the message itself is to be printed, line by line. A description of the algorithm by means of an iteration graph is

189

```
┌─────────────────────────────────────────────────────────┐
│  read  (Number-of-letters)                              │
├─────────────────────────────────────────────────────────┤
│  for I := 1 to Number-of-letters                        │
│  ┌───────────────────────────────────────────────────┐  │
│  │  read  (Message [I])                              │  │
├──┴───────────────────────────────────────────────────┴──┤
│  calculate the number of print columns required         │
│       to print the message, and check for overflow;     │
│  calculate the indentation needed to center             │
│       the message on the page                           │
├─────────────────────────────────────────────────────────┤
│  for Line := 1 to 5                                     │
│  ┌───────────────────────────────────────────────────┐  │
│  │  start a new print line;                          │  │
│  │  print the indentation in blanks;                 │  │
│  │  print one line of all letters of the             │  │
│  │       message                                     │  │
│  └───────────────────────────────────────────────────┘  │
└─────────────────────────────────────────────────────────┘
```

Most of the steps designated by the iteration graph are, if not elementary, either simple computations or are achievable by the iteration of an elementary step. Actual printing should be done by means of the Write procedure since many characters are to be printed, one at a time, on the same line. When a line is completed, a call to the procedure Writeln will tell the computer to insert an end-of-line marker.

A step which is not elementary is to print one line of all letters of the message. Apparently, this step requires iteration over the number of letters of the message, but the indices of the actual letters to be printed are to be obtained from the index array, Message. According to the data structure diagram, a line of the Ith letter of the message must be referred to by

Alphabet [Message [I], Line]

(A common mistake is to try to refer to the Ith letter of the alphabet, rather than to the letter indexed by the Ith element of Message.) The specification is not yet complete, however, for due to the fact that the large-font letters are of differing widths, the strings of Alphabet must be printed one character at a time, with the number of characters to be printed in a slice across each letter controlled by the corresponding value of Letterwidth. Thus, the printing of

190

characters in a line must be iterated first over the number of letters, and then, for each letter, must be iterated over the appropriate value of the width of that letter.

Expanding the final line of the preceding iteration graph, we represent it by a subsidiary iteration graph

print one line of each letter of Message:

```
┌──────────────────────────────────────────────────────────┐
│ for I := 1 to Number-of-letters                            │
│   ┌──────────────────────────────────────────────────────┐│
│   │ for L := 0 to Letterwidth [Message[I]]                ││
│   │   ┌──────────────────────────────────────────────────┐│
│   │   │print next character                              ││
│   │   └──────────────────────────────────────────────────┘│
│   └──────────────────────────────────────────────────────┘│
└──────────────────────────────────────────────────────────┘
```

With some attention to detail, the iteration graph can now be translated to a Pascal program. The details of initialization of the Alphabet are omitted.

```pascal
program PrintMessage (Input, Output);
   (*********************************************
   *   print letters of Alphabet as indexed by   *
   *   Message, in large-font pictorial letters  *
   *********************************************)
const
   Pagewidth = 132;
var
   Alphabet : array [0..26] of
                  array [1..5] of
                      packed array [1..6] of Char;
   Letterwidth : array [0..26] of 0..6;
   Message : array [1..30] of 0..26;
   Numberletters, I : 0..30;
   Line : 1..5
   Width, Indent, L : 0..Pagewidth;
begin
   (***** initialization of Alphabet and *****)
   (***** Letterwidth goes here          *****)
   Readln (Numberletters);
   Width := 0;
   for I := 1 to Numberletters do
       begin
           Read (Message [I]);
           Width := Width + Letterwidth [Message [I]];
       end;
```

```
if Width > Pagewidth then
    Writeln ('MESSAGE IS TOO WIDE FOR PAGE');
Indent := (Pagewidth - Width) div 2;
for Line := 1 to 5 do
    begin
        for L := 1 to Indent do
            Write (' ');
        for I := 1 to Numberletters do
            for L := 0 to Letterwidth [Message[I]] do
                Write (Alphabet [Message[I], Line, L]);
        Writeln;
    end
end.
```

Notice the use made of subrange types in the example program. Every numeric variable is used only for counting (except in computing an indentation) and therefore, its legitimate range of values can be bounded in advance. The use of subrange types, instead of type Integer, allows the Pascal compiler to check that the values actually assigned to these variables conform to our stated intentions.

The last example dealt with the printing of figures that were represented by a map of their images in an array in the memory of the computer. In an alternative representation of figures, each line is to be represented by a parametric equation. The exact values of the parameters, stored in the computer as the values of program variables, enable one to determine the coordinates of points on the line by computation. For instance, a straight line is represented by the parametric equation,

$$ax + by + c = 0,$$

in which the values of a, b and c determine exactly which line is represented. Sections of conic figures (circles, ellipses, parabolas, hyperbolas) are represented by second-degree equations,

$$ax^2 + bxy + cy^2 + dx + ey + f = 0,$$

and more complex curves by equations of higher degree. Any of these equations is of the form $F(x,y) = 0$, where F stands for some formula in two variables, and may contain a number of parameters. Every point on the curve is given by a pair of coordinates (x,y) that satisfy the equation. Points not on the curve have coordinates (x,y) for which $F(x,y)$ is not zero, but has some positive or negative value. If we were to plot a grid of the signs of the values of $F(x,y)$ on a rectangular array of points in the x-y plane, it would look something like this:

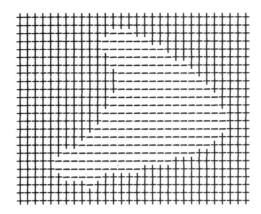

Obviously, since the values of F vary continuously with changes in x and y, points at which F is zero-valued must lie somewhere between each pair of adjacent points of the grid on which the signs differ. If we were to draw a continuous line on the grid, passing it between pairs of points of differing sign, we would have a pretty good approximation to the curve defined by the equation F(x,y) = 0. We can make use of this scheme in developing an algorithm to plot figures on a line printer when the equations of the figures are known.

The reason that a rectangular grid of points suggests itself is that a line printer only permits you to print at points that lie on such a grid. Each printable point must lie in a row that fixes its vertical position on the page, and in a column that fixes its horizontal position. In fact, we should not even speak of printable points but of printable areas, since each print character occupies a small, roughly rectangular area on the paper.

To give the impression that we are printing a line of characters, we can print a standard character such as "X", in each printable area that our mathematically defined curve would pass through. In order to determine whether or not the curve passes through a given area, evaluate the sign of the defining formula, F(x,y), on the points that form the corners of the rectangle. If there is a change of sign from one corner to another, then the curve must pass through the specified rectangle, and a character should be printed in it. Otherwise, that area can be left blank. Following this procedure, the print pattern determined from the grid of signs shown above would be:

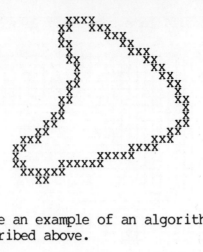

We can now give an example of an algorithm to print figures using the scheme described above.

<u>Example</u> 7.6.2 -- Curve plotting on a line printer

Suppose that one wishes to plot the curve whose points satisfy the equation $F(x,y) = 0$, where F is some computable, continuous function of two variables. The height and width of the plot are assumed to be given in units of lines and print columns by the values of Integer type variables, Height and Width. The value of Width must be less than or equal to 132, the number of columns that can be printed on a standard line printer. Our technique will be to keep track of the sign changes of the formula $F(x,y)$ that occur upon evaluation on successive corners of an individual printable area. For this purpose, think of a printable area as a small rectangle as shown in Fig. 7.4. Each edge of the rectangle links two adjacent corners, so a sign change can be considered to be a property of an edge. It is not necessary to check all four edges for sign changes; either two of the edges will have sign changes or none will. (We assume that the rectangular area is very small compared with the area of the figure to be plotted, so that a boundary line of the figure can pass through an individual printable area at most once.)

The sign changes of $F(x,y)$ can be recorded for each print row. For an individual printable area, imagine that we have already stored the values of the sign of F on its upper right and lower left corners, and that we posess one more piece of information, namely, whether or not the sign of F on the lower left corner is the same or different from the sign on the upper left corner. Now we shall evaluate the sign of the function on the remaining corner, the lower

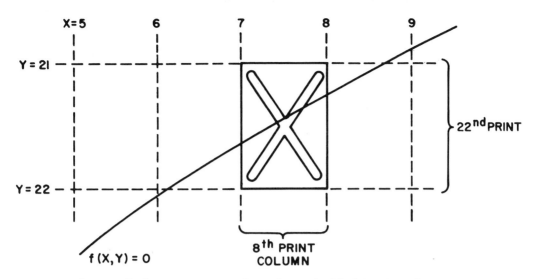

Figure 7.4 -- an example of an individual print
rectangle through which passes the
locus F(x, y) = 0

right. Check to see if this sign is different from that on
the upper right corner. If it is, then the curve must pass
through the printable area. If not, then check to see if the
newly computed sign of the lower right corner differs from
the sign of the lower left. That makes two sides checked. If
neither shows a sign difference, we check to see if the left
side of the rectangle showed a sign difference. If not, then
the curve could not have passed through the rectangle, for
three of the four sides have been checked.

Now the only information needed from previous computations are the signs of the function on the upper corners of
the rectangle, and the sign change, if any, on the left
side. The sign change on the left side can be saved from the
immediately preceding computation performed on the rectangle
to the left in the same row. The signs of the function on
the upper corners must be saved from the computations of
sign on the lower corners of rectangles in the preceding
row. But notice that by this argument, it is only necessary
to store a single row of sign information, and not the sign
information for the entire grid of points! An algorithm to
accomplish the printing of a figure follows. This algorithm
is not quite a complete Pascal program, because the function
to be plotted has not been given as a Pascal function (see
Chapter 8) but is instead represented by the symbol F,
denoting any function of two integer arguments.

195

```
program Plots (Output);
    (**********************************************
     * will plot the locus of F(x,y) = 0 when F is *
     * given a suitable definition as a function    *
     * of type Real or Integer. The variables Sign,*
     * Newsign, and Signchange are used to record   *
     * the algebraic sign of the function as it is  *
     * evaluated on different points.               *
     **********************************************)
const
    Width = 132;
    Height = 60;
var
    Newsign, Signchange : Boolean;
    Sign : array [0..Width] of Boolean;
    Col : 0..Width;
    Row : 1..Height;

(* the declaration of the function F goes here *)

begin
    (**********************************************
     * Initially, determine the sign of F at points *
     * along the upper boundary of the first print   *
     * row. Then print all rows.                    *
     **********************************************)
    for Col := 1 to Width do
        Sign [Col] := F(Col, 0) >= 0;
    for Row := 1 to Height do
        begin
            (**********************************************
             * Initialize a new print row. Determine the   *
             * change of sign on the corners of the left    *
             * edge of the first print rectangle.          *
             **********************************************)
            Newsign := F(0, Row) >= 0;
            Signchange := Newsign <> Sign [0];
            Sign [0] := Newsign;
            (**********************************************
             * for each print rectangle in the row, deter-*
             * mine whether or not to print a word, accor-*
             * ding to the change of sign along the right  *
             * edge, bottom edge, and left edge of the     *
             * rectangle.                                  *
             **********************************************)
```

```
      for Col := 1 to Width do
          begin
              Newsign := F(Col, Row) >= 0;
              if Newsign <> Sign [Col] then
                  begin
                      Signchange := True;
                      Write ('X');
                  end
              else
                  begin
                      if Signchange or
                          (Newsign <> Sign [pred(Col)]) then
                          Write ('X')
                      else
                          Write (' ');
                      Signchange := False;
                  end;
              Sign [Col] := Newsign;
          end;
      end;
  end.
```

In the preceding example, we have assumed that the coefficients of the formula F(x,y) are such that the figure to be
plotted will be neither too small nor too large to be displayed
on the printed page, when the units of x and y are print columns
and print rows, respectively. Naturally, the scale of the figure
will not be correct by accident any more than all objects of the
real world can be drawn life-sized on a sheet of 8 1/2 by 11 inch
paper. It is necessary to scale the plotting of figures to make
sure that they will fit onto the available page, yet will not be
too small for details to be seen. The same is true of architec-
tural drawings and photographs taken through a microscope. The
problem of scaling has been ignored in the example for the reason
that we will not be able to understand algorithms that do too
many different things at once. We prefer the point of view that
scaling requires a separate algorithm which must be used in
conjunction with the plotting algorithm in order to produce
successful displays of figures.

In the next two chapters, we shall see how to combine
several algorithms in order to solve difficult problems, and how
to decompose problems in order to find simple algorithms for
their separate parts.

EXERCISES FOR CHAPTER 7

7.1 Design a Pascal program to print a bar chart of the U.S. cost-of-living index from 1966 to the present. The bars are to be printed vertically to a scale of 12 units per inch. Each bar should be four print columns wide, with two columns of blanks serparating adjacent bars. The chart should have a title and captions indicating the year represented by each bar.

7.2 a) Design a program to print messages in large-font type, 12 print lines in height. Have it print your name and address.

b) Modify the program to have it scale the letters automatically to any size. Have the computer print an eye examination chart, using scaled letters of heights 60, 36, 24, 12, 8, 6, and 4 print lines high. At what size do the scaled letters become indistinguishable?

7.3 To print the time schedule of Section 7.5, the computer should read the information from cards, and print it in the desired format. Design a program to read cards in the format given below, and print it as shown in Figure 7.2.

columns:	contain:
1 -- 5	"H" in column 1 if the information on the card is a program or department heading; call number if the card gives information about a particular course section;
6 -- 80	program heading, if column 1 contains "H";

otherwise,

6 --11	three-letter department or program code and course number
12 --13	number of credits
14 --41	course name or abbreviation
44 -- 45	section number (if there is only a single section of the course, this field may be left blank);
46 --48	mode of instruction (LEC, REC, LAB, etc.)
49 --54	days (MWF, T-Th., etc.)
55 --65	hours (3:00 - 4:15, etc.)
66 -- 80	name of instructor

7.4 Design a program to print a monthly circulation report of a college library, including the following data:

    a) a title;
    b) date of report;
    c) month and year reported on;
    d) the following statistics, both broken down by library branches, and given in aggregate form:
        number of borrowers
        number of volumes borrowed
        number of volumes returned
        number of volumes in circulation at month's end
        number of volumes reported lost or missing
        number of overdue notices issued
        number of new volumes cataloged

7.5 Design a program to scale and print figures represented by equations of the form $f(x,y) = 0$. Plot, using the line printer, to a scale which makes the height of each figure 50 print lines:

    a) a square;
    b) a circle;
    c) a circle with an inscribed square;
    d) a square whose sides are diagonal to the edges of the paper, and containing an inscribed circle.

7.6 Have the computer print a line diagram of the daily fluctuations of the New York Times Stock Index daily closing price over a two month period. Include axes at the left side and the bottom of the diagram, print registration marks on the axes, and label the registration marks to indicate values along each of the coordinates.

8 COMPUTATIONS WITHIN COMPUTATIONS

As we gain experience in programming and attempt to design algorithms for more ambitious tasks, we can easily arrive at a state of semi-confusion, where our program involves too many variables, contains too many nested control statements, and spans too many pages. If the concepts that you try to capture on paper can no longer be clearly identified and distinguished in your mind, then the chances of composing an error-free program, or even of eliminating the errors in a prototype program, are small indeed.

The limit on the number of concepts that can be kept in mind at one time seems to be a constraint of our human intellectual equipment, just as a juggler can only keep a limited number of balls in the air at once. Psychologists have studied the phenomenon at length. They tell us that the number of simple, but distinct ideas we can successfully manage at one time is seven, plus or minus two. Perhaps the difference between nine and five is all that separates a genius from a moron!

Certainly there are known computational algorithms that embody more than seven elementary concepts. How, then, are they composed? The single most powerful tool that we have for managing the potential complexity of algorithms is abstraction. By abstraction, we mean the process of collecting all of the relevant details that support the development of an important concept, and binding these details into a package that embodies the concept. A good measure of the value of a programming language is how well it supports the process of abstraction.

In Pascal, we have seen one form of abstraction of concepts associated with data, realized by use of <u>record</u> type declarations in Chapter 5. Another facility is that of procedural abstraction, which we are going to explore in this chapter. The procedural abstraction mechanism of Pascal allows us to define our own functions and computational procedures, to give them names, and to refer to them subsequently by name, whenever we wish to have them evaluated. Procedures are very much like subsidiary programs, with one important distinction; they can have parameters which provide a means of communication with their environments.

The definition of functions and procedures is a very natural occurrence if a program is developed by the process of stepwise refinement. In stepwise refinement we attempt to deal with the interaction of a few abstract concepts, then subsequently with the elaboration of these concepts. But the detailed elaboration of a concept is exactly the process that one must go through in composing a procedure definition. At that point, the desired interactions of the procedure with its environment will already have been taken into account, and what remains is to tell how its specifications are to be realized.

The use of procedural abstraction also can help us to control the number of variables that we must deal with at one time. For in a procedure definition, those variables needed only for the immediate computation represented by the procedure can be kept within the package, and have no existence outside. Insofar as we can use these local variables to hold the data used by a procedure, the details of the transformations that go on during evaluation of the procedure are of no concern in the outside environment.

8.1 Block structure

In conjunction with procedure definition, Pascal employs a convention concerning the definitions of identifiers known as <u>block</u> structure. A block is the textual scope in which a group of identifiers have their definition and use. In Pascal, a program constitutes a block, and the definition of each procedure or function constitutes another block, nested within the program block. Syntactically, a block consists of a heading, defining identifiers to be used for communication, some declarative paragraphs in which labels, constants, types, variables, and internally nested procedures or functions are defined, and a statement part defining its algorithmic activity.

An identifier is considered to be defined, and is therefore available for use within a block, for one of two reasons. Either the identifier is declared in one of the paragraphs that precedes its use in the same block, in which case the identifier is said to be _locally_ defined, or else its definition is inherited, by virtue of its being defined in the text of a surrounding block. In the latter case, the identifier is said to be defined _globally_ to the block. The concepts of local and global definition are relative; a variable defined locally in a block will be globally defined in the body of any procedure whose declaration lies in the same block.

In case an identifier has both a local and a global definition, the local definition takes precedence. This is the only way in which a globally defined variable can be rendered inaccessible within a block. Of course, anywhere in the text outside of the block, the global definition is the one in effect.

For example, in the following nonsense program

```
program Main (Input);
    var
        X, Y : Real;
        Z : Boolean;

    procedure Swap;
        var
            Z : Real;
        begin
            Z := X;
            X := Y;
            Y := z;
        end;   (* Swap *)

    begin   (* Main *)
        Read (X, Y);
        if X > Y then
            Swap;
        Z := True;
    end.
```

the variables X, Y, and Z have their declarations in the block of the main program, and hence, are locally defined there. In fact, any variable that appears in the statement body of the main program must be locally defined in that block, since no block surrounds it.

The same variable names also are used in the statement body of the procedure Swap. Here, however, the variable Z is different from the one defined in the main program block; this identifier has been given another definition in the block of the procedure, identifying it with a new variable local to Swap. The local variable called Z does not even have the same data type as does the variable of the same name in the main program block. X and Y refer to the same variables defined in the main program; these are global variables as they are used within Swap.

As we have mentioned, local and global definitions can apply not only to the names of constants, types, and variables, but also to procedures and functions themselves. This is because the definition of a procedure is also its declaration. Thus a procedure definition can be nested in the text of some surrounding procedure or program block. The algorithm represented by the procedure definition is not executed at the point of its declaration, however, but at a point in the program where it is referred to by name. Most frequently, the way that a procedure will be made known for use within another procedure will be by global definition.

Although the scope rules of block structure allow us to define local identifiers for use within the body of a procedure, and unknown without, they do not provide any means for restricting the access of statements to global identifiers within the body of a procedure. In fact, the innermost nested procedure block will contain the largest number of defined variables; it has its own local variables, plus those of all surrounding blocks, excepting those that have been preempted by redefinition. Great care in programming is required in the use of global variables, to ensure that their uses in different procedures do not conflict.

Self-check questions:

1. What is meant by a block? Why is block structure used?

2. What determines whether a variable is locally or globally defined within a block? Does the concept of local or global definition apply to named objects other than variables?

3. Consider the following program outline:

```
program Main (Input, Output);
   var
      A, B : Integer;
      C : Char;

   procedure P;
      type
         B : 1..10;
      var
         D : B;
      begin
         .
         .
         .
      end;

   begin
      .
      .
      .
   end.
```

① ⟶ (at the point in procedure P body)

② ⟶ (at the point in Main body)

At point ①, what names are declared and what are their types? What names are declared at point ② and what are their types?

8.2 Communicating data to procedures

The simplest way that values of program variables can be communicated to a procedure is by referring to the names of globally defined variables, within the statement part of the procedure body. However, if this were the only way to pass data to a procedure, it would be very limiting. In functional notation as used in mathematics, the idea is that a function defines a mapping from one set of objects to another. The arguments of a function are expressions that take values from a specified domain. Similarly, it is convenient to allow computational procedures to have arguments that can be any expressions belonging to the data types declared for that procedure. In defining the program text that is the body of a procedure, we need to have names for arguments that the procedure is to receive. The actual arguments (called actual parameters) cannot be known at the time the procedure is defined, but only when it is invoked. Therefore in the definition of the procedure, some dummy arguments are defined (known as formal parameters in the nomenclature of Pascal). These formal parameters may be thought of as locally defined names used in the definition of the procedure body to represent variables or expressions that will be specified when the procedure is actually invoked.

In Pascal, there are two simple conventions that can be used in defining formal parameters. If the intended use of a formal parameter is to receive the value of an expression that is to be provided as an actual parameter when the procedure or function is called, then one simply declares the name and data type of the formal parameter, as in

```
function Max(X, Y : Integer) : Integer;
   begin
      if X > Y then
         Max := X
      else
         Max := Y
   end:
```

In such a case, the formal parameters are actually local variables of the procedure, but they are asigned initial values each time the procedure is called. Thus the statement

```
A := Max (10, 2*B)
```

becomes equivalent to executing the compound statement

```
begin
   X := 10;  Y := 2*B;
   if X > Y then then
      Max := X
   else
      Max := Y;
   A := Max
end
```

The actual parameters may be of any types that could legitimately be assigned to the formal parameters in an assignment statement.

The alternative parameter convention is used when the purpose of a procedure is to act upon one or more variables of the environment from which it is called, possibly changing their values. In declaring a formal parameter for such a use, the formal parameter name is preceded by the keyword var, designating it as a pseudonym for an actual variable to be supplied in the procedure call. An example is:

```
procedure Readchar (var F : Text; var Ch : Char);
    const
      Blank = ' ';
    begin
      repeat
        Ch : F↑; Get (F);
      until Eof (F) or (Ch <> Blank);
    end;
```

This procedure would be called to obtain a non-blank character
from a text file. Its actual parameters must be variables: expressions will not suffice. The data types of its actual parameters must match those of its formal parameters; no conversion of
values, as from Integer to Real, or from Integer to a subrange,
can be performed. The actual parameters corresponding to formal
parameters with the var attribute cannot be constants,
either.

The effect of calling a procedure with var parameters is
as though the actual parameters had been substituted for the
formal parameters in the procedure body. Thus,

    Readchar (Input, A)

is equivalent to

```
    begin
      repeat
        A := Input↑; Get (Input);
      until Eof (Input) or (A <> ' ');
    end
```

The syntax of a Pascal function heading is given by the
following chart. A procedure heading is similar, except for the
omission of the final colon and type .

function heading

```
```

where parameter list has the syntax chart

parameter list

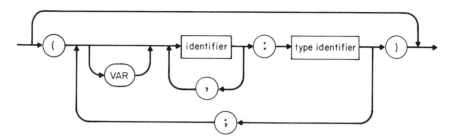

There is one more convention of communication between Pascal functions and their environments that needs explanation. This is the value return mechanism, and misunderstanding this convention can lead to serious programming errors. The name of a function can appear on the left side of an assignment statement within the statement part of the function. It is a pseudo-variable. The value returned by the function will be the last value dynamically assigned to the function pseudo-variable.

A word of caution is in order, however. If the function name is used in an expression within the function body, it is not a pseudo-variable, and does not produce the last value that was assigned to it. Instead, it is a recursive call of the function itself. Recursive function invocation will be discussed in Section 8.4.

Example 8.2.1 - A function for greatest common divisor

The algorithm of Example 4.1 can easily be translated into a Pascal function, by providing a suitable heading, and assigning the final value to the function pseudo-variable.

```
function GCD (M, N : Integer) : Integer;
   begin
      while M <> N do
         if M > N then
            M := M - N;
         else
            N := N - M;
      GCD := M;
   end;
```

We can illustrate the use of some simple procedures by considering computations on rational numbers. A rational number can be represented by a pair of integers, interpreted as the numerator and denominator of a fraction. We shall only deal with non-negative numbers. There are several computations that one might wish to do with rational numbers, but we shall consider only one of the simplest — the comparison of two rationals, to determine if one is greater than the other.

Example 8.2.2 — Comparison of two rational numbers

In this example, we are given four positive integers representing a pair of rational fractions, and we are to determine whether the first is larger than the second. The value to be returned is Boolean, True if the first rational is the larger, False otherwise. If the rational numbers are a/x and b/y, then the comparison could be effected by comparing a*y with b*x. However, there is a disadvantage to this, for then the ability to compare rational fractions will be severely restricted by the size of the largest integer number that can be represented in the computer. It may be that the two denominators, x and y, contain a common factor. If so, then this factor should be extracted before multiplying the numerators by the opposite denominators, in order that the products will not be larger than is necessary to make the comparison. The common factor of the denominators can be found by using the GCD function. Assuming that the function GCD of the previous example has been defined globally to the function we are about to write, the comparison algorithm can be given as:

```
function IsGreater (A, X, B, Y: Integer) : Boolean;
   var
      G := Integer;
   begin
      G := GCD (X, Y);
      IsGreater := A*(Y div G) > B*(X div G);
   end;
```

Here the integer variable G has been defined locally to the function to hold the value of the greatest common divisor.

Another possible representation for rational numbers is by a triple of integers, the first standing for the integral part of a rational number, and the second and third for the numerator and denominator of a fractional part, as in 2-1/4. In this representation, there is a reduced form of any rational number, in which the fractional part is less than unity in value, and the greatest common divisor of the numerator and denominator of the fractional part is unity.

Example 8.2.3 - Computing the reduced form of a rational number

A procedure to compute the reduced form of a rational number given as a triple of integers will differ from those of the preceding examples, in that it does not compute a single value as its result. Instead, it computes a transformation on the triple of values it is given, yielding in its place another triple that represents the same rational value. To accomplish this, the formal parameters of the procedure are declared to have the attribute var.

```
procedure Reduce (var M, A, X : Integer);
   (**********************************************
    *   if A is non-zero, extract the integral   *
    *   part of the fraction A/X, then reduce the  *
    *   fraction by eliminating common factors.    *
    **********************************************)
var
   G : Integer;
begin
   M := M + A div X;
   A := A mod X;
   G := GCD (A, X);
   A := A div G;
   X := X div G;
end;
```

Finally, we shall give as an example a complete Pascal program that uses the functions and procedures defined in the preceding examples to find and print in reduced form the greater of two rational numbers that are read as triples of integers.

Example 8.2.4 -- Comparing and reducing rational numbers

```
program Rational (Input, Output);
   var
      I1, A1, X1, I2, A2, X2 : Integer;
```

209

```pascal
function GCD (M, N : Integer) : Integer;
    begin
        whileM <> N do
            if M > N then
                M := M - N
            else
                N := N - M;
        GCD := M;
    end;

function IsGreater (A, X, B, Y : Integer) : Boolean;
    var
        G : Integer;
    begin
        if (X > 0) and (Y > 0) then
            G := GCD (X, Y)
        else
            G := 1;
        IsGreater := A * (Y div G) > B * (X div G);
    end;

procedure Reduce (var M, A, X : Integer);
    var
        G : Integer;
    begin
        M := M + A div X;
        A := A mod X;
        G := GCD (A, X);
        A := A div G;
        X := X div G;
    end;

begin (* body of main program *)
    Read(I1, A1, X1, I2, A2, X2);
    if (I1 < 0) or (A1 < 0) or (X1 <= 0) or
       (I2 < 0) or (A2 < 0) or (X2 <= 0) then
        Halt; (* can't use negative values *)
    Reduce (I1, A1, X1);
    Reduce (I2, A2, X2);
    Write ('THE LARGER RATIONAL NUMBER IS');
    if (I1 > I2) or (I1 = I2) and
        IsGreater (A1, X1, A2, X2) then
            Writeln (I1, A1, '/', X1)
    else
            Writeln (I2, A2, '/', X2);
end.
```

This algorithm illustrates several aspects of the use of procedures. As we progress to the consideration of more complex problems, we shall find that most of the individual algorithms we develop will be written as Pascal procedures.

Self-check questions:

1. Which are the local variables and which are the formal parameters of the procedure IsGreater of Example 8.2.2?

2. Why are the parameters of the function GCD in Example 8.2.1 not given the attribute var? What would be the consequence of declaring these as var parameters? Would it affect the use made of GCD in Examples 8.2.2 and 8.2.3?

3. Are any global variables used in the examples of section 8.2? Are the names of procedures or functions communicated as global identifiers in these examples?

8.3 Side effects

Since the global variables defined in surrounding blocks are available for use in the statements of a procedure, it may be that a procedure not only refers to the values of global variables, but also assigns new values to some of them. When this happens, it is called a side effect of the execution of a procedure, for it cannot be anticipated by looking only at the statement that invokes the procedure. One must look at the procedure declaration as well to discover possible side effects. Side effects are a perfectly legitimate function of a procedure, but since they are not always apparent from the text of an algorithm statement, one must be expecially careful to document side effects by the use of comments in the Pascal text.

The principal use of side effects is to enable procedures to manipulate the global data structures used in an algorithm. Since a local variable cannot retain its value from one invocation of a procedure to the next, any values that are to exist for a longer time than does a single invocation of a procedure must be held in a data structure that is global to the procedure. Of course, other procedures or program statements can also manipulate these global data.

Conversely, if a globally defined variable is used to store temporary values needed only for a single execution of a procedure, then it is possible that an unintended side effect may occur. This could happen if the same variable is used to store a value in the program segment from which the procedure is invoked. After invocation of the procedure, the global variable may have had its value changed, although that fact will not be apparent by reading only the program segment in which the procedure invocation appears. This kind of side effect is undesirable and can be avoided by following a policy of using local variables whenever possible.

Another possible consequence of a side effect is that the repeated invocation of a procedure may not produce an identical result, even if it is given the same actual parameters in each invocation. An example of such a procedure is the standard Pascal procedure Read.

In the following example, global variables are used solely in order to obtain persistence of the values they hold.

Example 8.3.1 -- Decomposition of integers into prime factors

Every integer has a unique decomposition as a product of prime factors, according to the fundamental theorem of arithmetic. Let us devise an algorithm that will read successive integers from an input file and print each integer together with its factorization. For this purpose, we shall need to be able to refer to a list of prime numbers, but as we do not know in advance how many primes will be needed, we must have an algorithm to generate primes. The algorithm Prime2 of Example 6.1.1 will accomplish this task. However, it is not necessary to recompute all of the primes previously generated, each time Prime2 is invoked. It would be more efficient to keep a list of all primes generated by previous invocations, and only generate new primes if the list needs to be lengthened. In order to do this, we shall make a procedure out of Prime2, but shall let the list of primes (contained in the integer array Prime) and the variable PrimesFound that gives the length of the list, be globally defined so that their values will be retained from one invocation of the procedure to the next.

In constructing an algorithm, the first task will be to initialize the global variables that are to be used by Prime2. Since the algorithm is to accept a sequence of numbers as input, some means of controlling the iteration must be provided. However, our algorithm is only intended to work

212

with positive integers, and so a means of control would be to terminate the list of data with an invalid value, that is, zero or a negative integer. An iteration graph describing this control is

```
initialize global variables;
Read (Number);
─────────────────────────────────────────────
while Number > 0
    ┌──────────────────────────────────────
    │ determine the prime factors of Number
```

The task of determining prime factors requires the prime numbers be examined, in order, to see if each one will divide Number. Whenever a prime factor is discovered, it should be extracted from Number by a division, reducing the value of Number at each factorization. Finally, when the value of Number has been reduced to 1, all of its factors will have been discovered. In carrying out this strategy, we must be careful to account for possible multiple factors, by extracting as many instances of each prime as will successively divide Number, before going on to test any succeeding primes. In the following iteration graph, N is used as an index to the primes, and the Nth prime is obtained by invoking the procedure Prime2. This strategy is summarized in the following iteration graph

determine the prime factors of Number:

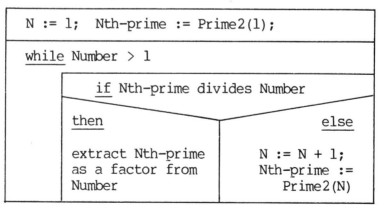

These iteration graphs are easily translated into a Pascal program:

213

```pascal
program PrimeFactors (Input, Output);
(****************************************
*  find and print all the prime factors  *
*  of a positive integer.                 *
****************************************)
type
    Indextype = 1..1000;
var
    Number, N, NthPrime : Integer;
(**** the following are global variables  ****)
(**** for use by the function Prime2      ****)
    PrimesFound : Indextype;
    Primes : array [Indextype] of Integer;

function Prime2 (N : Indextype) : Integer;
(*******************************************************
*  computes the Nth prime number by the algorithm  *
*  of Example 6.1.1. Global variables PrimesFound   *
*  and Primes require initialization in the sur-     *
*  rounding program block.                           *
*******************************************************)
var
    J : Integer;
    M : Indextype;
    NotaFactor : Boolean;
begin
    J := Primes[PrimesFound] + 2;
    while PrimesFound < N do
        begin
            M := 2;  NotaFactor := True;
            while NotaFactor and (Sqr(Primes[M]) <= J) do
                begin
                    NotaFactor := J mod Primes[M] <> 0;
                    M := succ(M);
                end;
            if NotaFactor then
                begin
                    PrimesFound := succ(PrimesFound);
                    Primes[PrimesFound] := J;
                end;
            J := J + 2;
        end;
    Prime2 := Primes[N];
end; (* Prime2 *)
```

```
begin (* PrimeFactors *)
    Primes[1] := 2;  Primes[2] := 3;
    PrimesFound := 2;
    Read (Number);
    while Number > 0 do
        begin
            Write (Number, ' HAS THE PRIME FACTORS');
            (**********************************************
            * Let N be an index to the primes. Starting with *
            * the first prime, test Number for divisibility  *
            * by the Nth prime. If divisible, then factor    *
            * outthe prime and print it. Don't advance the   *
            * index N until the Nth prime is no longer a     *
            * factor of Number, so as not to miss any re-    *
            * peated factors.                                *
            **********************************************)
            N := 1;  NthPrime := 2;
            while Number > 1 do
                if Number mod NthPrime = 0 then
                    begin
                        Write (NthPrime);
                        Number := Number div NthPrime;
                    end
                else
                    begin
                        N := succ(N);
                        NthPrime := Prime2(N);
                    end;
            Writeln;  Read (Number);
        end;
end.
```

8.4 Recursion

Some mathematical functions can be defined in a very concise way in terms of their own properties. For example the factorial function of a positive integer is given very neatly in terms of the factorial function of the next smaller integer,

Factorial(N) = N * Factorial(N-1)

The definition appears at first hand to be circular, but it is not necessarily so, for the argument of the defining expression on the right is not the same as the argument of the expression defined. Of course, in order to complete the definition, one must

215

also give an actual value for the function on some particular value of the argument. For the factorial function, we give

    Factorial (Ø) = 1,
    Factorial (N) = N * Factorial(N-1), for N > Ø.

This defines the function for all non-negative integers. A definition of a function in terms of its own properties is said to be <u>recursive</u>.

A recursive definition may also provide a means of computing values of the function, provided that one has available a programming language in which recursive computation is allowed. Pascal is such a language. Since the name of a procedure is defined in the block in which the procedure declaration appears, that name is automatically made known within the procedure body as a globally defined identifier. Thus, it is perfectly legal within the procedure body to re-invoke that very same procedure by mentioning its name! The process is not so mysterious as it sounds, for each invocation of the procedure is a separate computation.

A simple illustration of a recursive computation can be furnished by giving a Pascal function to compute Factorial:

```
function Factorial (N : Integer) : Integer;
    begin
        if N = Ø then
            Factorial := 1
        else
            Factorial := N*Factorial(N-1);
    end;
```

To see how the recursion works, let us follow the computation of Factorial(3) by this algorithm. We can follow the computation by substituting, on successive lines, the body of the procedure each time it is invoked with the value of its argument substituted for the formal parameter N. We omit the assignments for brevity.

<u>Factorial (3)</u>   (first invocation)

if 3 = Ø then 1 else 3 * <u>Factorial (2)</u>   (second invocation)

if 3 = Ø then 1 else 3 *
   (if 2 = Ø then 1 else 2 * <u>Factorial (1)</u>) (third invocation)

216

```
if 3 = 0 then 1 else 3 *
    (if 2 = 0 then 1 else 2 *
        (if 1 = 0 then 1 else 1 * Factorial (0)))
```
(fourth invocation)

```
if 3 = 0 then 1 else 3 *
    (if 2 = 0 then 1 else 2 *
        (if 1 = 0 then 1 else 1 *
            (if 0 = 0 then 1 else 0 *
                Factorial (-1))))
```
(evaluation of
fourth invocation)

```
1f 3 = 0 then 1 else 3 *
    (if 2 = 0 then 1 else 2 *
        (if 1 = 0 then 1 else 1 * 1))
```
(evaluation of
third invocation)

```
if 3 = 0 then 1 else 3 *
    (if 2 = 0 then 1 else 2 * 1)
```
(evaluation of
second invocation)

```
if 3 = 0 then 1 else 3 * 2
```
(evaluation of
first invocation)

Although the computer does not literally expand the text of the program in the way it has been done above, it does carry out the procedure invocations and evaluations in exactly the order indicated.

For the simple example of the factorial function, an iterative algorithm equally as simple could also be given. However, this is not always the case. Although it is always possible to give an iterative algorithm for a function that can be computed by a recursive procedure, there are some functions for which the invention of an iterative algorithm will be much more difficult than the invention of a recursive algorithm. The converse is also true; for other functions, an iterative algorithm will be easier to compose.

Let us examine another function that we know how to compute, and compare recursive and iterative procedures for its evaluation. Euclid's algorithm for he greatest common divisor of a pair of integers was given as a procedure in Example 8.2.1. A recursive procedure computing the g.c.d. is:

```
function GCDR (M, N : Integer) : Integer;
   begin
      if N = M then
         GCDR := M
      else if N > M then
         GCDR := GCDR (M, N - M);
      else
         GCDR := GCDR (M - N, N);
end
```

Tracing the evaluation sequence of GCDR(6,8) shows it to call for the evaluation of GCDR(6,2), which in turn calls for GCDR(4,2), which calls for GCDR(2,2). The evaluation of each of these calls is held in abeyance awaiting evaluation of the next, until upon reaching GCDR(2,2), evaluation is possible without further procedure calls. The result of evaluating GCDR(2,2) is then passed back along the line, becoming the value of GCDR(4,2), then of GCDR(6,2), and finally of GCDR(6,8).

For any pair of positive integers, the results of evaluating GCDR and the iterative procedure GCD will be identical. In case either of the arguments is not positive, execution of GCD will loop forever on the while statement, whereas GCDR will embark upon an unending sequence of recursive procedure calls, and will never return any result! In this sense, both procedures correspond to the notion of a mathematical function that is undefined on zero or negative arguments.

Initially, while we are getting used to the concept, most of the recursive procedures we study will simply substitute recursion for iteration. Later, we will encounter examples for which recursion provides an important aid to the conceptual development of an algorithm.

Example 8.4.1 -- A recursive sorting algorithm

As another easy example, let us revisit the insertion sorting algorithm of Section 6.4. In that example, the basic operation was the insertion of a new value into an already sorted initial segment of an array. The actual insertion was accomplished by the program segment

```
        J := pred(LastIndex);   Item := LastIndex;
        while Item < List [J] do
            begin
                List [succ(J)] := List[J];
                J := pred(J);
            end
        List [succ(J)] := Item;
```

which was applied when the array segment List [1..LastIndex]
was sorted.

Another perspective on the use of this program segment is
that it constitutes a procedure to perform Sort(LastIndex)
in terms of an array that has already been partially sorted
by Sort(pred(LastIndex)). The condition terminating the recursion occurs when LastIndex is one. We can easily make a
recursive procedure out of the program segment:

```
        procedure Sort (LastIndex : Indextype);
            var
                J : Indextype;
                Item : Integer;
            begin
                if LastIndex > 1 then
                    begin
                        Sort (pred(LastIndex));
                        J := pred(LastIndex);
                        Item := List[LastIndex];
                        while Item < List [J] do
                            begin
                                List[succ(J)] := List [J];
                                J := pred(J);
                            end;
                        List[succ(J)] := Item;
                    end;
            end
```

The iteration accomplished by the for loop in the
example of Section 6.4 has been replaced by the recursive
call to Sort, with its argument decremented each time. To
utilize this procedure, it must be embedded in a program
that initializes the list to be sorted and sets the sentinel
value in the zero-indexed element of List. We give this
program in outline:

```
program InsertionSort2 (Input, Output);
   const
      N = 25;
   type
      Indextype = 0..N;
   var
      List : array [Indextype] of Integer;

   procedure Sort (Lastindex : Indextype);
         ⋮

   begin
      (**** initialize List [1..N] ****)

      List[0] := -Maxint; (*set the sentinel value*)
      Sort (N);

      (**** print the sorted list ****)
   end.
```

The use of recursion in the last example was straight-forward, but achieves no real simplification over the iterative solution. In such cases it is usually preferable to use itera-tion, as it is slightly more efficient. Next, we shall consider an example for which it is difficult to compose an iterative algorithm, but comparatively easy to find a solution using recursion.

Example 8.4.2 -- Evaluating the determinant of a square matrix

When a small system of linear equations is to be solved by computation, one of the calculations often made is the determinant of a matrix whose elements are the coefficients of terms of the equations. The determinant is a single number defined as the sum taken over all permutations of the columns of the matrix, of the products of elements appearing on the principal diagonal of the permuted matrix. The sign with which each of these terms is added to the sum is posi-tive or negative according to whether the permutation of the columns is even or odd.

No one actually computes a determinant of a matrix larger than 3 by 3 by generating all permutations of the columns and evaluating the products of diagonals. Usually, one uses the method of expansion of cofactors. If a_{ij} denotes the matrix element in the ith row and jth column, then the cofactor of a_{ij} is the matrix obtained from the original matrix by deleting its ith row and jth column. The determinant of a matrix can be evaluated by summing over the column indices the products of the elements of any given row with the determinants of the cofactor matrices. The sign of each term of the sum is given by $(-1)^{i+j}$, where the indices i and j are numbered from 1 up to the dimension of the matrix. Symbolically, this formula for evaluation of the determinant of an N by N matrix can be written as follows:

$$\text{Det}(A) = \sum_{j=1}^{N} (-1)^{i+j} * A_{ij} * \text{Det}(\text{Cofactor}_{ij}(A))$$

where the choice of the row index, i, is arbitrary so long as it is within the range of 1 to N. This formula is a recursive definition of the determinant, since it gives the determinant of an N by N matrix in terms of the determinants of a set of N - 1 by N - 1 matrices, the matrices designated as $\text{Cofactor}_{ij}(A)$. In order for the recursive definition to be complete, it must have a termination condition telling explicitly how to get the determinant for a matrix of some fixed size. An obvious special case is the matrix consisting of only a single element, for which we specify that

Det(A) = A_{11}, when N = 1.

We can be guided by the outline of the recursive definition to obtain an iteration graph such as the following:

Det (A, N)

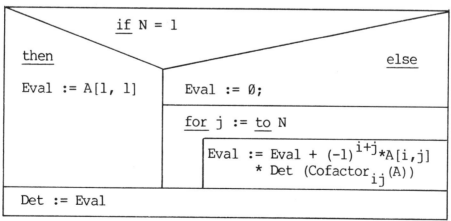

where the assignment operator on the last line designates the value to be returned by the function Det.

The part of the computation not yet specified by this iteration graph is the formation of the cofactor matrix. This is to be an N - 1 by N - 1 square matrix, obtained from the matrix A by deleting one row and one column. Since the row which is to be deleted can be selected arbitrarily, let us choose the Nth row, letting the index i of the iteration graph equal N. Also, since the result is independent of the order in which summation over the column indices is done, let us reverse the order of summation, letting j start from N and go in steps of -1 until 1. The initial relation of the cofactor matrix to the host matrix A is shown in the diagram below.

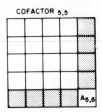

This particular choice of the order in which to iterate over the columns of A is in no way crucial to the success of the algorithm; it merely serves to simplify the calculation of indices in forming the cofactor. Cofactor$_{N,N}$(A) is formed simply by copying the first N - 1 columns of each of the first N - 1 rows of A.

For a value of the column index that is intermediate between 1 and N, the relationship of the cofactor matrix to the host matrix is as shown below

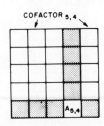

Notice that to transform $Cofactor_{N,j+1}(A)$ to $Cofactor_{N,j}(A)$, only a single column of the cofactor matrix needs to be replaced. The jth column of the cofactor matrix should be replaced by the first N - 1 elements of the j+1st column of A.

The final modification of the iteration graph that we shall make is to account for the sign of the cofactor expansion by alternation, rather than by raising -1 to an integral power. The transformations of the original iteration graph have altered it significantly, and we shall redraw it before proceeding to translate it into a procedure.

Det (A,N)

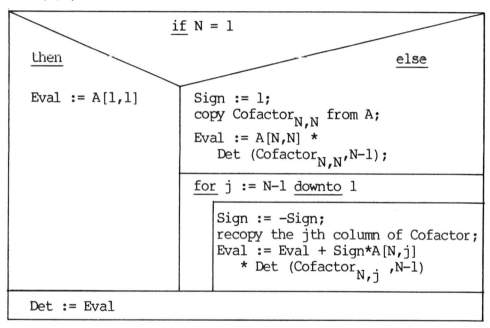

The iteration graph is translated into the procedure Det in the following program. The procedure has been embedded in a program block that also reads data, applies the procedure to the data, and prints a result.

```
program TestDeterminant (Input, Output);
    const
        Nmax = 12;
    type
        Indextype = 1..Nmax;
        IndexVectortype = array [Indextype] of Indextype;
```

```pascal
var
    A : array [Indextype, Indextype] of Real;
    Columns : IndexVectortype;
    N, Row, Col : Indextype;

function Det (Columns : IndexVectortype;
              N : Indextype) : Real;

var
    Eval, Sign : Real;
    CofactorColumns : IndexVectortype;
    Col, C : Indextype;
begin
    if N = 1 then
        Det := A[1, Columns[1]]
    else
        begin
            Sign := 1.0;  Eval := 0.0;
            for Col := N downto 1 do
                begin
                    for C := 1 to pred(Col) do
                        CofactorColumns[C] := Columns[C];
                    for C := Col to pred(N) do
                        CofactorColumns[C] := Columns[succ(C)];
                    Eval := Eval + Sign*A[N, Columns[Col]]
                                    * Det(CofactorColumns, N);
                    Sign := -Sign;
                end;
            Det := Eval;
        end;
end;


begin (*** TestDeterminant ***)
    Read (N);
    for Row := 1 to N do
        begin
            for Col := 1 to N do
                begin
                    Read (A[Row, Col]);
                    Write (A[Row, Col]);
                end;
            Writeln;
        end;
    Writeln;
    Writeln ('THE DETERMINANT EVALUATES TO: ',
             Det (Columns, N));
end.
```

224

8.1   Complete the specification of the algorithm of Example 3.8.1 for finding the intersection of a pair of lines, as a Pascal procedure. Do not neglect to specify how the parameters giving the lines are to be passed to the procedure, and how the coordinates of any intersection which has been found are to be returned. Compose a surrounding block of Pascal text to enable the procedure to be tested.

8.2   When the computer reads input lines on which are encoded the text of a Pascal program, its first task in interpreting the text is to recognize the reserved words, identifiers, and constants of the language. Compose a procedure called Scan to perform this function. It may, of course, employ other procedures local to itself to carry out specialized tasks.

Upon each successive call, Scan is to locate the next word or operator symbol of the text, returning the word as the value of a global variable called Word Scanned. The type of Word Scanned should be
packed array [1..80] of Char
Another global integer variable, WordLength, is to contain the number of characters in the scanned word.

The several reserved words and operator symbols of Pascal are to be assigned index numbers, and Scan is to return the appropriate index number as the value of a global variable, ReservedIndex. Assign the index number values 1 for any identifier, 2 for any numerical constant, 3 for any Boolean constant, and 4 for any character constant. Let illegal constructions (such as 12.ABC) be given the index number 0.

The problem can be simplified significantly by adding the restriction that no word is allowed to be broken across the boundary between lines of input. Don't forget to let the procedure scan to the end of a comment.

8.3   In many computational applications, a sequence of randomly generated numbers is utilized to simulate randomly occurring events. It is, of course, impossible to generate a truly random sequence by means of a finite, deterministic algorithm, but one can generate sequences that satisfy the simplest statistical tests of randomness quite easily. Some of these generators actually produce repetitive sequences of numbers, having a long period of repetition. For example, two such generators are described by:

X1 := (509 + 67*X1) mod 4096

X2 := (2*X2) mod 4096 + (X2 + X2 div 4 + X2 div 2048) mod 2

(in the second generator, X2 cannot be given initial values of 0 or 4095.)

Give Pascal procedures for each of these pseudo-random sequence generators (the variables X1 and X2 must be global to the procedures in order to have their values saved from one invocation to the next). Perform the following tests on both generators:

a) determine the period of repetition.

b) determine the distribution of values by counting the number of values generated in each interval of 100, from 0 to 4095, as the generator cycles through a complete period.

c) determine the mean of the values generated.

d) determine the covariance of values separated by intervals of 1, 2, and 5 in the sequence. The covariance of values separated by an interval I is given by

$$\frac{1}{N} \sum_{i=1}^{N} (X_i - mean)*(X_{i+I} - mean)$$

where N is the period of the generator.

Pseudo-random sequence generators of the first type (with any values of the constant parameters) are called multiplicative congruence generators; those of the second type are called linear congruence generators, or shift-register-sequence generators.

8.4 Give a procedure that will compute and print a calendar for any month, past or future, that is given as an argument. Note that leap year occurs every fourth year, but only every fourth whole century.

8.5   The Fibonacci function is defined by a recursion formula involving two previous values,

$$F(n) = \begin{cases} 1, & \text{if } n = 1; \\ 1, & \text{if } n = 2; \\ F(n-1) + F(n-2), & \text{otherwise.} \end{cases}$$

If this formula is implemented directly as a recursive Pascal procedure, it is needlessly inefficient in that many computations are repeated. For instance, in the computation of F(6), the evaluation sequence would be

```
 F(6)     compute F(5), then F(4)
 F(5)     compute F(4), then F(3)
 F(4)     compute F(3), then F(2)
 F(3)     compute F(2), then F(1)
 F(2) = 1
 F(1) = 1
 F(3) = 1 + 1 = 2
*F(2) = 1
 F(4) = 2 + 1 = 3
*F(3) = compute F(2), then F(1)
*F(2) = 1
*F(1) = 1
*F(3) = 1 + 1 = 2
 F(5) = 3 + 2 = 5
*F(4)     compute F(3), then F(2)
*F(3)     compute F(2), then F(1)
*F(2) = 1
*F(1) = 1
*F(3) = 1 + 1 = 2
*F(2) = 1
*F(4) = 2 + 1 = 3
 F(6) = 5 + 3 = 8
```

Out of the 22 steps of the execution sequence, the 12 marked with asterisks are duplications of previous steps. As the argument of the Fibonacci function is increased, the inefficiency grows much worse.

a) Can you give a simple iterative procedure for computing the Fibonacci function, which does not needlessly repeat computations?

b) Can you give a recursive algorithm that does not cause repetition of previous computations?

227

9 SOLVING HARD PROBLEMS

Even after we have learned to use most of the standard tools of computation, it is still not easy to generate an algorithm when faced with the specification of a problem to be solved. We often encounter the difficulty that when starting to think of the steps required in a possible solution, we may be swamped by a tidal wave of details, all seemingly interrelated, that must be taken into account. If only the problem could be reduced in its complexity by taking just one step at a time, then an algorithm might be developed by a process of orderly analysis. It is this difficulty of complexity that we are about to tackle in this chapter.

9.1 Top-down problem solving

There is one concept of dealing with problems in a large organization that says you should always start at the top. If you can get the attention of the person who has overall responsibility for the organization, and present your problem to him, he then will determine the general course of action to be taken and will delegate the responsibility for carrying out this action to appropriate second-level executives within the organiztion. They may, in turn, have some of the details taken care of by employees under their jurisdiction. The solution to the problem begins at the top, and details are allowed to filter down to the workers by a process of delegation.

This process works in many human organizations, and it is not a bad thing to imitate in the organization of a computational algorithm. We can make it a little more specific by giving a recursive procedure for this type of problem solving. (This is informal, not a Pascal procedure).

SOLVE (Problem):
1. Obtain a precise statement of the specifications to be met.
2. Formulate a simple, iterative solution, naming as subproblems any trouble spots encountered along the way.
3. While any subproblem remains unsolved, SOLVE(Subproblem).

We shall attempt to follow this procedure in generating algorithms for the examples in this chapter. You may already recognize that the ability to define procedures in a programming language is of enormous importance in carrying out this plan of attack, for the algorithm solving each identified subproblem can be given as a Pascal procedure.

Example 9.1.1 -- Printing a column of text

A computer printout is to be prepared from text obtained from an input file. The printout is to appear as a sequence of numbered pages of text, in lines no more than 60 characters wide, with a left margin of 15 print spaces, an upper margin of 6 print lines, and up to 50 printed lines appearing on a page. Words are not to be broken at the ends of the lines, as the computer does not know all of the rules of syllabification of English. There is to be a blank line left between paragraphs, and the first line of each new paragraph is also to have an identation of five spaces from the left margin.

The input is to be in the form of lines from a file of characters, with words to be separated by one or more blanks, or by an end-of-paragraph character '@' optionally followed by blanks, or by an end of record. Words are not to be broken from one line to the next. A word will be any sequence of non-blank characters except for the end-of-paragraph character. Thus, if the text consists of ordinary English, the punctuation marks following any word will be treated as though part of the word, and will not be separated. If a word ends with a period, a question mark, or a colon, it is to be separated from the following word on the print line by two blank spaces, regardless of the separation that occurs in the input text. If a word ends with any other symbol, it is to be separated from the following word by a single space. Printing of the text is to continue until an end-of-text symbol '@@' is encountered.

We begin composing an algorithm according to our top-down method by giving a control program whose function is merely to identify subtasks and assign them to other procedures. This control program will also contain the declarations of global variables and procedures, but since we do not yet know what they shall be, we cannot write them.

```
begin
    Initialize;
    while not EndOfText do
        PrintPage
end.
```

As you can see, the top-down design philosophy makes it very easy to get started. So far, the algorithm calls for some form of initialization to be performed by a procedure yet to be specified, followed by the printing of pages until some condition arises to cause the logical variable EndOfText to become false. Since we don't yet know what to initialize, our next step will be the composition of PrintPage.

The task assigned to PrintPage is to begin a new page of output with an upper margin of six blank lines in which is embedded a page number, then to print 50 lines of text. It must also take responsibility for updating the page number in preparation for the printing of a page that may follow. At this point, we realize that the original specification of the problem did not say how the page number should appear; we must make that decision at this point in order to complete the specification of the task for PrintPage. Let us say that the page number is to be bracketed by dashes to set it apart, and centered on the second (otherwise blank) line from the top of the page.

There are some integer variables that must be declared globally to PrintPage. One is to keep track of page numbers; call it PageNumber. We shall also use several constant parameters of the application; these are Margin, giving the width of the left margin, LineWidth, the maximum width of a printed line and PageLength, the number of printed lines on a page.

A Pascal procedure to print a page is:

```
procedure PrintPage;
    var
        LineCount : 1..PageLength;
    begin
        Page; (****starts a new print page****)
        Writeln;
        WritePageNumber; Writeln;
        Writeln; Writeln; Writeln; Writeln;
        for LineCount := 1 to PageLength do
            PrintLine (LineCount);
        PageNumber := PageNumber + 1;
    end;
```

Most of the work involved in printing a page has been relegated to other procedures, WritePageNumber and PrintLine. The first of these converts the value of PageNumber to a sequence of numerals and centers it on a line.

```
procedure WritePageNumber;
    var
        I : 1..LineWidth;
        Numerals : array [1..4] of Char;
        NumeralIndex: 0..4;
        N : Integer;
    begin
        (****  convert the page number to a numeral string  ****)
        NumeralIndex := 0; N := PageNumber;
        while N > 0 do
            begin
                NumeralIndex := succ(NumeralIndex);
                Numerals[NumeralIndex] :=
                        Chr(N mod 10 + Ord('0'));
                N := N div 10;
            end;
        (****  center and print the numerals  ****)
        for I := to Margin +
                        (LineWidth - NumeralIndex - 2) div 2 do
            Write(Blank);
        Write('-');
        for I := NumeralIndex downto 1 do
            Write(Numerals [I]) ;
        Write ('-');
    end;
```

Now we must deal with the printing of individual lines of text. There are several special cases, for if the last line printed ends a paragraph, then the next line is to be left blank, unless it occurs at the top of a page. Also, the beginning of a line is to be indented if it is the first line of a paragraph. To summarize these cases, an iteration graph will be useful.

PrintLine:

if end of paragraph			
then			else
if at top of page		if beginning a new paragraph	
then	else	then	else
begin a new line;	leave a line;	begin a new line;	begin a line;
indent; finish printing the line;		indent; finish printing the line;	finish printing the line;

The several conditions controlling the course of execution of PrintLine depend on circumstances outside its area of responsibility, and must somehow be communicated to it. Determining that the line to be printed is the first on a page can be done by testing the condition LineCount = 1, since LineCount is a parameter whose value is passed to PrintLine. To record conditions of having ended a paragraph or of being ready to begin a new one, we shall use global, Boolean variables. These variables will have to be declared in the outermost block, that of the control program, but part of the job of maintaining their values correctly will fall to PrintLine. We are now ready to compose this procedure.

```
procedure PrintLine (LineCount : Integer);
    (* local variable and procedure declarations go here *)
    begin
        if EndParagraph then
            begin
                if LineCount = 1 then
                    begin
                        StartLine;  Indent;  WriteLine;
                    end;
```

232

```
        else
            begin
            (**************************************
            *   leave a blank line and indicate   *
            *   that a new paragraph is to follow  *
            **************************************)
                Writeln;
                ParaBegin := True;
            end;
        EndParagraph := False;
    end
else
    begin
        StartLine;
        if ParaBegin then
            begin
                Indent;
                ParaBegin := False;
            end;
        WriteLine;
    end;
end; (* PrintLine *)
```

Again, most of the work has been left to other procedures, StartLine, Indent, and WriteLine. We see that the use made of the flag, ParaBegin, has been simply to remember, following the termination of one paragraph, that the next line printed is to be indented to begin another paragraph. After this action has been taken, the flag is reset to False until it is needed again. Both the flags, EndParagraph, and ParaBegin will have to be set in the initialization procedure in order that PrintLine will work correctly the first time that it is called.

The two procedures StartLine and Indent are very simple in function. StartLine is to begin the printing of a new line, set the left margin, and initialize a variable called RestOfLine that will indicate how many characters can be printed before the end of the print line is reached. Indent is to fill the indentation space with blank characters, and record the fact that fewer characters remain to be printed before encountering the end of the line. The variable RestOfLine must be global to both of these procedures and to WriteLine, but it need not be known or remembered outside of a single execution of PrintLine. Therefore, we can add its declaration to those local to PrintLine, which are:

233

```pascal
var
    RestOfLine : 0..LineWidth;

procedure StartLine;
    var
        I : 1..LineWidth;
    begin
        for I := 1 to Margin do
            Write (Blank);
        RestOfLine := LineWidth;
    end; (*StartLine*)

procedure Indent;
    begin
        Write ('     ');
        RestOfLine := RestOf Line - 5;
    end; (*Indent*)

procedure WriteLine;
    (**********************************************
    *  unless the paragraph has ended, print the   *
    *  next word, if it will fit on the print line *
    **********************************************)
    begin
        while not EndParagraph and
                (WordLength <= RestOfLine) do
            begin
                PrintWord;
                ReadNextWord;
                (*****************************************
                *  WordLength is to be set by side effect  *
                *  of ReadNextWord, which must be called   *
                *  before WriteLine is first executed      *
                *****************************************)
            end;
        Writeln;
    end; (*WriteLine*)
```

We now get down to the definition of two procedures that do most of the work. Let us consider ReadNextWord first. Its function is to obtain the next word from the input text. It must scan over blank characters if there are any, until it comes to a non-blank character. If in the process it encounters the end of one line of input, then it is to call for another. When a string of non-blank characters is found, it is to be saved in a global variable called Word, and its length is to be recorded as the

234

value of WordLength. The data type of Word must be an array of characters.

In case a word is found to be terminated by the end-of-paragraph character, ReadNextWord must recognize that fact and pass over the character. And, if a word is terminated by a punctuation mark indicating that two blank spaces are to follow it, that fact also must be noted. For this purpose, a variable Nblanks will indicate the number of spaces to follow the word.

There is one additional requirement of ReadNextWord that we can discover by careful analysis of the operation of the procedures already written. The value of WordLength that it returns must never be greater than the parameter LineWidth. WriteLine will never put a word on a line if the length of the word is more than RestOfLine, and the largest value that RestOfLine can have is the value of LineWidth. If too large a value of WordLength is ever set the algorithm will fail to terminate, with new lines continually being started, and WriteLine stubbornly refusing to print anything on them because they aren't long enough. Since nothing has been said about this contingency in the original specification of the problem, we shall make an arbitrary decision that if a word is encountered whose length exceeds LineWidth, it will be split into two with the first part having WordLength equal to LineWidth, and the remainder will be given as the next word.

On the next page, we give an iteration graph to specify the algorithm in informal terms.

In the algorithm ReadNextWord, when the end-of-paragraph character '@' has been found, we might have been tempted to set the flag EndParagraph. However, the use made of EndParagraph in previously composed procedures has been to indicate that the processing of one paragraph has been completed. ReadNextWord can know only that the end of a paragraph has been detected in the input; completion of processing for that paragraph is outside the jurisdiction of ReadNextWord, and so it should not be allowed to set this flag. In particular, printing of the last word of the paragraph will probably not have been completed when ReadNextWord detects the terminating symbol. If ReadNextWord were allowed to overstep its jurisdiction and set EndParagraph to True when the symbol '@' was encountered, then WriteLine might terminate a line without having called PrintWord to print the last word of a paragraph, which would be an error.

ReadNextWord:

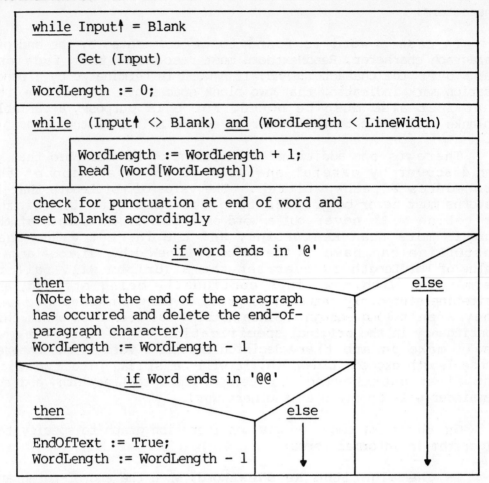

A safe course of action is to define a new Boolean variable, a flag called IsLastWord, which will be set by ReadNextWord whenever the end-of-paragraph character is encountered. Since this variable is to be used by other procedures as well, it must be declared globally.

The Pascal text of ReadNextWord can now be given.

```
procedure ReadNextWord;
    begin
        while Input↑ = Blank do
            Get (Input);
        WordLength := 0;
        while (Input↑ <> Blank) and
                (WordLength < LineWidth) do
            begin
                WordLength := WordLength + 1;
                Read(Word[WordLength]);
            end;
        if Word[WordLength] in ['.', '?', ':'] then
            Nblanks := 2
        else
            Nblanks := 1;
        if Word[WordLength] = '@' then
            begin
                IsLastWord := True;
                WordLength = WordLength - 1;
                if (WordLength > 0) and
                        (Word[WordLength] = '@') then
                    begin
                        EndOfText := True;
                        WordLength := WordLength - 1;
                    end;
            end;
    end; (*ReadNextWord*)
```

The other working procedure is PrintWord. Its task is to print the sequence of characters stored in the array Word, and whose length is given by WordLength. Also, if there is enough room, the word is to be followed in the print line by one or two blank characters as determined by the value of Nblanks. The variable RestOfLine, which records the number of character spaces remeining in the print line, must be decremented by the length of the word printed and the number of blanks that were left. And finally, if PrintWord happens to print the last word of a paragraph, then the processing of that paragraph is complete, so it becomes the responsibility of PrintWord to set the flag EndParagraph to True in such a case. It is a straightforward matter to compose a Pascal procedure to accomplish this task.

```
procedure PrintWord;
    var
        J : 1..LineWidth;
    begin
        for J := 1 to WordLength do
            Write (Word[J]);
        RestOfLine := RestOfLine - WordLength - Nblanks;
        if RestOfLine > 0 then
            for J := 1 to Nblanks do
                Write (Blank);
        if IsLastWord then
            begin
                IsLastWord := False;
                EndParagraph := True;
            end;
    end; (* PrintWord *)
```

All that remains is to give the initialization procedure. As a guide, we can examine the use made of each global variable, determining whether it requires initialization, and how this is to be accomplished.

PageNumber must be set initially to 1;
IsLastWord, EndParagraph and EndOfText must be initialized to False;
ParaBegin must be initialized to True;
Word, WordLength and Nblanks must be set by an initial call to ReadNextWord.

We have now specified the task of Initialize.

```
procedure Initialize;
    begin
        PageNumber := 1;
        EndOfText := False;
        EndParagraph := False;
        IsLastWord := False;
        ParaBegin := True;
        ReadNextWord;
    end;
```

The final step needed to complete the algorithm is to fill in the declarations of the global variables. This step was deferred until the end in order that we could determine exactly what variables were needed. The following outline of a Pascal program gives the global variable declarations and also indicates the scope of each procedure declaration.

238

```pascal
program PrintText (Input, Output);
   const
      Margin = 15; LineWidth = 60; PageLength = 50;
      Blank = ' ';
   var
      PageNumber : Integer;
      WordLength, Nblanks : 0..LineWidth;
      Word : array [1..LineWidth] of Char;
      EndOfText, EndParagraph, ParaBegin,
         IsLastWord : Boolean;

   procedure PrintPage;
      var
         LineCount : 1..PageLength;
      procedure WritePageNumber;
            ⋮

      procedure PrintLine (LineCount : Integer);
         var
            RestOfLine : Integer;
         procedure StartLine;
               ⋮

         procedure Indent;
               ⋮

         procedure Printword;
               ⋮

         procedure WriteLine;
               ⋮

      end; (* PrintPage *)

   procedure ReadNextWord;
         ⋮

   procedure Initialize;
         ⋮

begin (* body of PrintText *)
   Initialize;
   while not EndOfText do
      PrintPage;
end.
```

In addition to its utility in composing algorithms, there is another significant benefit to the use of top-down organization in the design of a computational program. Since functional responsibility for a single task is localized, insofar as possible in a single procedure, it is usually not difficult to fix the blame for malfunction when something goes wrong. When a program does not work as anticipated, the search for an error can be limited to that segment of the program whose assigned function was not carried out properly. Of course, the top-down design philosophy demands that you pay special attention to specifying the task to be performed by each procedure, in advance of beginning the composition of that procedure. Errors in the overall program can also occur because the specification of a task is given incorrectly or incompletely.

Example 9.1.2 -- Generating an alphabetical list of permutations

Suppose that as part of a word game we want to generate all words that can be made by permuting a given string of letters. Also, in order to test the generated words in an orderly way, say by comparing them to entries in a dictionary, we shall require the permutations to be listed in alphabetical order. Since it would be of no use to have the same word listed more than once, we only wish to generate distinct permutations. To perform this task, we want a computational algorithm to read a string of characters from a line of input, and to generate and print in alphabetical order, all distinct permutations of the character string.

There is an obvious brute-force strategy for an algorithm to meet these specifications. That is, to read in an input string, generate and store a list of all possible permutations of the string, then sort the list into alphabetical order and print the entries on the list, skipping successive repetitions of words. However, this approach has some serious disadvantages, not the least of which is that it requires us to represent in the computer an enormous list of strings and to sort that list - an expensive operation if the list is long. And no economy can be realized from possible redundancies in repeated permutations as the brute-force strategy requires that all permutations must be generated before the distinct ones can be picked out. Thus, there would not likely be enough room in the computer to store the list of 362,880 possible permutations of the string 'AAAAAAAAB', although the number of distinct permutations is only 9.

So the brute-force approach has disadvantages which make us want to think further. We do not actually have an algorithm at

hand to generate permutations; perhaps it is not much more difficult to generate distinct permutations in alphabetical order,
than it is to generate all possible permutations in an arbitrarily chosen order. If we could do this, then it would not be
necessary to store a list of the permuted strings; they could
just be printed as they were generated. If such an algorithm
could be invented, then an algorithm to accomplish the overall
task might have the iteration graph:

```
┌─────────────────────────────────────────────────┐
│  get a string from the input;                    │
│  sort it into a string of least                  │
│      aphabetical order;                           │
├─────────────────────────────────────────────────┤
│  while the last permutation printed              │
│  is not in greatest alphabetical order           │
│   ┌──────────────────────────────────────────┐   │
│   │  print the string;                        │   │
│   │  replace the string by                    │   │
│   │      its NextPermutation                  │   │
│   └──────────────────────────────────────────┘   │
└─────────────────────────────────────────────────┘
```

In the informal description above, we have introduced the
notion of least and of greatest alphabetical order. A string
is in least alphabetical order if the letters of the string
satisfy the relation:

$$letter_i \leq letter_{i+1},$$

where i ranges from 1 to the length of the string minus 1, for
then no permutation can precede this one in alphabetical order.
Conversely, by greatest alphabetical order, we mean the
permutation in which the letters satisfy the relation:

$$letter_i \geq letter_{i+1}.$$

Let us consider a concrete example in order to discover an
algorithm for generating the next permutation in alphabetical
order. Suppose we consider the string 'LITTLE'. Seeking the next
permutation in order, we will need to restrict the interchange of
letters to a substring as far to the right as possible. The next
permutation of 'LITTLE' will obviously have no change made in the
initial letter, the one occupying the position of greatest significance. However, notice that the terminal substring 'TTLE' is
already in greatest order. Thus, there is no possible permutation
of this substring alone that will increase the order of 'LITTLE'.

Apparently then, the letter 'I' in the second significant position, is the leftmost letter that must be changed in the next permutation.

What letter should replace 'I' in the second position? It must be one of the letters of the substring 'TTLE', since we have agreed that the letter to the left of the 'I' is to be left unchanged. We must choose from the terminal substring that letter which will result in the smallest increase in the order of the permuted word. Replacing the 'I' by the 'E' would decrease the order, and replacing it by a 'T' would increase the order more than would replacement by the 'L'. Suppose we now exchange the 'I' with the 'L' in 'LITTLE' and stop to consider what we have got. The resulting word is 'LLTTIE'. What we desire is the word least in order among all those permutations beginning with 'LL'. We do not have it yet, for in fact, the terminal substring 'TTIE' is in greatest order, not least order. Rearranging it into least order produces 'LLEITT', which is the next permutation of these letters following 'LITTLE' in alphabetical order.

Let us try to generalize the steps that we followed in generating the next permutation from 'LITTLE', being careful to determine what about each step is an instance of a more general rule. We begin by stating the task to be accomplished by each step.

1) From the given string, determine the longest terminal substring that is in greatest order. Let I denote the index of the letter just to the left of this substring.

2) From the terminal substring to the right of the Ith letter, pick out the letter least among those that are greater in order than the Ith letter. Let J be the index of this letter.

3) Exchange the Ith and Jth letters in the string.

4) Reorder the substring to the right of the Ith letter so as to produce a substring in least order.

Giving names to the procedures that will carry out each of these tasks, we have an initial design for a procedure to find the next permutation:

```
procedure NextPermutation;
    var
        I, J : Indextype;
    begin
        I := Locate;
        J := MinMax (I);
        Exchange (I, J);
        Reorder (succ(I));
    end;
```

The definition given for a string to be in greatest alphabetical order suggests an algorithm for the first subtask. Suppose the letters of the permuted string are stored in an array variable, Letter, and that another variable, WordLength, records the number of letters in the string. A Pascal function to locate the index of the letter to the left of the maximal length substring in greatest alphabetic order is

```
function Locate : Indextype;
    var
        K : Indextype;
    begin
        K := WordLength - 1;
        while Letter[K] >= Letter[succ(K)] do
            K := pred(K);
        Locate := K;
    end;
```

There is a hazard to the use of Locate as given above. If the permuted string is already in greatest alphabetic order, then Locate will continue to decrement I until it runs right off the end of the string, with I = 0. One cannot predict what it will do after that. In this case the difficulty can be avoided by specifying that Letter[0], which is not part of the permuted string, will serve as a sentinel. We can give the sentinel the value of the character least in order among type Char, by assigning it Chr(0). Then it will be safe to use Locate on any string that contains at least one alphabetic or numeric character.

In the function MinMax, which is to perform the second task listed above, one would ordinarily be obliged to search the entire substring from Letter[I + 1] through Letter[WordLength], keeping track of the best candidate so far discovered in order to assure that the letter that is found satisfies the specification completely. In the algorithm NextPermutation, however, MinMax is always executed immediately following Locate, and there is some

243

additional information that can be used to advantage. It is certain that the substring to the right of the Ith letter contains at least one letter that is greater in order than Letter[I], for the I+1st letter is one example. Also, we know that the substring from Letter[I+1] to Letter[WordLength] is in greatest alphabetic order, that is, its letters are arrayed in non-increasing order. Therefore, a satisfactory procedure to follow in MinMax would be to scan the substring from left to right until encountering the first letter that is less than or equal to Letter[I] in order. This letter will be one position to the right of the one desired.

```
function MinMax (I : Indextype) : Indextype;
   (****************************************************
   *   Since Letter[I+1] is known to be greater in      *
   *   order than Letter[I], the search can begin       *
   *   from Letter[I+2]. The search proceeds through    *
   *   a sequence of letters in declining order, stop-  *
   *   ing when one is found to be less than Letter[I].  *
   *   The preceding letter is then the least that is   *
   *   greater in order than Letter[I].                 *
   ****************************************************)
   var
      J : Indextype;
   begin
      J := I + 2;
      while Letter[J] > Letter[I] do
         J := succ(J);
      MinMax := pred(J);
   end;
```

In the form given, MinMax also lacks a condition to guarantee termination. We can employ a sentinel, just as was suggested for termination of Locate. Let us specify that Letter[WordLength + 1] is always to be defined and shall have the constant value Chr(0). Then if the value of J in MinMax ever reaches WordLength + 1, the termination condition must hold.

We shall defer giving a procedure to exchange letters in the string. The final subtask to be performed is that of reordering the terminal substring into least order. If nothing was known about the order of the terminal substring at this point, then a sorting algorithm would be required. But once again there is additional information that can be used. Just prior to the exchange of the Ith and Jth letters, the terminal substring from Letter[I+1] to Letter[WordLength] was known to be in greatest

244

order. Then, one of its letters, Letter[J] was pulled out and replaced. However, it is known that Letter[J-1] is greater in order than the letter to be inserted in the Jth position (if Letter[J-1] is, in fact, in the substring at all), and also it is known that the letter being inserted is not greater in order than Letter[J+1]. Therefore, the substring remains in greatest alphabetic order, even though one of its letters has been replaced. To reorder a string that is initially in greatest alphabetic order into one in least order requires only a reversal. Hence, the reordering procedure becomes:

```
procedure Reorder (First : Indextype);
    var
        K : Indextype;
    begin
        for K := 0 to (WordLength - First - 1) div 2 do
            Exchange (First + K, WordLength - K);
    end;
```

The procedure to accomplish the interchange of a pair of characters is similar to ones we have seen before.

```
procedure Exchange (I, J : Indextype);
    var
        TempChar : Char;
    begin
        TempChar := Letter[I];
        Letter[I] := Letter[J];
        Letter[J] := TempChar;
    end;
```

All that now remains now is to complete the specification of the control program. As a termination condition, it requires that the last permutation printed should be in greatest alphabetic order. We could test for this condition and keep a record of it, but upon a little reflection, you will see that if the permuted string is already in greatest order when NextPermutation is executed, then we have the unique circumstance that will cause the index I to run off the left end of the string when Locate is executed. Therefore, when NextPermutation is presented with the permutation in greatest order, it will record that fact by setting the variable I to zero. All that is necessary in order to test this condition in the control program is communicate the value of the local variable I to the surrounding block. For this purpose, let us define a global variable, Index, and allow it to be set by side effect of a call to NextPermutation. We insert an assignment statement into this procedure as its last line,

>   Index := I

The control program can now be given as a Pascal program:

```pascal
program AlphabeticPermutations (Input, Output);
   const
      MaxLength = 25;
      Blank = ' ';
   type
      Indextype = 0..MaxLength;
   var
      WordLength, L, Index : Indextype;
      Letter : array [Indextype] of Char;

   (*  procedure declarations go here  *)

begin
   WordLength := 0;
   repeat
      WordLength := succ(WordLength);
      Read(Letter[WordLength]);
   until Input↑ = Blank;
   Letter[0]  := Chr(0);
   Letter[succ(WordLength)]  := Chr(0);
   Write ('THE ORIGINAL STRING IS: ');
   for Index := 1 to WordLength do
      Write (Letter[Index]);
   Writeln; Writeln;
   Writeln ('THE PERMUTATIONS ARE:');
   SortLetter;
   (*********************************************
   *  obtain all permutations of Letter. After  *
   *  the maximally ordered permutation has been *
   *  printed, NextPermutation will set the value *
   *  of Index to zero.                          *
   *********************************************)
   Index := 1;
   while Index > 0 do
      begin
         Write ('       ');
         for L := 1 to WordLength do
            Write(Letter[L]);
         Writeln;
         NextPermutation;
      end;
end.
```

246

The sorting procedure is executed only once and on an array of not more than 80 elements. The simple insertion sort agorithm studied in Section 6.3 will be sufficient for this purpose,

```
procedure SortLetter;
    var
        I, J : Indextype;
        NewChar : Char;
    begin
        for I := 2 to WordLength do
            begin
                NewChar := Letter[I];
                J := pred(I);
                while NewChar < Letter[J] do
                    begin
                        Letter[succ(J)] := Letter[J];
                        J := pred(J);
                    end;
                Letter[succ(J)] := NewChar;
            end;
    end;
```

One deficiency of a textbook as a vehicle for learning how to design algorithms is that it makes everything look unnaturally easy. Each step is presented as though it follows from previous steps in a manner so logical that it is hard to conceive that the design could have progressed in any other way. When one attempts to design algorithms on his own, however, he immediately finds that this is not the case. Instead, the final design of an algorithm is the end result of a sequence of iterations, involving many false starts and the correction of a multitude of errors along the way. The process of trial and error, and of progressive refinement of detail in successive versions of an algorithm is a perfectly natural one, a process by which our own perception of the problem is sharpened and the steps to be taken in its solution are clarified. What we must do is to make this process of refinement orderly enough that it eventually comes to a successful conclusion.

In this respect, the process of top-down design is of great help, for it permits one to defer the consideration of details until larger concepts have been worked out, and it enables one to refine portions of an algorithm by trial and error without having to scrap the entire previous effort each time an error is discovered in one part. It is hard to overemphasize that careful and

247

detailed specification of the task to be performed is the key to success in top-down design. There is a tendency, particularly evident in computer programmers without much experience, to let the specification of the task be defined by the result of designing the procedure, instead of the other way around.

9.2 Using trial and error methods

Most complicated tasks derive their complexity from the fact that there is a very large number of possible courses of action that may be taken. Some courses will lead to a satisfactory solution and some will not, but at the outset, we cannot predict with any accuracy which will be the successful alternatives. When faced with such a problem, we usually resort to trial and error methods. This is exactly the situation that faces us in many of the games we play for recreation. In chess or checkers, for example, there are no secrets concerning the actual state of the board at any point. Unlike card games, all of the raw information is right there, staring you in the face. But the number of possible outcomes from a given board position is astronomical, and so you try in your mind various possible moves, attempting to evaluate the relative worth of each. When you find a move that has the potential of improving your position (or when you can no longer avoid commitment because of the timer's clock), then you go ahead.

In a one-person game such as solitaire, the trial and error process can be extended from alternatives considered in the mind to alternatives tried on the board. If a chosen course of play turns out to yield an undesirable outcome, then the board position can be restored to its previous state, and a different move tried. In solitaire, this is regarded as cheating, but in actual problem solving it can be a very useful tactic, if one is allowed the luxury of retreating to a previous position from which to choose a less disastrous next move. In computational algorithms there is no notion of cheating, and it is usually possible to restore the computation to a previous state, provided the possible need to do this has been anticipated beforehand. The tactic is known as backup.

Of course, in designing algorithms for the solution of complicated problems, it is necessary to try to minimize the complexity of each individual procedure by employing top-down design. Thus, the manager of a large organization, when faced with the need to carry out a large task in which there are many possible courses of action, will attempt to identify subtasks corresponding to a course he wishes to try. He may hire employees to perform these subtasks, and instruct each employee to report on his success when he has completed the assigned task. When an employee reports success, then the manager can proceed with his chosen course of action, discharging the employee to await the next call to duty. If an employee reports failure, then he is discharged and the manager may be forced to modify his original course of action. The manager himself will report on his success to his own employer, whenever he either succeeds through the efforts of his employees or fails, having exhausted all courses of action open to him.

By way of analogy with the manager directing his employees toward the accomplishment of a task, we can employ top-down design of an algorithm to perform a computational task, using trial and error methods. The analogy to the employee's report will be the value of True or False returned by a Pascal procedure to indicate whether or not it was able to perform its assigned task. The actual performance of the task may be accomplished as a side effect of the procedure, that is, by setting values of variables that are defined globally to the procedure rather than being passed as arguments. This technique is illustrated in the next example.

Example 9.2.1-- The eight queens problem

In the game of chess, the queen is the most powerful single piece on the board. She is allowed to move any number of squares along any of the forward-backward or transverse files of the chessboard, or along the 45-degree diagonals. This suggests the folllowing puzzle. Is it possible, with no other pieces on the 8-by-8 chessboard, to position 8 mutually antagonistic queens in such a way that no queen can reach any other queen in a single move? Quite obviously, it is impossible to position more than 8 queens on the board without conflict, for no two queens can occupy the same column, and there are only 8 columns. But it is not obvious that even as many as 8 can be placed on the board in a 'safe' disposition. This is the sort of problem that a human can solve in a few minutes by trial and error methods and by using his amazing power of geometric perception. It fascinates computer scientists to try to enable a computer to solve problems like this, and the eight queens problem has received a lot of attention. The solution given here draws on algorithms developed by Professors E. W. Dijkstra and N. Wirth. Both Dijkstra's algorithm and the version given here make use of a recursive procedure, whereas Wirth's algorithm is completely iterative. It will be worth your time to make a trip to the library to read about his alternate method of attack.†

For the sake of elegance, we shall add to the specification of the problem that the placement of the eight queens, if one is found, is to be printed on a replica of a chessboard.

A trial and error algorithm works by generating candidates for a solution, and testing each candidate to see whether or not it satisfies the problem specification. The process continues until either a satisfactory solution is found, or all candidates for a solution have been tried and found wanting. However, if the number of possible configuration to be tried is very large, a little intelligence must be applied to reduce the number of possible configurations. For instance, the number of possible ways to place eight queens on a chessboard is $\binom{64}{8}$, or $4,426,165,368$ although some of these configurations are equivalent to one another by rotating the chessboard through 90 or 180 degrees. But since we already know that no configuration having two or more queens in a single column can succeed, we could restrict the candidate configurations to include only those in which each queen occupies a separate column, and if a solution is to be found at all, it wll be found among this set of restricted configurations. The reduction in the number of candidates is appreciable; there are only 8^8, or $16,777,216$ such configurations.

Moreover, it is not even necessary to generate all of the configurations having one queen per column. A board configuration can be generated by placing the queens one at a time. A partially generated configuration, one in which fewer than eight queens have been placed, can be regarded as representing a set of candidate configurations, namely all those fully generated configurations that can be formed by placing the remaining queens. If a partially generated configuration is tested and found to be unsatisfactory, then all of the fully generated configurations that could be obtained by completing it must also be unsatisfactory. Obviously, the generation of a particular candidate configuration can stop as soon as it is discovered that one of its partial configurations is unsatisfactory.

---

† N. Wirth, Programming by Stepwise Refinement, Communications of the ACM, vol. 14, p. 221, April, 1971.

This last concept, that of generating and testing partial configurations, suggests a recursive procedure for finding a solution to the eight queens problem. Suppose that a partial configuration has been generatd, one in which J - 1 queens have been placed in non-conflicting positions. A procedure is required that will place the Jth queen in a position that does not conflict with those previously placed, and such that it will also be possible to place all of the remaining queens without conflict. A procedure to accomplish this task might undertake on its own the placement of the Jth queen. However, to determine whether or not the remaining queens can be successfully placed, it will need an answer to the same problem that it itself has been faced with, except that the number of queens remaining to be placed will be one fewer. This suggests a recursive call upon the procedure. It is as if a manager has a task to delegate which requires all of the same capabilities as does his own task, except that it is slightly smaller in scope. His solution may be to hire, as the cmployee to perform this task, one of his college classmates, a replica of himself.

In informal notation, the control procedure will have the iteration graph

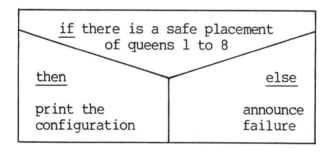

A procedure to determine a safe placement of the Jth through 8th queens is now needed. We have determined that it should be a recursive procedure, and a termination condition is needed to halt the recursion. A suitable way to halt it is to observe that after all eight queens have been successfully placed, the procedure might be called with a value of J greater than 8. In such a case, there is no work to be done, and the procedure could immediately report success, thereby halting the recursion. Let us call this procedure Place, and pass to it as an argument the column number of the next queen to be placed. The queens will be placed in columns successively from column 1 to column 8 of the chessboard. An iteration graph for the procedure is:

Place (J)

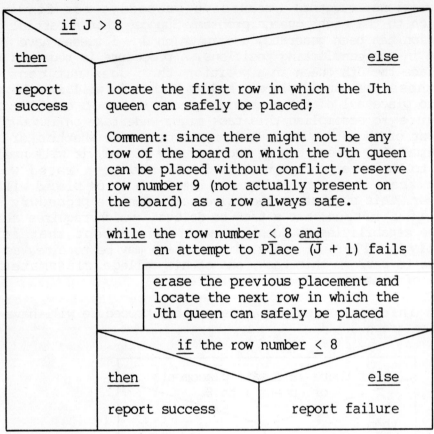

In order to locate a row in which a queen in the Jth column can safely be placed, another procedure will be needed. Since we have provided a dummy row 9 in which a queen will always be safe from attack, there is no need for this procedure to report success or failure; it can always succeed. A possible iteration graph for it is:

SafeRow (I)

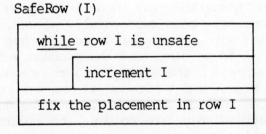

At this point we can avoid no longer the decision as to how to represent the data giving the position of the queens already placed and the areas that they might reach in one move. A first thought might be to represent the chessboard by a two-dimensional array of logical variables. One could use the value True to represent a position occupied by a queen already placed, and False to represent a vacant square. However, we should quickly recognize that imitating the layout of the chessboard offers no advantage to the computer. We humans make use of our facility of visual perception to take advantage of the array of squares on a chessboard, and can immediately visualize from it the domain of influence of a queen. (If we cannot, then our chess games will be of short duration.) But for the computer to make direct use of the chessboard in order to determine whether a given square comes under the influence of a given queen, it would have to simulate the movement of the queen along one of the paths she might travel. This makes no sense at all.

Since only the occupied squares are of any real interest in this algorithm, an alternative representation might be to keep an array of eight integers, representing the row indices of squares occupied by queens in each of the eight columns. Suppose such an array is named Row. Then, to determine whether a square whose indices are (X, Y) is subject to attack by the queen in column J, one could ask the following questions.

1) Is Y = J?   (square in column J)

2) Is X = Row[J]?   (square in the same row as the Jth queen)

3) Is X - Row[J] = Y - J?   (square subject to diagonal attack)

4) Is Row[J] - X = Y - J?   (square subject to attack on the perpendicular diagonal)

Although these questions are sufficient to determine whether or not a square is safe from attack by a particular queen, what we must be able to calculate is whether a square is safe from attack by _any_ previously placed queen. Using this method of representation, the questions must be asked successively concerning every previously placed queen before the status of the square under consideration can be determined.

Another possibility, yet further in abstraction from the idea of simulating the chessboard, is to represent the domains of influence of the queens. Although each queen commands a row, a column, and two perpendicular diagonals of the board, in all there are only eight rows, eight columns, and 15 diagonals of each inclination on the chessboard. So instead of recording the domain of influence of <u>each</u> queen, one might instead record which of these lines on the board is under the control of <u>some</u> queen. The columns are already taken care of by the convention that only those partial configurations will be generated in which the queens are all in separate columns. The required information can be recorded in three Boolean-valued arrays, that we shall call Row, UpDiagonal, and DownDiagonal. To determine in which diagonals a given square lies, it is only necessary to take the sum and the difference of its row and column indices. To find out whether or not a square is safe we can evaluate the expression

Row[I] <u>or</u> DownDiagonal[J-I] <u>or</u> UpDiagonal[J+I]

where I represents the row number and J is the number of a column not yet occupied by a queen.

We are now ready to consider the detailed composition of an algorithm as a Pascal program. The main program block provides declarations of the global variables in which the status of the board positions will be recorded, and of the procedures that are to do the work. Its statement body is a brief control program that calls these procedures.

```
program EightQueens (Output);
(*************************************************
*    global variables are:                       *
*        Queen - records the row number in which  *
*                the queen of each column is placed *
*        Row - a Boolean array indicating rows    *
*                subject to attack by previously   *
*                placed queens                     *
*        UpDiagonal, DownDiagonal - Boolean arrays *
*                indicating the diagonals subject to *
*                attack                            *
**************************************************)
type
    Columntype = 1..8;
var
    Queen : array [Columntype] of Columntype;
    Row : array [Columntype] of Boolean;
    UpDiagonal : array [2..16] of Boolean;
    DownDiagonal : array [-7..7] of Boolean;
    Success : Boolean;
```

254

```
(*************************************************
* The procedure Place will find a solution to   *
* the problem of placing the queens, if one     *
* exists.  The procedure acts by side effect    *
* to set values of the global variables as it   *
* places each queen.  Final placements will be  *
* recorded in the array Queen for use by the    *
* output procedure PrintBoard Place also notes  *
* its success or failure by setting a value in  *
* the global variable Success.                  *
*************************************************)

(*  procedure declarations go here  *)

begin
    InitializeBoard;
    Place(1);
    if Success then
        PrintBoard
    else
        Writeln
        ('NO SOLUTION TO THE 8 QUEENS PROBLEM HAS BEEN FOUND');
end.
```

The next step is to compose the recursive procedure that does most of the work.

```
procedure  Place (J : Integer);
    (*************************************************
    * The argument J gives the column number of the *
    * next queen to be placed.  This variable will   *
    * be global to all procedures defined within     *
    * this one.  Placement is a temporary variable   *
    * indicating the row occupied by the Jth queen.  *
    * The outcome of the attempt to find a solution  *
    * is returned in the global variable Success     *
    *************************************************)
    var
        Placement : Integer;

(* declarations of SafeRow and DeletePlacement go here *)

begin
    if J > 8 then
        Success := True
```

```
            else
                begin
                    (**** Place the Jth queen, then attempt to ****)
                    (**** place the others                       ****)
                    Placement := SafeRow (0,J);
                    Success := False;
                    while (Placement <= 8) and not Success do
                        begin
                            Place (J+1);
                            if not Success then
                                (*move the Jth queen and try again*)
                                begin
                                    DeletePlacement(Placement, J);
                                    Placement := SafeRow (Placement, J);
                                end;
                        end;
                end;
    end; (*Place*)
```

In order to locate a safe placement of the queen in the Jth
column, it will be necessary to scan the squares of the column,
checking to see if each square is under the influence of some
previously placed queen. When a square is found that is not
subject to attack, the row number of that square gives a safe
placement for a queen in column J.

```
function SafeRow (RowIndex, ColIndex : Integer) : Integer;
    (**************************************************
     *  The RowIndex is initially either zero or the   *
     *  last row in which the Jth queen was placed.    *
     *  The task is to advance RowIndex until the      *
     *  square (RowIndex, ColIndex) is not threatened  *
     *  by any previously placed queen                 *
     **************************************************)

    (*** declarations of IsSafe and FixPosition go here ***)

    begin
        repeat
            RowIndex := RowIndex + 1
        until IsSafe;
        if RowIndex <= 8 then
            FixPosition;
        SafeRow := RowIndex;
    end; (*  SafeRow  *)
```

256

Finally, we have reached the point at which we must use the arrays in which the status of rows and diagonals of the board are recorded.

```
function IsSafe : Boolean;
    begin
        if RowIndex > 8 then
            IsSafe := True
        else
            IsSafe := not (Row[RowIndex]
                    or UpDiagonal[ColIndex + RowIndex]
                    or DownDiagonal[ColIndex - RowIndex]);
    end;

procedure FixPosition;
    begin
        Queen[ColIndex] := RowIndex;
        Row[RowIndex] := True;
        UpDiagonal[ColIndex + RowIndex] := True;
        DownDiagonal[ColIndex - RowIndex] := True;
    end;
```

Notice that FixPosition can only be applied to a square for which IsSafe is True. Therefore, the values of Row, UpDiagonal, and DownDiagonal for that square are all false before FixPosition is applied, and are changed to true values to place a single queen. No other queen previously or subsequently placed can lie in the row or either of the diagonals dominated by the Jth queen unless she is first moved to a different square. Therefore, to move her it will suffice to restore the truth values marking her row and diagonals to False, and there is no danger that in so doing the domain of any other queen will be inadvertently affected. The procedure to delete the placement of a queen is therefore very simple.

```
procedure DeletePlacement;
    begin
        Row[Placement] := False;
        UpDiagonal[ColIndex + Placement] := False;
        DownDiagonal[ColIndex - Placement] := False;
    end;
```

The hard part of the algorithm is now done. It is also obvious what needs to be initialized; it is only the status of the domains of influence. Although Success is also a global variable, it does not require explicit initialization, since it is always

257

set by a call to Place before it is tested.

```
procedure InitializeBoard;
    var
        I : Integer;
    begin
        for I : = 1 to 8 do
            Row[I] := False;
        for I := -7 to 7 do
            DownDiagonal[I] := False;
        for I := 2 to 16 do
            UpDiagonal := False;
    end;
```

All that remains is to print the display of the board with the final placement of the queens. This is accomplished by an iterative procedure. To print horizontal lines, one can use the underscore character '_'. The vertical bar '|' can be arrayed on the paper to create vertical lines. If we choose a square of the chessboard to be five print columns wide and three print lines high, it will come out to be nearly square on the output listing. A board square that is to contain a queen will have 'Q' printed in its center, while other squares will be left blank.

```
procedure PrintBoard;
    var
        I, J : 1..8;
    begin
        (*********************************************
        *  First, print a horizontal line of under-  *
        *  scores to mark the top boundary of the    *
        *  board. Then, print rows of squares        *
        *********************************************)
        Writeln ('A SOLUTION TO THE 8 QUEENS PROBLEM IS:');
        Writeln; Write(' ');
        for J := 1 to 8 do
            Write ('____ ');
        Writeln;
        for I := 1 to 8 do
            begin
                (***************************************
                *  print the first third of the verti- *
                *  cal line separating the squares      *
                ***************************************)
                Write('|');
```

258

```
                  for J := 1 to 8 do
                     Write ('     |');
                  Writeln;
                  (****************************************
                  *   print the middle third of each      *
                  *   square, containing a 'Q' if occupied *
                  ****************************************)
                  Write ('|');
                  for J := 1 to 8 do
                     begin
                        Write (' ');
                        if Queen [J] = I then
                           Write ('Q')
                        else Write (' ');
                        Write ('  |');
                     end;
                  Writeln;
                  (****************************************
                  *   print the bottom third of each sqare *
                  *   including the lower boundary line     *
                  ****************************************)
                  Write ('|');
                  for J := 1 to 8 do
                     Write ('____|');
                  Writeln;
               end;
          end; (*PrintBoard*)
```

The resulting display is shown in Figure 9.1, representing the first of 92 possible solutions to the eight queens problem.

In the examples of this chapter, a methodology of computational problem-solving has been displayed. Although the methods may not yet be your methods, with time and a little practice they can become yours. The keys to simplifying hard problems are the choice of a suitable data representation and the decomposition of a large task into more or less independent subtasks. Top-down design of algorithms is an attempt to systematize the process of decomposition into subtasks, and the composition of subordinate algorithms to accomplish those subtasks. There has not, as yet, been developed quite such a systematic approach to defining data representations, but a good principle to follow is to avoid commitment to a particular choice of representation for as long as possible. In this way, crucial choices can be deferred until one understands the problem and the form of the intended solution better than is possible at the outset.

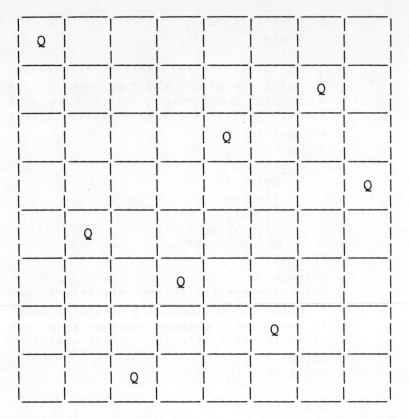

Figure 9.1 -- A solution to the eight queens problem

In the remaining chapters of this book, we shall learn more about how computers do their work and more about techniques useful in particular applications. However, the basic tools of programming and algorithm composition are already in our hands.

EXERCISES FOR CHAPTER 9

9.1 Design a Pascal program that will accept as input the text of any program written in Pascal, and will print a listing of the program with proper indentations of declarations, compound statements, conditionally executed statements, the bodies of iteration loops, text of comments, etc. The line-width and indentation should be parameters of the program. If you have done Exercise 8.2, you may find the procedure Scan defined there to be a useful component of your program.

9.2 Design a Pascal program to determine all the triangles that are formed by a finite set of line segments. Each straight line segment is defined by a pair of real numbers. Three lines form a triangle if each pair intersects, and if the intersections do not all coincide. You may find the algorithm given in Example 3.8.2 to be helpful in determining whether two line segments intersect.

Test the program on the following two sets of data:

Input for the first case consists of 12 line segments whose endpoints are

X1	Y1	X2	Y2
50.0	−50.0	−60.0	60.0
1.0	901.0	1.0	−927.0
−837.0	1.0	843.0	−1.15
−50.5	37.0	325.0	−401.0
−51.1	−50.0999	87.3	88.3001
−6.1	6.1	6.1	−6.1
−.00001	999.0	99.0	−.0001
1.0	3.0	9.0	27.0
881.0	343.0	2.0	4.0
7.0	49.0	−8.0	−16.0
98.765	−87.654	−76.543	65.432
−999.0	0.0	999.0	0.0

Input for the second case consists of eight lines

X1	Y1	X2	Y2
−4.	4.	4.	4.
−4.	4.	−4.	−4.
−4.	−4.	4.	−4.
4.	−4.	4.	4.

0.0	5.656	5.656	0.0
0.0	-5.656	-5.656	0.0
5.656	0.0	0.0	-5.656
-5.656	0.0	0.0	5.656

9.3 Give a recursive procedure for generating that permutation of a vector of characters, that will immediately precede the given vector in lexical order.

9.4 In the game of poker, a hand consists of five cards dealt from a deck of 52, comprising 13 ranks in four suits. The hands are valued as follows, from best to worst:

A <u>straight flush</u> consists of 5 cards of the same suit, in sequence.

<u>Four of a kind</u> is any hand containing four cards of the same rank.

A <u>full house</u> is three cards of one rank, and a pair of another rank.

A <u>flush</u> is five cards all of the same suit, but not in sequence.

A <u>straight</u> is five cards in sequence, but not all of the same suit.

<u>Three of a kind</u> is any hand containing three (but not four) cards of the same rank, and two other cards not a pair.

<u>Two pair</u> is a hand containing two distinct pairs of the same rank (but the ranks of the pairs differ).

<u>One pair</u> is a hand containing one pair of the same rank, but no other pair.

<u>No pairs</u> is a hand containing no two cards of the same rank, but not in sequence nor all of one suit.

Within each category given above, hands are ordered by the rank of the largest tuple (four, three, pair), then by the ranks of the largest single card, then the second largest single card, The number of distinct hands possible in each of the major categories is:

Straight flush	36
Four of a kind	624
Full house	3,744
Flush	5,112
Straight	9,180
Three of a kind	54,912
Two pair	123,552

| One pair | 1,098,240 |
| No pair | 1,303,560 |

Design a Pascal program to accept as input the description of up to seven poker hands, all presumably dealt from the same deck, to check the hands for validity (names of rank and suit must be valid, and no two cards in the deal can be identical), print a description of each hand along with the category to which it belongs, and tell which hand (or hands) is the best of those dealt.

9.5 The knight's tour.
In the game of chess, there are several different sorts of playing pieces that are allowed different moves on the 8 by 8 grid of squares that constitutes a chessboard. The piece having the most interesting move pattern is the knight, whose move allows him to advance exactly one square along a horizontal or vertical file and exactly two squares along a perpendicular file. The possible moves of a knight on an open board can be represented as ordered pairs, whose elements give the number of squares advanced along rows and columns of the board. The eight possible moves are: (1,2), (2,1), (2,-1), (1, -2), (-1,-2), (-2,-1), (-2,1), (-1,2).

An old problem, one reputedly solved by the German mathematician Gauss at age four, is to find a sequence of moves of the knight, starting from a given square on the board, that will eventually visit every square exactly once. That is, no square previously visited in the sequence is to be reoccupied. Compose a Pascal program that, when given the coordinates of an initial square, will find a knight's tour from that square if one exists.

9.6 The stable marriage problem.
Suppose there are two finite sets, each of N elements, and that we are to make a one-to-one assignment or correspondence between elements of one set and elements of the other. Such an assignment we shall call, by way of analogy, a marriage. Let us call the sets M and F, for want of better names. Note that what we mean here by a marriage is a multiple assignment of N pairs, not just a single pairing.

To complicate matters, let there be associated with each element a vector of values indicating the relative affinity of that element for each element of the opposite set. The affinity is indicated by an integer from 1 to N, and all affinities of a given vector must be distinct numbers. By convention, let 1 stand for the greatest affinity, N for the least. Thus for instance, if N = 10, the affinity vector for element M[5] might be (3,10,5,6,2,9,1,8,7,4), indicating that the greatest preference of M[5] is for F[7], the least is for F[2].

We can now define some plausible notions of a stable marriage, subject to the affinities expressed by the vector elements.

a) M-stability: We shall define stability by the absence of instability. If the marriage contains pairs (i,j) and (k,h) for which both

M[i] prefers F[h], the spouse of M[k],to F[j], his own spouse,

and

M[k] prefers F[j] to his own spouse, F[h],

then the marriage assignment is called M-unstable, otherwise it is M-stable. Obviously, the notion of M-stability takes no notice of the preferences of the elements of set F; hence it is only a model of marriage rules in certain societies. Give an algorithm for finding an M-stable marriage

b) F-stability: A marriage is said to be F-unstable if the marriage contains pairs (i,j) and (k,h) for which

M[i] has greater affection for F[h], who is M[k]'s spouse than does M[k] himself

and

M[k] finds M[i]'s spouse, F[j] more attractive than M[i] does.

A marriage is F-stable if it contains no F-unstable pairs. This notion of stability also depends only on the affinity vectors of set M, but F-stability and M-stability are nevertheless independent; one does not necessarily imply the other. Give an algorithm for F-stable marriage assignment.

c) M-F stability: A notion of stable assignment that utilizes both sets of affinity vectors is the following. A marriage is said to be M-F unstable if there are pairs (i,j) and (k,h) in the marriage such that both

M[i] prefers F[h] to his own spouse,

and

F[h] prefers M[i] to her own spouse.

264

A marriage assignment is said to be M-F stable if it contains no M-F unstable pairs. Obviously M-F stability is independent of either M or F stability since it depends on additional affinity data. It is also somewhat more difficult to produce. Give an algorithm to find an M-F stable marriage

9.7 When a message is transmitted over a communications system, the format of the message must ordinarily be checked to ensure that it observes the protocol required for proper functioning of the system. You are to design, write and test a Pascal program to check messages and compute their cost on the simulated telegraph system described below.

A message is any sequence of 200 or fewer words, preceded by a header and followed by the unique terminating string 'STOPSTOP'.

A header is a message prefix consisting of a type (one of 'STANDARD', 'URGENT', or 'NITE MAIL') and two zones (a zone is an integer between 1 and 20), regarded as the origin and destination of the message.

A word is a sequence of one to sixteen alphabetic characters, other than the terminating sequence 'STOPSTOP'.

An input message that contains punctuation marks is not to be rejected, but punctuation marks are to be replaced by words,

'.' = STOP
',' = COMMA
'?' = QUESTNMARK

Any word in the message regarded (by you) as profanity is to be replaced by a nonsense word.

The maximum message length of 200 words applies only to NITE MAIL. STANDARD type messages are limited to 100 words, URGENT to 50.

Cost is calculated by the following formulas. A STANDARD type message, within the same zone (origin equals destination) is charged $3.00 for the first 20 words, $0.10 for each additional word. For crossing zones, there is a surcharge of $0.01 per word for each zone crossed. An URGENT message is charged 300% of the cost of a STANDARD message. For NITE MAIL, the cost is 75% of that for STANDARD type.

Your program is to read telegrams in succession, print the type, zones and cost of each, and print an edited version. Each telegram is to appear on a new page of output.

10 SIMULATING THE REAL WORLD

So far, the problems that have been studied have been sufficiently simple that we could think in terms of directly composing
an algorithm to give a solution. The most difficult problem yet
encountered was the eight queens problem of Section 9.2. There we
were forced to use trial-and-error methods to grope toward a
solution, retracing steps whenever it was discovered that a false
start had been made. There are worse problems. There are some
situations in which our understanding of the process at work is
so incomplete that there seems to be no recourse open to us in
order to predict an outcome, other than to perform an experiment
to see how the result will turn out. Of what use can computation
be in dealing with a problem like that?

It sometimes is the case, in dealing with very complex
problems, that doing an actual experiment is unfeasible because
of danger, cost, time limitations, or possible catastrophic outcome if a wrong choice is made in determining the initial parameters. In such cases, we would like to be able to simulate the
conditions of a real experiment, but to do the simulation under
conditions of comparative safety, at low cost, in a reasonably
short time, and without having to bear the consequences of an
unfavorable outcome. This is where the computer can help. For if
the underlying laws governing the actual process are known with
sufficient precision, then the computer can be used to model the
dynamic behavior of the process, calculating the state of the
model from one instant to the next as the process unfolds from
beginning to end. If the computer model has been carefully made,
and no important details left out, then the conclusions drawn
from the simulated experiment will also apply to the real-world
situation that generated the original problem.

10.1 Simulating deterministic processes

The easiest processes to simulate are those in which the outcome is deterministic, that is, there is no unpredictable event, or element of chance, that enters into the laws that govern the process. Examples of such processes are the orbital motions of planets or of space vehicles, the flow of water past the hull of a moving ship, and the transformation of one chemical isotope into another by a process of radioactive decay. One might think that in such problems, mathematical analysis would be able to provide formulas from which solutions could be directly calculated, and that there would be no need to simulate the process in order to predict its outcome. Although this is often possible, it also happens that for many deterministic processes the mathematical description is so complicated that mathematical analysis is not a very attractive way to get a solution. For instance, in studying the orbital motion of planets, in a system in which the gravitational attraction of three or more bodies must be considered simultaneously, mathematical analysis becomes extremely difficult; but computational simulation is not complicated in any profound way by increasing the number of bodies beyond two. In the following example, we consider a relatively simple problem, one for which a fairly sophisticated mathematical analysis could provide an answer. However, simulation will also provide an answer, and very little mathematics will be required.

Example 10.1.1 -- A pursuit problem

On his way to school each day, a farmer's son must pass by a rectangular fenced field, as shown in Figure 10.1. His route can take him around a corner of the field, or he can climb through the fence and walk diagonally across the field. If he goes around the field, outside the fence, he must cross a swampy area near the corner, and he always steps in water over his boot tops. On the other hand, if he crosses the field, his feet stay dry, but the field is inhabited by a very large and ill-tempered bull who will certainly try to run him down. So on each school day, the farmer's son must observe the position at which the bull is grazing the field and estimate his chances of crossing the field that day without being caught. Can you help him?

The details of the problem specification are as follows. The field is 100 meters wide from north to south, and 200 meters wide from east to west. The path that the farmer's son uses has its starting point in the middle of the south

267

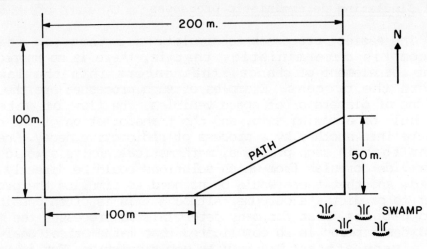

Figure 10.1

side, 100 meters from the southwest corner, and its end in the middle of the east side, 50 meters from the southeast corner. The boy can run at a rate of 5.5 meters per second, carrying his school bag, and the bull has a top speed of 7.5 meters per second. The bull, not being very bright, never anticipates the boy's route to try to cut him off, but instead runs straight at the boy, at each instant that he is within the boundaries of the fence. We will neglect the time it takes for either the bull or the boy to accelerate to full running speed, and we further assume that, if the bull gets to within 2 meters of the boy's position at any instant, the bull's attack is successful. (At least the boy will have to abandon his school bag.)

Let us measure distances from the southwest corner of the field, letting any point in the field be designated by an ordered pair (x, y) denoting meters north and east of the reference point, respectively. The problem we wish to solve is this: Given an initial location (x_o, y_o) of the bull in the field, if the boy began to run across the path, would the bull's attack succeed?

In any simulation, we must have some uniform measure of the evolution of the simulated process. Very often, this uniform measure is best provided by a time scale. The state of the simulated process can be evaluated at discrete, equal intervals of time, and once evaluated, the data of the state at one instant form the basis for the evaluation of the state of the process at the succeeding instant. Selection of the uniform time interval is an important and often critical decision to be made in setting up a simulation. The time interval must be small enough that any change in the state of the process during a single interval is also small, relative to the total change that may occur during the lifetime of the process. On the other hand, very little additional accuracy is ordinarily gained by making the interval smaller than is needed, and the cost of running the simulation will be inversely proportional to the time interval selected.

In the example we are dealing with here, a suitable time interval can be guessed at by examining the physical capabilities of the participants in the chase. The boy is expected to run in a straight line at a constant speed, and so his trajectory is completely insensitive to the interval chosen. On the other hand, the bull's trajectory is unknown but will ordinarily be some curved path. His path will be approximated by a series of straight line segments, each segment being the distance he will have run in a single interval of time. If the length of the bull's stride in full gallop is about 2 meters, we might guess that he cannot change his direction very abruptly in any shorter distance; so approximating his path by a succession of 2-meter straight line segments should be quite satisfactory. Since he moves at a speed of 7.5 meters/second, it will take him 0.26667 seconds to cover 2 meters, and in this way we arrive at a reasonable time interval.

The next step is to formulate a system of simple equations that tell how to make the transition in the state of the process from one time interval to the next. Such a system of equations is very easy to give in vector notation. Let P_1 and P_2 be vectors (in this case, ordered pairs) denoting the positions of the boy and the bull, respectively. Let V_1 and V_2 be vectors denoting their respective velocities, and let $\Delta t = 0.26667$ be the time interval in seconds. Then

$$P_1(t + \Delta t) = P_1(t) + V_1(t) * \Delta t$$
$$P_2(t + \Delta t) = P_2(t) + V_2(t) * \Delta t$$

The equations given in this notation illustrate the general nature of simulation equations; values for the next time instant are calculated from values given for the present time.

Since the time intervals are uniform, we can multiply the velocities of the boy and of the bull by the constant time interval to convert them into positional increments. The equations become

$$P_1(t + \Delta t) = P_1(t) + \Delta P_1(t)$$
$$P_2(t + \Delta t) = P_2(t) + \Delta P_2(t)$$

The positional increment for the boy is the ordered pair $(\Delta x, \Delta y)$ giving the distance he has moved in 0.26667 seconds in components of direction northward and eastward, respectively. From his path, it is easy to see that the northward and eastward components of his progress must be in the ratio of 1 to 2, and from his running speed and the time interval, it is also evident that the total distance covered must be 1.4667 meters. Since the geometry of a right triangle tells us that the total distance covered is the sum of the squares of the perpendicular components, the vector positional increment of the boy's position is given by

$$P_1 = 1.4667 * (1/\sqrt{5}, 2/\sqrt{5}) = (0.6559, 1.3118)$$

The positional increment traversed by the bull in any single time interval is not quite so easy to obtain, for although he moves a constant distance of 2 meters, his direction may change from one instant in time to the next. In fact, his direction will always be that of a line drawn form his own position to that of the boy. This line has a northward component of $x_1 - x_2$ and an eastward component of $y_1 - y_2$, as shown in Figure 10.2.

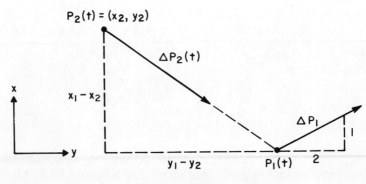

$P_2(t) = (x_2, y_2)$

$\Delta P_2(t)$

x

$x_1 - x_2$

y

$y_1 - y_2$

ΔP_1

$P_1(t)$

1

2

Figure 10.2

270

Its total length is

$$\text{Distance} = \sqrt{(x_1 - x_2)^2 + (y_1 - y_2)^2},$$

where the x's and y's are the components of the two position vectors at the time instant t. The positional increment of the bull in the this interval of time will be

$$2 * ((x_1 - x_2)/\text{Distance}, (y_1 - y_2)/\text{Distance}).$$

With this amount of preliminary analysis out of the way, we are prepared to begin the composition of an algorithm for simulation. An iteration graph describes informally the steps to be carried out.

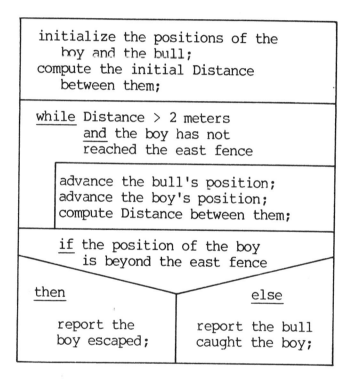

A translation of the iteration graph into a Pascal program is given on the next page.

```pascal
program Pursuit (Input, Output);
    (*********************************************************
    * Simulates a bull pursuing a boy across a pasture.     *
    * (X1, Y1) are coordinates of the boy's position;       *
    * (X2, Y2) are coordinates of the bull's position.      *
    * The size of the pasture is 100 by 200 meters.         *
    * The boy always starts from a point 100 meters along   *
    * the south boundary and runs to a point 50 meters      *
    * along the east boundary. The time interval is that    *
    * in which the bull travels 2 meters.                   *
    *********************************************************)
const
    BoysSpeed = 5.5;      (* meters per second *)
    BullsSpeed = 7.5;     (* meters per second *)
    LengthOfBullsStride = 2.0;      (* meters *)
var
    X1, Y1, X2, Y2, BoysMoveNorth, BoysMoveEast,
    Distance, TimeInterval : Real;
begin
    (***** initialize variables *****)
    TimeInterval := LengthOfBullsStride/BullsSpeed;
    BoysMoveNorth := BoysSpeed * TimeInterval/Sqrt(5);
    BoysMoveEast := 2 * BoysMoveNorth;
    Read (X2, Y2); (* initial position of the bull *)
    Writeln ('THE BULL STARTS FROM', X2, Y2);
    if (X2 < 0) or (X2 > 100) or (Y2 < 0) or (Y2 > 200) then
        begin
            Writeln ('THE BULL IS OUTSIDE THE FIELD');
            Halt;
        end;
    Distance := Sqrt(Sqr(X1 - X2) + Sqr(Y1 - Y2));
        (**** Simulate the pursuit ****)
    while (Distance > LengthOfBullsStride) and (Y1 < 200) do
        begin
            (**** advance the bull first, since his direction *)
            (**** depends on the previous position of the boy *)
            X2 := X2 + LengthOfBullsStride * (X1 - Y2)/Distance;
            Y2 := Y2 + LengthOfBullsStride * (Y1 - Y2)/Distance;
            X1 := X1 + BoysMoveNorth;  Y1 := Y1 + BoysMoveEast;
            Distance := Sqrt(Sqr(X1 - X2) + Sqr(Y1 - Y2));
        end
    if Y1 >= 200 then
        Writeln ('THE BOY ESCAPES THE BULL')
    else
        Writeln ('THE BOY IS CAUGHT AT', X1, Y1);
end.
```

10.2 Growth of populations

One of the intriguing uses to which simulation can be put is the study of the growth of populations of man or other species. Various phenomena, such as changes in the availability of food supply, predators, epidemics, the effect of population density on mating patterns, and the reduction of fertility in birds due to DDT poisoning can be introduced into the simulation model to determine the effect on population growth. Upon first consideration, it is not clear that a population model is a deterministic one, and indeed it is not if the behavior of individuals must be simulated, as would be the case in very small populations. But when one is dealing with very large populations, he need not consider individuals at all; he can rely on the statistics of group behavior. For example, the school board of a large city does not ordinarily feel it necessary to send out queries to all women residents of childbearing age, asking them whether or not they anticipate having new children within the year, in order to estimate the probable size of enrollment in first-grade classes six years hence. Instead, it can obtain an equally reliable estimate by simply counting the number of women of childbearing age and multiplying by the current birthrate for the community. The contribution of any individual, only weakly predictable in any case, is unimportant when averaged with that of a large number of similar individuals.

Example 10.2.1 -- Growth of a rabbit population

Everyone knows that rabbits are capable of impressive rates of reproduction, for as long as the lettuce holds out, so a rabbit population may provide a good model for studying growth. Suppose that, on the average, each pair of rabbits produces four surviving offspring per year. With such a phenomenal rate of growth, we will calculate the replacement rate on a monthly basis, as

4 (offspring)/2 (parents)/12 (months)
= 0.167 new rabbits per adult per month

Life is not all eating and reproducing for a rabbit, however. It has its hazards. Let us suppose that the toll taken by owls, foxes, weasels, and shotguns is 50 per thousand per month. With these data, we can write a small simulation program to study the growth of a rabbit population for a year. The logic of an elementary simulation program is often quite simple, as illustrated by the following iteration graph:

273

```
┌─────────────────────────────────────────────────┐
│  initialize the population;                        │
├─────────────────────────────────────────────────┤
│  for each successive month, up to                 │
│       the duration of the simulation              │
│    ┌────────────────────────────────────────────┐│
│    │ calculate the number of                     ││
│    │ individuals added, the                      ││
│    │ number lost, and the                        ││
│    │ total population                            ││
│    └────────────────────────────────────────────┘│
└─────────────────────────────────────────────────┘
```

A program to carry out the simulation is:

```pascal
program Rabbits (Input, Output);
   (*********************************************************
    * A simulation of growth in a population having constant *
    * replacement and loss rates.                           *
    *********************************************************)
   const
       ReplacementRate = 0.167;   (* per individual per month *)
       LossRate = 0.05;           (* per individual per month *)
       Duration = 12;             (* months *)
       InitialPopulation = 1000;
   var
       NumberAdded, NumberLost, PopulationSize : Integer;
       Month : 0..12;
   begin
       Writeln
           ('A SIMULATION OF GROWTH OF AN INITIAL POPULATION OF',
           InitialPopulation :6, ' INDIVIDUALS');
       Writeln
           ('WITH REPLACEMENT RATE =', ReplacementRate :6:3,
           ' AND LOSS RATE =', LossRate :6:3);
       Writeln; Writeln;
       Writeln
           ('    MONTH    POPULATION      ADDED        LOST');
       Writeln;
       PopulationSize := InitialPopulation;
       for Month := 0 to Duration do
           begin
               NumberAdded := Round(ReplacementRate * PopulationSize);
               NumberLost := Round(LossRate * PopulationSize);
               Writeln (Month :10, PopulationSize :12,
                       NumberAdded :12, NumberLost :12);
           end;
   end.
```

274

The function Round referred to in the calculation of NumberAdded and NumberLost is a predefined procedure of Pascal. It rounds the floating-point number given it as an argument to the nearest whole integer. Upon executing this small program, the computer prints the following table:

A SIMULATION OF GROWTH OF AN INITIAL POPULATION OF 1000 INDIVIDUALS WITH REPLACEMENT RATE = .167 AND LOSS RATE RATE = .050

MONTH	POPULATION	ADDED	LOST
0	1000	167	50
1	1117	186	56
2	1247	208	62
3	1393	232	69
4	1556	259	78
5	1737	289	87
6	1939	323	97
7	2165	361	108
8	2418	403	121
9	2700	450	135
10	3015	503	151
11	3360	560	168
12	3752	625	188

As is often the case when we try to make simplified models of real-world processes, the model of the preceding example is sure to be criticized. It tacitly assumes that newborn bunnies spring to maturity in a period of one month, immediately ready to participate in the procreation of young, and it similarly ignores the fact that the mortality rate of young rabbits is greater than that for adults. nevertheless, the model illustrates the nature of population growth when birth and death rates are not in balance. The rate at which a population increases is proportional to some constant times the population itself, at least until some environmental or behavioral factors act to alter the birth or death rates. For the values of replacement and loss rates assumed in the model, you can see that the rabbit population will have doubled in approximately 6-1/2 months, and furthermore it will continue to double again in each 6-1/2 month period unless the growth rates should change. You may recognize this law of expansion, for it is the same law that governs the growth of capital given compound interest, as well as many other natural phenomena.

In the next example, we will refine a population growth model to take into account the fact that birth and death rates vary with the ages of individuals. A new factor then enters into the population study. How many individuals will there be in each age group of a population? The exact distribution of ages cannot be easily predicted by mathematical analysis, but it can be found as a result of simulation.

Example 10.2.2 — Distribution of ages in a human population

Unlike animals of most other species, humans require a relatively long period of time, nearly 20% of a life span, to reach sexual maturity. On the other end of the time scale, humans tend to outlive their prime reproductive years by 25 to 40 years. Also, since humans have few predators (other than fellow humans), the rate of loss of individuals is not nearly uniform with respect to age, but tends to be much higher among older members of a population than among younger. Thus, the use of a constant replacement rate, the number of births per year per 1000 individuals, and a constant death rate, ignoring the distribution of individuals by ages, provides a very crude model by which to simulate the growth of a human population. A somewhat better model can be obtained if birth and death rates are given by age bracket.

Suppose that we are given birth and death rates by ten-year age brackets for a human populaton. However, the age distribution, or relative number of individuals in each of these age brackets, is unknown. This distribution will actually be determined from the simulation, and remarkably, it will be substantially independent of the assumed age distribution of the initial population!

If the simulation proceeds with time intervals of 1 year, then the number of individuals of age k years will be determined by the number of individuals who were of age k - 1 in the preceding year, less the number of that age who were lost during the year. The replacement of individuals occurs entirely at age 0, however. The number entering the population as infants is given by the sum over all ages, of births produced by each age group during the preceding year.

As results of the simulation, let us ask for the population growth rate, the expected doubling time, and the final distribution of population by ages. Since the number of

276

individuals finally calculated is not of primary interest,
let us obtain the final distribution in 10-year age brackets, normalized to a sample population of 1000. Similarly,
let the initial population be given by specifying numbers of
individuals at ages of whole decades, since we do not expect
to gain much precision by any more detailed specification.
With these requirements given, the simulation algorithm can
be designed.

The constants governing population growth will be birth
and death rates. Since these are needed for 10-year age
brackets between 0 and 99 years, 10-element vectors will be
provided to hold these constants.

    var (BirthRate, DeathRate) : array [0..9] of Real;

In order to access the correct birth rate for a
population sample whose age is given by the value of an
integer variable Age and lies between 0 and 99, the index
can be calculated by dividing Age by 10, as in

    BirthRate [Age div 10].

Internal to the algorithm, the number of individuals of
each age from 0 to 99 will be kept in array:

    var N : array [0..99] of Integer;

We will also need an integer variable to record the number
born in each year.

At the heart of the simulation algorithm must be a program segment that gives the distribution of individuals in
each age group by calculating the number of survivors from
the year before. It must also accumulate the number of new
births. This calculation requires an iteration over the ages
0 to 99. However, since the computation of N[Age] will
depend on the value of N[Age - 1] from the previous year, we
should not compute a new value of N[Age - 1] until a new
value of N[Age] has first been evaluated. The easiest way to
impose this ordering on the sequence of computations of
array elements will be to iterate over the array indices
from greatest to least. The following program segment will
accomplish the task.

```
NumberBorn := 0;  (* initialize before counting *)
for Age := 99 downto 1 do
    begin
        (*** calculate births from parents of each age group *)
        NumberBorn := NumberBorn +
            Round(BirthRate[Age div 10] * N[Age]);
        (**** calculate survivors from the previous year ****)
        N[Age] := Round(N[Age - 1] *
                DeathRate[N[Age - 1] div 10]);
    end
```

In the program segment, the Pascal built-in function Round
has been used to round the total of individuals born or
surviving to the nearest whole number. This rounding will
not adversely affect the simulation so long as the population is large enough that individual behavior is not
important.

Note, however, that if the population were to be chosen
so small that it became essential to simulate the behavior
of individuals, then this algorithm would fail completely.
For instance, suppose the value of the birth rate is given
to be 0.1 births per year per individual (which is fairly
high, given that only half of the individuals can bear
children). Then if the simulation was begun with an initial
population of 2 (Adam and Eve), the value of Round (0.1 * 2)
would always be zero, denying the existence of any progeny.

To obtain a complete simulation program, all that remains
is to provide means of iterating the above program segment
over a number of one-year intervals, and of reading initial
data and printing results.

```
program Humans (Input, Output);
    const
        MaxAge = 99;
        MaxDecade = 9;
    var
        Age : 0..Maxage;
        Decade : 0..MaxDecade;
        N : Array[0..MaxAge] of Integer;
        TotalNumber, NumberLastYear, NumberBorn, Duration,
            Year : Integer;
        BirthRate, DeathRate : Array[0..MaxDecade] of Real;
        GrowthRate, NormalizationCoeff : Real;
```

278

```pascal
begin
   for Decade := 0 to MaxDecade do
      Read (BirthRate[Decade]);
   for Decade := 0 to MaxDecade do
      Read (DeathRate[Decade]);
   for Age := 0 to MaxAge do
      if Age mod 10 = 0 then
         Read (N[Age])
      else
         N[Age] = 0;
   Read (Duration);
   Writeln
(' S I M U L A T E D   P O P U L A T I O N   G R O W T H');
   Writeln ('      AGE', '     0-9', '    10-19',
         '   20-29', '   30-39', '   40-49', '   50-59',
         '   60-69', '   70-79', '   80-89', '   90-99');
   Writeln;
   Write ('BIRTH RATE: ');
   for Decade := 0 to MaxDecade do
      Write (BirthRate[Decade] :8:3);
   Writeln; Writeln;
   Write ('INIT POPULAT');
   for Decade := 0 to MaxDecade do
      Write (N[Decade * 10] :8);
   Writeln; Writeln;

   (***** initialize the simulation to start at year 0 *****)
   TotalNumber := 0;
   Writeln (0:4, TotalNumber:8);
   for Year := 1 to Duration do
   begin
      NumberBorn := NumberBorn +
            Round(BirthRate[Age div 10] * N[Age]);
      N[Age] := Round (N[Age-1] *
            (1 - DeathRate[(Age-1) div 10]));
      TotalNumber := TotalNumber + N[Age];
   end;
   GrowthRate := TotalNumber/NumberLastYear - 1.0;
   Writeln ('THE RATE OF POPULATION GROWTH IS',
         100*GrowthRate :6:2, ' PERCENT PER YEAR');
   Writeln ('THE POPULATION WILL DOUBLE IN',
         Ln(2)/GrowthRate :6:1, ' YEARS');
   Writeln;
   Writeln ('THE FINAL DISTRIBUTION OF POPULATION BY AGES,',
            ' NORMALIZED TO A SAMPLE POPULATION OF 1000, IS:');
   Writeln;
```

```
Writeln ('   AGE','      0-9', '  10-19',
     '  20-29', '  30-39', '  40-49', '  50-59',
     '  60-69', '  70-79', '  80-89', '  90-99');
Write ('NUMBER');
(***************************************************
*   accumulate the distribution into ten-year age    *
*   brackets; normalize to a population of 1000, and  *
*   print the normalized distribution.               *
***************************************************)
for Age := 0 to MaxAge do
   if Age mod 10 <> 0 then
      N[Age - Age mod 10] := N[Age - Age mod 10] +
                                         N[Age];
NormalizationCoeff := 1000/TotalNumber;
                      (* real number division *)
for Decade := 0 to MaxDecade do
   Write (Round (N[Decade*10] * NormalizationCoeff) :8);
end.
```

You may have noticed that the model for the simulation
program given above takes no account whatsoever of centen-
arians. This is based on the assumption that so few reach
the age of 100 that they will have no effect on the statistics of the population as a whole. Alternatively, we might
say to those who are interested in the statistics of longe-
vity that our model, which cannot account for distinctions
between individuals, is not sufficiently refined to yield
meaningful results about the small segment of population
over 100 years old.

If the program is now run with the data given below:

Birth rates: 0 .030 .124 .005   0   0   0   0   0   0

Death rates: .004 .003 .003 .005 .010 .018 .030 .050 .075 .100

Initial
  population: 0   0 1000   0   0   0   0   0   0   0

Duration: 200

then the final results that will be printed are:

THE RATE OF POPULATION GROWTH IS 1.64 PERCENT PER YEAR
THE POPULATION WILL DOUBLE IN 42.3 YEARS

AGE	0-9	10-19	20-29	30-39	40-49	50-59	60-69	70-79
NUMBER	235	194	160	130	105	75	52	30

80-89	90-99
13	5

It is seen that the final distribution of population bears no resemblance whatsoever to the assumed initial population of 1000 20-year-olds. If the final distribution of population obtained in the first run of the simulation is now used as initial data, with the birth and death rates remaining the same as before, and the simulation is rerun, the final output is:

THE RATE OF POPULATION GROWTH IS 1.62 PERCENT PER YEAR
THE POPULATION WILL DOUBLE IN 42.7 YEARS

And the final distribution by ages is virtually the same as it was before, to within rounding errors:

AGE	0-9	10-19	20-29	30-39	40-49	50-59	60-69	70-79
NUMBER	236	195	159	130	105	75	52	30

80-89	90-99
13	5

We see that the final results are not much affected by the initial choice of a population distribution, so long as the initial population is young enough to reproduce itself.

An interesting use that can be made of the population growth model of the preceding example is to study the composition (by age) and growth rate of a population in case birth and death rates should change. As you might anticipate, a reduction of birth rates tends to produce not only a slower rate of population growth, but also a population containing a higher percentage of old people. See Exercise 10.3 for some examples.

There are many applications other than the one we have studied in which simulation is used to predict the outcomes of possible courses of action. Simulations are used to anticipate the possible effects of changes in predator-prey populations in wild species, and to investigate strategies for control of population sizes of wild game species by establishing hunting quotas. They are also used to model such phenomena as the migration of families from cities to suburbs and the effects of government economic policies on a national economy, and to plan strategies for the use of capital and industrial capacity in commerce.

10.3 Probabilistic simulations

In all of the simulation examples considered so far, we have assumed that we know accurately the relations between elementary data and dependent quantities. In the case of population models, although it is not possible to predict with certainty when a single pair of individuals will produce offspring, our models relied on measurable average birth rates that could be used with confidence when the total number of individuals in the population was large.

However, there are some simulation problems in which, although only statistics for the population as a whole are desired as answers, the behavior of individuals cannot be ignored. In the example that follows, the statistics of individual behavior in an unconstrained environment are assumed to be accurately known. However when constraints are placed on the environment, the consequences of individual behavior can no longer be predicted accurately from a knowledge of the average behavior. It is not satisfactory to apply the constraints to average behavior; it is necessary to take an average over constrained behavior. Exactly what is meant by this last sentence should become clear from the example.

Example 10.3.1 -- The drunken sailors

The navy of the Republic of Inebria has a single naval vessel. Each year, when the navy holds exercises, the vessel puts to sea for several days, making a stop at the port of Firewater, in the Booze Islands. The sailors are there given shore leave, during which they invariably visit the local bars and become intoxicated. Upon returning the their ship, they must walk the length of a dock, at the end of which the ship is moored.

If sober, this would be no problem; but an intoxicated Inebrian sailor is not in complete control of his faculties, and when he is trying to walk forward in a straight line, he sometimes staggers one step to either side, or one step backwards. The ship's physician has gathered extensive statistics on drunken Inebrian sailors and has concluded that the probability that a drunken sailor's next step will be forward is 0.7, that it will be backward is 0.1, and that the probabilities are 0.1 that it will be to either side. Also, he determined that the length of a sailors stride is uniformly 1 yard.

The dock at Firewater harbor is 20 yards long and 4 yards wide. In walking the dock, a sailor can deviate from the center line of the dock by as much as 2 yards to either side, but if he goes further off line than 2 yards, he will fall off the dock. Also, a sailor who backs off the dock into the street will decide to spend the rest of the night in town and will be AWOL (Absent With Out Leave). Only those sailors who traverse the entire length of the dock without falling into the water or going AWOL will successfully return to the ship. Our problem is to determine, for a drunken sailor who arrives at the entrance to the dock, on its center line, with the intention of returning to his ship, what are his relative chances of successfully returning, of falling off the dock, or of going AWOL.

A first, naive approach might be to determine the average behavior of a sailor and apply it to the problem. Since the probability of deviating from a straight path to the right is the same as that of deviating to the left, the average path followed by a large populaton of sailors on open ground will be down the middle. Also, since the probability of moving forward is higher than that of moving backward, the average path will be straight forward. If this average path were to be applied to try to answer the question posed above, the conclusion would be that a sailor is certain to return to his ship sucessfully. However, we know that this answer does not make sense, for in truth, almost no individual sailor will follow the average path.

Thus we are forced to consider the actual paths that different sailors might follow, and to determine the fate of each, following such a path. After experimenting with many individual sailors, the probability of each of the three outcomes can be determined approximately by taking the quotient of the number of trials ending in that outcome with the total number of trials of the experiment. But how is an actual path traversed by a drunken sailor to be computed? One way is to simulate the behavior of a sailor. This can be done by recording his position as he takes one step after another. At each position, we must make a random choice, governed by the probabilities established by the ship's physician, of the direction of the sailor's next step.

How does one get a deterministic computer to make a "random" choice? In this case, what we mean by a random choice is one in which the relative frequency of occurrence of each choice in a long series of trials is consistent with the probabilities given, and such that, in any sequence of choices, there is no easily discernable rule by which the next choice can be predicted from the results of the several most recent choices. We can use the computer to generate a sequence of choices that will satisfy this weakened notion of randomness. In order to obtain the desired probability of making each choice, let us use the computer to generate a sequence of decimal digits, such that each digit from 0 to 9 will occur equally often in a long sequence. Then we can equate the various choices with the occurrence of various digits, as follows:

0	- step to the left
1	- step backward
2	- step to the right
3-9	- step forward

It is easy to obtain a generator of a sequence in which each digit occurs equally often. For instance, the following generator, in which N is a global variable, used to record the state of the sequence generator from one call to the next, will satisfy the stated requirement on distribution of values:

```
function DigitSequence : Integer;
    begin
        N := N + 1;
        DigitSequence := N mod 10;
    end
```

Successive calls to this generator, begun with an initial value of N = 0, will produce the sequence

1 2 3 4 5 6 7 8 9 0 1 2 3 4 5 6 7 8 9 0 1 2 ...

As you can see, this sequence does not satisfy our second criterion for randomness, as it is easy to predict the next element from the preceding one. This is hardly surprising, since the rule used by the generator to obtain the next digit depended only on the previous one. How could we obtain a sequence in which the next digit depended on more than just the immediately preceding one?

It is useful for our purpose to consider a number simply as a sequence of digits. Then the operation of multiplying the number by 10 just shifts the whole sequence one place left, putting a zero in the rightmost place. Conversely, the operation of division by 10 moves the sequence right one place. Also, if N is any integer, N $\underline{\text{mod}}$ 10000 represents the sequence of the four least significant digits of N. Suppose we let ABCD stand for some four-digit sequence. If we want to obtain a new digit, depending on the digits of ABCD, one way would be to take a linear combination of these digits, as

$$(c_1 {*} A + c_2 {*} B + c_3 {*} C + c_4 {*} D) \ \underline{\text{mod}} \ 10$$

where c_1 through c_4 are constant coefficients. The final operation, $\underline{\text{mod}}$ 10, selects the least significant digit of the linear combination as the result. Let us adopt this strategy for generating a new digit.

What are we to do with the digits of the previous sequence? We should save them, except for the greatest significant digit, which can be discarded. Accordingly, to save the three least significant digits and discard the fourth, we could take

   10 * (ABCD $\underline{\text{mod}}$ 1000)

producing the sequence BCD0. Upon combining the newly formed digit with the ones saved, we get a new four-digit sequence, whose computational formula is

   10 * (ABCD $\underline{\text{mod}}$ 1000) + ($c_1 {*} A + c_2 {*} B + c_3 {*} C + c_4 {*} D$) $\underline{\text{mod}}$ 10

The sequence ABCD can be called a <u>predictive</u> sequence, for it is used to determine the next digit of the longer, pseudorandom sequence in which it appears.

In the following sequence generator, RandomN is a global, integer variable used to represent the predictive sequence of digits as a number. It must be global in order that its value will be retained from one invocation of the procedure to the next.

```
var
   RandomN : Integer;

function RandomDigit : Integer;
   var D : Integer;
   begin
      D := (RandomN + 7*(RandomN div 10)
                    + 7*(RandomN div 1000)) mod 10;
      RandomN := 10*(RandomN mod 1000) + D;
      RandomDigit := D;
   end;
```

Upon calling RandomDigit successively, the following sequence is generated

   1 8 5 8 0 2 7 7 6 9 0 2 3 1 9 0 1 8 8 4 7 1 6 ...

Although it is not evident from such a short sequence that the digits are generated with equal probability, this fact can be confirmed by the generation of longer sequences. The sequence does not show any discernible regularity, although it will actually repeat itself regularly. Its utility is due to the fact that the period of this repetition may be long, compared to the duration of a simulation. Notice that this generator will not work at all if the initial value of RandomN is set to any sequence in which all digits are zeros or fives (0000, 5555, 5050, etc.).

With the generator RandomDigit available as a tool, we can now return to the problem of simulating the staggering footsteps of a drunken sailor. Let us record the position of the sailor by a pair of coordinates, (X, Y), whose values are given in units of yards. Suppose that the end of the dock at the street is represented by the line $X = -10$, the ship is at the end represented by $X = 10$, and the two sides of the dock are bounded by the lines $Y = 2$ and $Y = -2$. The sailor is to begin his walk at the dock entrance, $X = -10$, $Y = 0$. We shall follow his journey until he leaves the dock by one of its four sides, and then record the outcome of his journey by printing the result and by incrementing one of the counts NumberAWOL, NumberShipped, or NumberDrowned. The simulation of a single sailor is given as a procedure, with the intent that it may be executed several times by a control program that accumulates statistics by performing independent trials of the sailor's walk.

```
procedure DrunkenSailor;
    var
        X, Y, Nsteps : Integer;
    begin
        X := -10;  Y := 0;  Nsteps := 0;
        while (Abs(X) <= 10) and (Abs(Y) <= 2) do
            case RandomDigit of
                0 : Y := Y - 1;
                1 : X := X - 1;
                2 : Y := Y + 1;
                3, 4, 5, 6, 7, 8, 9 :
                    X := X + 1;
            end;
        if X < -10 then
            begin
                NumberAWOL := NumberAWOL + 1;
                Write ('   THE SAILOR HAS GONE A.W.O.L.');
            end
        else if X > 10 then
            begin
                NumberShipped := NumberShipped + 1;
                Write
                    ('   THE SAILOR RETURNED TO HIS SHIP');
            end
        else
            begin
                NumberDrowned := NumberDrowned + 1;
                Write ('   THE SAILOR FELL OFF THE DOCK');
            end
        Writeln (' IN', N :3, ' STEPS.');
    end
```

Now that we know how to simulate the path taken by one
sailor, how can the paths taken by several be simulated? We
are accustomed to procedures that will yield the same result
upon successive executions. However, notice that in this
case there is a global variable that controls the choices
made at each step of the way. This is the variable RandomN
that is used to remember the previous four digits from the
pseudorandom sequence. Two executions of DrunkenSailor will
only yield the same result for certain, if the values of
RandomN are the same when the procedure is invoked in the
two trials. This suggests a way to make the successive
trials of the sailor's walk independent of one another. If
the period in which the sequence generated by RandomDigit
repeats itself is long enough, then a succession of trials

of DrunkenSailor can be run, letting the final value of RandomN at the end of one trial be the initial value for the next. If the value of RandomN does not repeat itself, then the sequence generated by RandomDigit will not force repetition in the behavior of DrunkenSailor during the course of a fixed number of trials.

Assuming that the period of the pseudorandom sequence is long enough to permit 100 trials to be run without a forced repetition of outcome, the control program that governs the conduct of the experiment and the summary of the outcomes is:

```
program Inebria (Input, Output);
  (**************************************************
  *  Determine the relative numbers of Inebrian      *
  *  sailors who are able to return along a dock to   *
  *  shipboard, who fall off the dock along the way,  *
  *  or who leave the dock by the shore end, going    *
  *  Absent WithOut Leave                             *
  **************************************************)

  var
      Trial, Ntrials, NumberAWOL, NumberShipped,
      NumberDrowned, Random N :                    Integer;

  (****   procedures RandomDigit, DrunkenSailor ****)
  (****   are to be declared here                ****)

begin          (****  simulation control program   ****)
    RandomN := 1; (*   initial value must not be 0 ***)
    NumberAWOL := 0; NumberShipped := 0; NumberDrowned :=0;
    Read (Ntrials);
    Writeln (Ntrials :4,
              ' DRUNKEN SAILORS RETURN FROM SHORE LEAVE');
    for Trial := 1 to Ntrials do
        DrunkenSailor;
    Writeln; Writeln;
    Writeln('OF THE', Ntrials :4, ' SAILORS,',
            NumberAWOL :3, ' WENT A.W.O.L.',
            NumberShipped :3, ' RETURNED TO THEIR SHIP, AND',
            NumberDrowned :3, ' DROWNED.');
end.
```

All that remains to do is to check the assumption we have made that the period of the pseudorandom sequence generator is sufficiently long. Since the path to the ship will re-quire at least 20 paces, but it may take fewer than that number to fall into the water, one might guess that 20 paces will approximate the length of an average walk on the dock. Since there are 100 trials to be run, the period of repetition of the pseudorandom sequence should exceed 20*100, or 2000. To determine the period of the sequence generator implemented by the procedure RandomDigit, we can run the following test program:

```
program Period (Output);
   const
      InitialN = 1;
   var
      RandomN, Dummy, Count : Integer;

   (***** declaration of RandomDigit goes here ****)

begin
   RandomN := InitialN; Count := 0;
   repeat
      Dummy := RandomDigit;
      Count := Count + 1;
   until RandomN = InitialN;
   Writeln('THE PERIOD OF THE SEQUENCE GENERATOR IS',
         Count :6);
end.
```

When this test program is run with the sequence generator RandomDigit, it gives the result that the period is 4368. This period considerably exceeds the number of steps anti-cipated in 100 trials of the simulation. Obtaining a gener-ator with a long period of repetition usually involves a certain amount of trial and error to select suitable values of the coefficients.

When the simulation is run for 50 sailors of the Inebrian navy, the conclusions yielded by the program are:

OF THE 50 SAILORS, 9 WENT AWOL, 20 RETURNED TO THEIR SHIP, AND 21 DROWNED.

On the basis of this simulation, it is apparent that the captain of the ship has a problem on his hands!

EXERCISES FOR CHAPTER 10

10.1 Recode the simulation of Example 10.1.1 as a procedure. Use it in a program that will determine the boundary between safe and unsafe initial positions of the bull in the field, and plot the boundary on an image of the field as the output of the program.

10.2 Modify the assumptions of Example 10.1.1 to account for the limited agility of an old bull. Suppose that the bull can change his direction by at most 10 degrees at any single 2-meter stride. Modify the criterion for successful attack to be

(Distance < 2 meters) and
   (required change of direction < 10 degrees)

Include in the simulation program the capability to plot a map of the field, indicating by printed numerals the successive positions of the boy and the bull. Choose a few initial positions of the bull that were unsafe under the original conditions of Example 10.1.1, and repeat the simulations using the modified assumptions about the bull's agility.

10.3 Investigate the effects of various social factors on population growth and distribution by ages, using the simulation program of Example 10.2.2.

(a) Suppose that the average age at which people marry is advanced, altering the birth rates to:

Age	0-9	10-19	20-29	30-39	40-49	50-59	60-69...
BirthRate	0	.010	.112	.036	.006	0	0...

(b) Suppose that free availability of contraceptives would affect the birth rate as follows:

Age	0-9	10-19	20-29	30-39	40-49	50-59	60-69...
BirthRate	0	.020	.100	.010	.001	0	0...

(c) Suppose that a combination of conditions (a) and (b) yields the following birth rates:

Age	0-9	10-19	20-29	30-39	40-49	50-59	60-69...
BirthRate	0	.003	.085	.018	.001	0	0...

(d) In societies in which medical care for infants is inadequate, infant mortality rates are often high. Rerun the simulation using the birth and death rates of Example 10.2.2, except that the death rate for ages 0-9 is altered to 0.040.

10.4 The life cycle of the salmon is an unusual one among saltwater fish. Salmon fry are hatched from eggs in the headwaters of streams and rivers, live their first year in fresh water, descend as yearlings to the sea, and grow to maturity at sea during the next two or three years. Then they return to the same rivers and streams from which they were hatched, swim upstream to the headwaters, spawn their eggs and die. Suppose that the following survival rates are known for salmon;

Age:	1 mo.-1 yr.	1-2 yrs.	2-3 yrs.	3-4 yrs.
Rate of survival:	20%	50%	70%	70%

Furthermore, suppose that of the surviving three-year-olds, 10% mature and attempt to spawn at that age, while 90% remain at sea. All four-year-olds are mature and attempt to spawn. Spawning is a hazardous endeavor, and only 80% of those adult fish that attempt it will live long enough to succeed. A successful female will drop 100,000 eggs.

The highest loss occurs from the time the eggs are dropped until the fry have hatched and reached one month of age. If the supply of eggs is scanty, then predators are not attracted, and the percentage that hatch and grow to one month is actually higher. An oversimplification of this phenomenon is given as follows. Suppose that for each river there is a fixed, limiting number of salmon fry that can be hatched and survive to one month - a maximum capacity of the stream to hatch salmon, if you will. Suppose that the number of fry who survive to one month, N_f, is given as a function of the capacity, C, and the number of eggs laid, N_e

$$N_f = \frac{0.005 \, N_e C}{\sqrt{0.000025 \, N_e^2 + C^2}}$$

(a) For C = 1000, determine the number of salmon that will enter the mouth of a stream to spawn each year.

(b) If a natural disaster occurred in 1973 to eliminate the entire batch of salmon fry from the stream in that year, in which of the years 1977, 1981, 1985, 1989, ... will the number of salmon returning to the mouth of the river to spawn have returned to 90 percent of normal?

(c) Coastal salmon fishing usually harvests the mature fish as they return to the mouths of the rivers preparatory to swimming upstream to spawn. Determine the size of the annual catch, for the stream having $C = 1000$, if the fishermen take 20 percent of the adult fish. What will be the catch if 50 percent are taken? 80 percent? 90 percent? 95 percent?

(d) Determine the percentage of adult fish that should be taken each year to assure the largest-size catch on a continuing basis.

10.5 In Example 10.3.1, suppose that the ship's captain puts up a rope along each side of the dock, altering the probabilities of a sailor's sideways motion at the edge of the dock.

probability at Y =	forward	backward	left	right
-2	0.7	0.1	0.02	0.18
-1, 0, or 1	0.7	0.1	0.1	0.1
2	0.7	0.1	0.18	0.02

Can you determine the effectiveness of the captain's safety measure?

10.6 A statistical knight's tour. In the knight's tour (Exercise 9.5), the task was to determine a sequence of moves to be made by the knight on a chessboard that would take him to every square on the board exactly once. Suppose we consider a knight who chooses his next move randomly with equal probability from the eight possibilities afforded him. For this knight, we define a tour to be a sequence of moves that does not leave the board and does not repeat any position previously visited. The tour ends when the knight's random selection results in a next move that would violate one of these conditions. For a knight starting at square (4, 4), determine the average length of his tours. Also, have the computer plot a bar chart showing the relative frequency of tours of each length, found in a series of 100 independent trials.

11 NUMERICAL COMPUTATION

Most of the computation done by scientists, including social scientists, and by engineers involves computing with numbers. The largest and fastest digital computers have been designed in order to make possible the numerical solution of some extraordinarily large systems of equations, such as the meteorological equations governing the movement of air masses, and whose solutions are used in long-range weather forecasting. The same basic techniques are used in designing algorithms for numerical computation as in other types of applications, but there are also some special considerations related to the limits of precision with which real numbers can be represented in a computer. The design of numerical algorithms relies heavily on the tools of mathematical analysis, and in this chapter you will have to make greater use of your mathematical knowledge than has been required in previous chapters.

When we talk about numerical computation, we usually mean that the computation is to be carried out with real (or sometimes complex) numbers, as distinguished from computation that can be done solely on integers or rationals. This is because in scientific applications we very often deal with continuously varying quantities: position, temperature, chemical concentrations, and the like. Because of the relative imprecision with which we are able to measure physical quantities in the real world (even the velocity of light is known to only a precision of about three parts in 10^9 and this is one of the most precisely known physical constants), for most of our purposes a finite approximation to real numbers, having only six to eight significant decimal digits, is sufficient. However, the range of numbers that must be represented is truly enormous. For example, the size of the universe is estimated to be of the order of 5 billion light years (approximately 10^{25} meters), whereas the diameter of the nucleus of a helium atom is approximately 10^{-15} meters. In order to meet these requirements, the numbers used in a computer to approximate real numbers are the so-called floating-point numbers. The notation was adapted from the notation used by scientists to represent values of physical quantities.

11.1 Computing with floating-point numbers

In scientific notation, a number is represented as a fixed-point decimal, followed by a multiplier which is a positive or negative power of 10. This notation saves the trouble of writing long strings of trailing zeros to represent a large number, or of zeros following a decimal point to represent a very small number. Equally important, it allows the scientist to indicate in a very simple way the precision with which the quantity represented by the number is known. This is indicated by the use of a fixed-point decimal having no surplus digits; if the scientist is honest, he lists just those digits of which he is certain. Thus a precisely measured interval of time might be given as $1.03622 * 10^3$ seconds, a distance measured by a survey as 753.1 meters, a voltage read from a portable voltmeter as 124 volts, and a concentration of mercury ion in water as $2 * 10^{-11}$.

The number of significant digits used in representing the modulus, or fixed-point portion of a number, is called the precision of the representation. In some computers the precision of number representation can easily be controlled by the programmer, but most machines allow a choice between only one or two predetermined levels of precision. There are two things to keep in mind when the numerical precision is arbitrarily set, rather than being set by the demands of the particular application. One is that, no matter how many significant figures can be printed on the computer output, the precision of an answer cannot be better than the precision of the input data. Too often, novices at scientific computation will present an answer given to the limit of numerical precision of the computer, such as a velocity of $2.74460 * 10^2$ meters per second, although the input data on which the computation is based may be known with a precision of only two or three decimal digits. The extra decimal digits of the answer, while printed by the computer, are completely meaningless in such a case.

The other danger in the use of fixed-precision arithmetic is that, although the precision of the number representation may be sufficient to cope with the input data, accuracy can be lost in an intermediate step of the computation. Since this is a process that can occur without the knowledge of the programmer, it is particularly dangerous, and we shall investigate it in some detail.

First, let us see how floating-point numbers are represented in a computer. As an example, we will use the representation in the IBM 360 and 370 series machines. The memory of these machines is divided into individually addressable units, called words. A word is a string of 32 bits, and in representing a floating-point number they are used as follows: the rightmost 24 bits represent the modulus as a fraction in radix-2 arithmetic. That is, the binary point is assumed to lie immediately to the left of these 24 bits. It is not necessary, therefore, to waste any of the precious bits to represent the point. The leftmost bit is used for the algebraic sign of the number. The remaining 7 bits, those in positions 2 through 8 counting from the left end of the word, are available to represent the exponent. Now there appears to be a problem, however. With 7 bits, we can only represent numbers from 0 to 127, or if one bit is used for the sign of the exponent, then the magnitude of the exponent can only be as large as 63, which is 2^6-1. If our floating-point number is expressed in radix-2 arithmetic, then an exponent of 63 will only suffice to represent a multiplier of 10^{19}, in round figures. Although this is indeed a large number, it may not be large enough for all purposes. A way out of this problem is to sacrifice a few bits of precision for the sake of the ability to represent larger multipliers. The way that this has been done on the IBM machines is to treat the modulus as though it were a fraction in radix-16 arithmetic, rather than radix-2 arithmetic. The bit patterns remain exactly the same except that some fractions will require 1, 2 or 3 leading zeros following the radix point in radix-16 representation. The advantage gained is that each of the precious units of the exponent now represents a power of 16, rather then a power of 2, and the exponent of 63 can stand for a multiplier of approximately 10^{76}, which should be sufficient for nearly any purpose. The sacrifice in precision is only 3 bits, slightly less than one decimal place.

To give you some feel for the representations of the modulus, here are a few fractions in their various forms:

Rational fraction	Fixed decimal	Radix 2 with exponent	Radix 16 bit pattern
1/2	.5000	.1000000000000000 E 0	.1000000000000000 E 0
1/4	.2500	.1000000000000000 E-1	.0100000000000000 E 0
1/16	.0625	.1000000000000000 E-3	.0001000000000000 E 0
1/64	.0078125	.1000000000000000 E-5	.0100000000000000 E-1
3/4	.7500	.1100000000000000 E 0	.1100000000000000 E 0
1/10	.1000	.1100110011001100 E-3	.0001100110011001 E 0
1/3	.3333...	.1010101010101010 E-1	.0101010101010101 E 0

The fractions 1/10 and 1/3 cannot be exactly represented by a
finite-length binary expansion, and have been truncated in the
representations above.

In the course of ordinary arithmetic, the operations
commonly performed on the exponent of a floating-point number are
addition, subtraction, and multiplication or division by a power
of 2. It turns out, for reasons we shall not go into here, that
the representation of the exponent as a signed magnitude is not
advantageous for these operations. In fact, it is not even
necessary to represent a zero exponent by a string of binary
zeros. It is equally satisfactory to regard the string of 7 bits
of the exponent as a positive integer between 0 and 127, and to
choose a middle value, 64, as representing an exponent of zero.
Thus, to get the actual power of 16 that is to be the multiplier
of the modulus, we take the integer represented by the 7 bits and
subtract 64 from it. This operation is easily done by the hard-
ware of the computer itself.

In the convention outlined above, the representation of the
number 125.1 would be as follows. The integer part, 125, has the
binary representation 1111101. The fractional part, .1, has the
binary representation .000110011001100110011... . Putting the
two together gives the binary fixed-point number:

1111101.000110011001100110011...

However, this number is in unnormalized form, that is, the
binary point does not appear at the left side of it. To normalize
it in binary arithmetic, we should slide the whole bit pattern to
the right 7 places with respect to the decimal, and record the
multiplier of 2^7. But since the normalization is required to be
with respect to radix-16 arithmetic, the only acceptable multipliers are powers of 16. Sliding the bit pattern one more place
to the right, so that a leading zero appears between the point

and the leftmost 1, will accomplish the task, and the multiplier will then be 2^8, or 16^2. The normalized modulus is then

.011111010001100110011001100110011...

There are only 24 bits allocated for the representation of the modulus, so the string of bits will have to be truncated. The easiest way to do this is to chop the string aff after the 24th bit, yielding .011111010001100110011001. Some computers do this, but it is not the most accurate way to abbreviate a number becauses it introduces systematic error: every time a number must be truncated, the value is made slightly smaller. A better way, which does not introduce systematic error, would be to round the number up or down to he nearest representable number. In binary representation his is very easy to do, for you simply test the first bit that is to be thrown away. If that bit is a 1, then add 1 in the least significant position of the number that is to be kept; otherwise, simply chop it off. The IBM 360 and 370 machines do rounding, and the modulus that will be retained will be .011111010001100110011010, since the first bit of the string thrown away was a 1. Finally, the floating-point representation of 125.1, in the machine, will be a word having the bit pattern

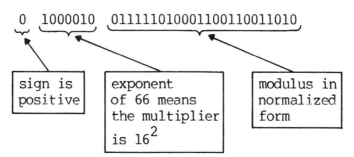

The limit of precision in the normal floating-point representation of the IBM computers is about 2^{-25} in absolute terms. However, because some numbers have three leading zeros in the bit positions of the modulus, the precision can be as poor as 2^{-22} – approximately one part in four million is susceptible to loss. Where the loss of accuracy due to the limitations of precision has its most obvious effect is in the comparison of numbers. When we ask whether or not two numbers are the same, we must be prepared to believe that they may be the same if they agree to within one part in two million. Similarly, in evaluating a sum, the accuracy of the result will obviously be limited by the precision with which the sum can be represented, but if the terms being summed are not all of one sign, then the accuracy of the sum may be further reduced by having subtracted quantities of like magnitudes.

For instance, in the algorithm of Example 3.8.2, a test to find out whether two lines are parallel consists of inquiring whether the determinant of a 2-by-2 matrix of coefficients is zero. The determinant is of the form A1*B2 - B1*A2, where the variables are of type Real and take values that are floating-point numbers. Given the limitations of a finite-precision representation, we cannot ask simply whether the determinant evaluates to zero, but we should ask whether it is smaller than one part in two million of one of the component terms. The test should be

if Determinant <= 0.5E-6 * A1 * B2 then

11.2 Evaluation of functions

There are many functions of analysis that recur frequently in the equations governing natural phenomena, and one of the primary tasks of numerical computing is the evaluation of these functions. During the 1930s, the U.S. National Bureau of Standards employed an army of mathematicians to evaluate many of the more commonly occurring functions, using desk calculators. From the results of their labors, tables of values were published, and the use of these tables was for many years the standard means of evaluating these functions when they were needed in scientific calculations. Today, tables are hardly used any more, at least by scientists who have access to a digital computer. Instead of publishing tables of values, people now publish computational algorithms for the evaluation of functions. It is less work to recompute a value, using an efficient algorithm, than it is to look up a value in a table and use an interpolation formula if the desired argument lies between a pair of argument values listed in the table.

Typical of the mathematical functions we have in mind are the exponential function, the natural logarithm, trigonometric functions, Bessel functions, and various distribution functions used in statistics. There are, of course, many more that have not been mentioned. Most are functions of one argument, although they may have one or more parameters as well. Only a few can be evaluated by a finite polynomial formula; more typically, they can most easily be defined in terms of an infinite series in ascending integral powers of the argument. Typical of these, in fact the quintessential power series, is that for the exponential

298

function:

$$e^x = 1 + x + \frac{1}{2} x^2 + \frac{1}{6} x^3 + \frac{1}{24} x^4 + \frac{1}{120} x^5 + \ldots = \sum_{n=0}^{\infty} \frac{x^n}{n!}$$

This power series is as well-behaved as one could wish for; it is uniformly convergent for all values of x. In case you have forgotten what this means, its implication is that, should you desire the value of the series for some fixed value of x to be given to any specified accuracy, say to within an absolute error of 10^{-6}, there exists some fixed, finite number of terms of the series that must be summed. The rest can be thrown away, for although there are infinitely many of them, they are so small that their total contribution is less than the specified limit of error. Now this fact makes a definition in terms of infinite series really useful, for all we are ever interested in is an evaluation to within some finite error, such as the limit of precision of our number representation.

For example, suppose we consider the special case when x = 1. Then

$$e = 1 + 1 + \frac{1}{2} + \frac{1}{6} + \frac{1}{24} + \frac{1}{120} + \frac{1}{720} + \frac{1}{5040} + \frac{1}{40320} + \ldots$$

Suppose we wish to evaluate the transcendental number e to a precision of six significant decimal digits. The first ten terms of the series given above will be sufficient. We shall prove this by giving a convincing demonstration. Let us expand each of the fractions, rounding the sixth digit to the right of the decimal. We get the sum:

$$
\begin{array}{r}
1.000000 \\
1.000000 \\
0.500000 \\
0.166667 \\
0.041667 \\
0.008333 \\
0.001389 \\
0.000198 \\
0.000025 \\
0.000003 \\
\hline
2.718282
\end{array}
$$

Rounding the sum to six significant figures gives the value of e to the specified precision, 2.71828.

But what about the terms that have been omitted? Each has a positive value; how can we be sure that the accumulation of these values will not have a large effect on the result? Note that the first term omitted has the value of the last term divided by 10, the next term is further divided by 11, and so on. Thus the remainder of the series is of the form

$$0.000003 * \left(\frac{1}{10} * \left(1 + \frac{1}{11} * (1 + \ldots)\right)\right)$$

This is certainly less than if each denominator of the continued fraction were 10, but in that case, the sum would be

$$0.000003 * \left(\frac{1}{10} * \left(1 + \frac{1}{10} * \left(1 + \frac{1}{10} * (1 + \ldots)\right)\right)\right)$$

$$= 0.000003 * 0.1111111\ldots = 0.000003333333\ldots$$

So we discover that there is a bound on the value of the discarded portion of the infinite sum, and that the bound is too small to affect the value of the sum, to the precision that we have required.

It might appear, then, that there are no computational problems involved in the evaluation of the exponential function by using the power series. This might be a true statement if computers used infinite-precision real arithmetic, but it is not true of computations done in finite-precision floating-point arithmetic. Suppose that the exponent is negative, say -10, and the desired precision of the result is six decimal digits. Fifty terms of the series will more than suffice to limit the error in the sum to the precision specified, if the remaining terms are simply neglected. However, the first few terms of the series are found to be

$$e^{-10} = 1 - 10 + 50 - 166.6667 + 416.6667 - 833.3333$$
$$+ 1388.889 - 1984.127 + 2480.159 - 2755.732$$
$$+ 2755.732 - 2505.211 + \ldots$$

The terms increase in magnitude until they reach $-10^9/9!$. The term that follows that one is $10^{10}/10!$, the same in magnitude, and from then on, successive terms are smaller in magnitude. However, the fact that such large numbers must be accumulated and subtracted means that, if our computer can retain only 7 decimal digits in a floating-point number (roughly the equivalent of a

24-bit modulus) whereas the result to be computed is actually 0.00004540, no significant digit of the result can be computed by this method! The difficulty has nothing at all to do with the convergence of the series, but has to do with the fact that the discrepancy in size between the largest individual terms in the alternating series and the result to be computed is some 8 orders of magnitude. Thus, the computational error made in rounding off one of the large terms to the precision of the internal number representation will be greater than the magnitude of the final result.

One way around the difficulty is to use extended-precision arithmetic. With a 56-bit modulus available, we could compute e^{-10} by direct evaluation of the series, but we could not compute e^{-20}. There is, however, a better way, a different algorithm, which we shall study in the following example.

Example 11.2.1 Evaluating the exponential function

Our task is to formulate an algorithm that will compute the exponential function for any real argument, yielding a result with six significant decimal digits of accuracy.

It has already been demonstrated that accuracy can be lost when we try to sum a series whose terms alternate in sign. Furthermore, the number of terms of the power series that must be included in the sum in order to attain the desired accuracy of the result is strongly dependent on the magnitude of the argument. And yet, if the exponent is an integer and the value of the constant e is known, the exponential function can be evaluated by a sequence of multiplications or divisions with no degradation in accuracy. Suppose that we were to write the argument of the exponential function as the sum of two parts.

x = integer part + fractional part

where the fractional part is between zero and one, and the integer part is a positive or negative integer. Then since the two components can be evaluated separately, we need not even use the same algorithm for the two evaluations. To compute the exponential of an integer argument, we can use iterated multiplication, while the exponential of a positive fractional argument can be evaluated if we sum the first few terms of the power series.

An obvious way to raise a number to an integral power is by repeated multiplication (or division if the power is negative). This suggests as a first version of an algorithm to compute the exponential function of an integer:

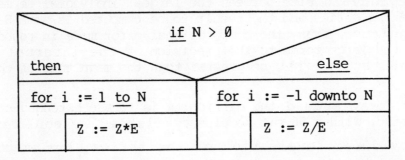

if N > 0	
then	else
for i := 1 to N	for i := -1 downto N
Z := Z*E	Z := Z/E

This naive procedure is not one that you would want to advertise for public use. First of all, negative powers of e can be treated in the same way as are positive powers, by selecting 1/e as the constant multiplier. Secondly, the naive algorithm uses unnecessarily many multiplications, in the general case. By way of illustration, consider the representation of e^{15} as

$$e^{15} = e*e*e*e*e*e*e*e*e*e*e*e*e*e*e$$

An alternate representation is

$$e^{15} = e^8 * e^4 * e^2 * e$$

Instead of requiring 14 multiplications, it appears that three will be sufficient if the second representation is used. However, there is a bit of cheating going on, for in the representation given above, it is assumed that the values of e raised to powers of 2 are freely available. But if these values are not known, it will require additional multiplications to determine them. The potential for saving computation lies in the observation that the values

$$e, e^2, e^4, e^8,$$

need only be obtained in succession, so that they can be computed by the formulas:

$$e^2 = e * e$$
$$e^4 = e^2 * e^2$$
$$e^8 = e^4 * e^4$$

This sequence adds only three more multiplications to the

process, making it possible to evaluate e^{15} by using only six multiplications. (To evaluate e^{16} is easier, requiring only four multiplications.) Incorporating this into an algorithm, we can give the iteration graph (for positive N only):

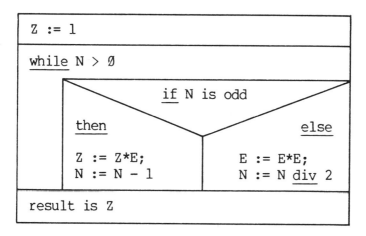

To translate this into a procedure, we need only make provision for negative values of N.

```
function IntExp (N : Integer) : Real;
   var
      E, Z : Real;
   begin
      Z := 1.0;
      if N >= 0 then
         E := 2.718282
      else
         E := 0.3678794;
      N := Abs(N);
      while N > 0 do
         if Odd(N) then
            begin
               Z := Z*E;
               N := N - 1;
            end
         else (* N is even and positive *)
            begin
               E := E*E;
               N := N div 2;
            end;
      IntExp := Z;
   end;
```

In evaluating the exponential of the fractional part, we already know a bound on how many terms of the series will need to be summed. The exponent must be smaller than 1, but even if it were as large as 1, then ten terms of the series would suffice to give the required accuracy. We have a choice; we can either take ten terms of the series in all cases, or we can test the size of successive terms, halting the computation when the remaining terms have become insignificant. The first course of action is simpler, while the second will be more efficient in most cases. We choose the latter.

```
function FractExp (X : Real) : Real;
   (**********************************
   * sums a series of the form:       *
   *           X**I / Factorial(I)     *
   **********************************)
   var
      Term, Sum : Real;
      I : Integer;
   begin
      I := 0;  Term := 0.0;  Sum := 0.0;
      while Term > 1.0E-7 do
         begin
            Term := Term * X/I;
            Sum := Sum + Term;
            I := I + 1;
         end;
      FractExp := Sum;
   end;
```

Now the two procedures need only to be put together within a control procedure that will separate the exponent into its integer and fractional parts. The integer part is obtained by applying the Pascal function Trunc.

```
function Exponential (X : Real) : Real;
   var
      FractPart : Real;
      IntPart : Integer;
   (* declarations of IntExp and FractExp go here *)
   begin
      IntPart := Trunc(X);
      FractPart := X - IntPart;
      Exponential := IntExp(IntPart) * FractExp(FractPart);
   end;
```

Other computational problems arise in the evaluation of functions whose series do not converge so rapidly. Consider, for example, an infinite power series representation for the natural logarithm,

$$\ln(x) = -\sum_{i=1}^{\infty} \frac{(1-x)^i}{i}$$

When x = 0, the sum is

$$\ln(0) = -(1 + \frac{1}{2} + \frac{1}{3} + \frac{1}{4} + \frac{1}{5} + \frac{1}{6} + \frac{1}{7} + \frac{1}{8} + \frac{1}{9} + \cdots$$

It is well known that this sum does not converge, for no matter what finite number of terms you might take as an approximation to the sum, there is no bound to the value of the sum of the terms remaining. This is true in spite of the fact that the magnitude of the individual terms approaches a limit of zero as the index of the terms approaches infinity.

On the other hand, for x = 2, we obtain a series whose terms have the same magnitudes as those of the series above, but whose signs alternate:

$$\ln(2) = 1 - \frac{1}{2} + \frac{1}{3} - \frac{1}{4} + \frac{1}{5} - \frac{1}{6} + \frac{1}{7} - \frac{1}{8} + \frac{1}{9} - \cdots$$

This sum converges to the value 0.693147 in the sense that there is a limit of the partial sums. However, in a very real sense, the sum cannot be computed. For example, suppose we attempt the computation in a straightforward manner, for instance by the Pascal program segment:

```
var
    Sum : Real;  J : Integer;
begin
    Sum := 0.0;
    for J := 1 to 10000000 do
        Sum := 1/J - Sum;
end
```

where the result is to be the magnitude of the final value of Sum. Even though ten million terms of the series have been summed, the accuracy of the answer will be to only three significant decimal digits. It is easy to see what happens if we consider successive pairs of terms to be added to the sum. When J

305

becomes as large as 2^{12}, or 4096, then the difference between $1/J$ and $1/(J + 1)$ will be less than 2^{-24}. Thus, when these terms are added to the sum, whose magnitude is about 0.6, the addition of successive terms is like

```
  0.6 ...
+0.0002441 40625
-0.0002440 81035
```

However, with approximately seven decimal digits of precision, the computer will round these numbers, and evaluate

```
  0.6 ...
+0.0002441
-0.0002441
```

so that the successive pairs of terms 1/4096 and −1/4097 actually contribute nothing to the computation! We might just as well have summed from J − 1 up to 4096, which obviously cannot yield better than three-place accuracy.

It may have occurred to you that the algorithm above is not the right one to use, and that we would be better off to combine adjacent terms of the series algebraically, so as to obtain a new series whose terms are all of one sign. In general, this is a good strategy to follow. In this case, the series would become

$$\ln(2) = \frac{1}{2} + \frac{1}{12} + \frac{1}{30} + \frac{1}{56} + \frac{1}{90} + \frac{1}{132} + \cdots$$

An algorithm to sum this series would be

```
var
    Sum : Real;  J, J2 : Integer;
begin
    Sum := 0.0;
    for J := 1 to 2048 do
        begin
            J2 := J*2;
            Sum := Sum + 1.0/(J2*(J2+1));
        end;
end
```

The sum is carried out until the individual terms have become smaller than 2^{-24}. Beyond that point, terms can no longer be added using floating-point arithmetic with a 24-bit modulus.

However, the result will still only be correct to three significant decimal digits! The reason is that the terms that have been thrown away, although small, do not decrease in size fast enough, and their total contribution is of the order of 1/4096, or 0.00024.

How then are we to evaluate the natural logarithm of 2? One way would be to use the algorithm above, but to use extended-precision arithmetic. Then, by summing approximately 2^{24} terms of the series, we could obtain a result accurate to seven digits. This would require several minutes of computation time, and we are motivated to look for a better way.

If we turn our attention once more to the power series for the natural logarithm, we can see that the series must converge more rapidly the nearer the argument of the logarithm is to 1. For when the magnitude of $1 - x$ is smaller than 1, successively higher powers assume decreasing values. Thus it should be easier to compute the logarithm of $2^{(1/2)}$ than to compute the logarithm of 2, using the power series. This is indeed the case. It requires only 17 terms of the series to calculate the logarithm of $2^{(1/2)}$ to seven-digit accuracy, and the easy way to evaluate ln 2 is by taking $2 * \ln 2^{(1/2)}$. This idea forms the basis for the algorithm of the following example.

Example 11.2.2 -- Evaluating the natural logarithm

We wish to compose an algorithm to evaluate the natural logarithm of a positive real argument, yielding accuracy commensurate with the precision of the floating-point number representation. In this algorithm, we will assume that the number representation is that used in the IBM 360 and 370 series machines, with a 24-bit modulus in normal-precision arithmetic, and each unit of the exponent representing a power of 16. The only significant way in which this information is used is in deciding on convenient multiplicative constants. With this type of number representation, multiplication or division by 16 affects only the exponent of a floating-point number, and so there is no reduction in accuracy due to rounding of the modulus.

The strategy of the algorithm is to bring an arbitrary positive number into the range $1/(2^{(1/2)})$ to $2^{(1/2)}$ by multiplying or dividing it by powers of $2^{(1/2)}$. Each time there is a multiplication or division by $2^{(1/2)}$, the constant value of $\ln 2^{(1/2)}$ is added to or subtracted from the result. In order to expedite matters if the number is very large or very small, powers of 16 and powers of 2 are first factored out. When the number, shorn of all integral powers of $2^{(1/2)}$, is within the desired range, its logarithm is evaluated by the following procedure, and added to the result.

```
function LogSum (X : Real) : Real;
    (*****************************************************
    *  X is a number whose magnitude lies between Sqrt(2) *
    *  and its reciprocal. The natural logarithm of X is  *
    *  to be evaluated by summation of terms of the form  *
    *        -(1-X)**J / J                                 *
    *  with summation index J.                            *
    *****************************************************)
    var
        Product, Sum : Real;
        J : Integer;
    begin
        J := 1;  Product := 1.0 - X;  Sum := Product;
        while Abs(Product) > 1.0E-6 do
            begin
                Product := (1.0 - X) * Product;
                J := J + 1;
                Sum := Sum + Product/J;
            end;
        LogSum := Sum;
    end;
```

The main procedure consists almost entirely of a sequence of tests to determine the range in which the argument lies and to add (or subtract) the appropriate constants to (from) the result.

```
function NatLog (X : Real) : Real;
    const
        Root2 = 1.4.4214;     (* Square root of 2 *)
        RootHalf = 0.707107;  (* Square root of 1/2 *)
        LR2 = 0.3465736;      (* Natural log of Root2 *)
        L2 = 0.6931472;       (* Natural log of 2 *)
        L16 = 2.7725887;      (* Natural log of 16 *)
        OneSixteenth = 0.0625;
```

```
var
    L : Real;     (* used to accumulate the result *)

(* the declaration of LogSum goes here *)

begin
    if X <= 0.0 then
        begin
            Writeln ('CANNOT TAKE THE LOG OF ZERO OR ',
                     'A NEGATIVE NUMBER');
            Halt;
        end;
    L := 0.0;
    if X > 1.0 then
        begin
            while X >= 16.0 do
                begin X := X/16.0;  L := L + L16 end;
            while X > 2.0 do
                begin X := X/2.0;  L := L + L2 end;
            if X >= Root2 then
                begin X := X/Root2;  L := L + LR2 end;
        end
    else
        begin
            while X <= OneSixteenth do
                begin X := X*16.0;  L := L - L16 end;
            while X <= 0.5 do
                begin X := X*2.0;  L := L - L2 end;
            if X <= RootHalf then
                begin X := X*Root2;  L := L - LR2 end;
        end;
    (***************************************************
     *   the remaining part of the logarithm is to be   *
     *   evaluated by summation of the power series.     *
     ***************************************************)
    NatLog := L + LogSum(X);

end; (* NatLog *)
```

The examples of this section have illustrated some of the common computational problems involved in the evaluation of mathematical functions. Many of the more subtle problems that one can encounter require a substantial knowledge of mathematical analysis in order to develop good algorithms.

11.3 Finding roots of equations

In the mathematical problems that arise out of science, it very commonly happens that the desired answer can be expressed as the root of an equation of one variable, also depending on one or more parameters. For example the radius of a circular orbit of an earth satellite is given by the solution of the equation

$$r^3 - \left(\frac{T}{2\pi}\right)^2 m_e g = 0$$

where r stands for the unknown radius, and the parameters T, m_e, and g refer to the period of the orbit, the mass of the earth, and gravitational constant, respectively. In some cases, we wish a solution to be given in analytic form as a specific function. Then, the behavior of the solution as the parameters are varied can be inferred from the mathematical properties of the function. However, it is also often the case that the solution cannot be given analytically as a simple function of the parameters. Polynomial equations furnish a good class of examples. Although there is a simple analytic formula for the solution to a quadratic equation in terms of its coefficients, the analytic formulas for cubic and quartic equations are so cumbersome that they are almost never used, and polynomial equations of higher degree than quartic do not admit analytic solutions in terms of algebraic formulas.

On the other hand, equations can be solved numerically even when the algebraic complexity of the formulas seems overwhelming. All that is required is that the component formulas of the equation are themselves computable, continuous functions of the unknown variable. In order to standardize the problem somewhat, all of the terms of the equation are collected together on one side of the equals sign, so that we can give this collection of terms a name, call it f(x). Roots of the equation are those values of x for which f(x) = 0. A numerical solution consists of searching out those values. This does not require that any explicit, analytical solution of the equation ever be found.

There are two more-or-less distinct parts of the problem of root-finding. First, we must locate an interval of values of the variable, x, within which we can be certain that a root is to be found. The second part is to obtain the exact location of the root within that interval, to the accuracy desired.

In order to locate an interval in which a root is certain to be found, we must acquire some knowledge of the behavior of $f(x)$. There are several possible ways that this might be done. We might know some properties of the function from mathematical analysis or from knowledge about a scientific problem from which the equation arose. Or we might plot the function to determine the approximate locations of its roots. The fundamental idea is that, if (x_1, x_2) is an interval for which $f(x_1)$ and $f(x_2)$ differ in algebraic sign, then there is at least one root of the equation $f(x) = 0$ within the interval. Since f is a continuous function of x, the curve representing $f(x)$ has to cross the zero axis somewhere between the two endpoints, as indicated in Figure 11.1(a). In fact, it is possible that there is more than one root of the equation within such an interval, as shown in Figure 11.1(b).

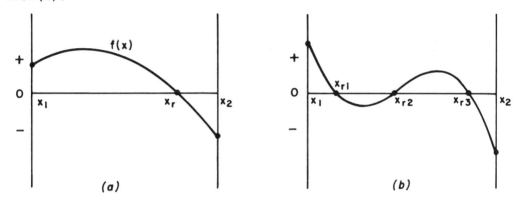

Figure 11.1 Roots of the equation $f(x) = 0$ are zero crossing points of the curves.

The converse of this observation is false. In an interval (x_1, x_2) for which $f(x_1)$ and $f(x_2)$ are of the same sign, we cannot be sure there is no root of $f(x)$. In Figure 11.2 are shown plots of three quadratic equations over the interval $(0, 2)$. In each case, $f(0) = f(2)$, so the signs of the endpoint values agree. Yet in the first case, $f(x)$ has two roots in the interval, in the second case, a double root at $x = 1$, and in the third case, none. Double roots, that is, two roots which coincide on a single point, are particularly difficult to locate accurately by purely computational methods, and we shall ignore them in the discussion that follows.

If we wish to locate intervals in which there can be no more than one root of an equation $f(x) = 0$, we can first locate the points at which f takes maximum and minimum values, that is, the

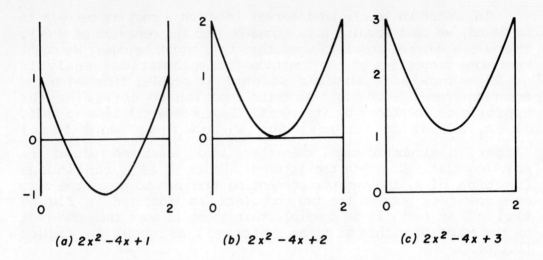

(a) $2x^2 - 4x + 1$ *(b)* $2x^2 - 4x + 2$ *(c)* $2x^2 - 4x + 3$

Figure 11.2 When the function has the same sign at both endpoints, there may or may not be roots of the
equation within the interval.

points at which the curve of $f(x)$ changes slope from positive to
negative, or vice versa. In any interval between a maximum point
and the next minimum point, $f(x)$ must have a negative slope.
Therefore, if it also happens to pass through zero in that
interval, this zero crossing will be the unique root of the
equation within the interval, as depicted in Figure 11.3. By
dividing the interval of values of x that are to be searched for
roots into subintervals between adjacent maximum and minimum
points of $f(x)$, and applying to each subinterval the test that
determines whether it contains at least one root, we can find a
set of intervals, each containing a single root of the equation
We will not dwell further on the process of locating intervals,
except to mention that an algorithm for locating maximum and

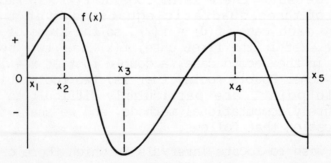

Figure 11.3 Single roots of the equation $f(x) = 0$ lie in each of
the intervals (x_2, x_3), (x_3, x_4), and (x_4, x_5).

minimum points of a function can be found in Forsythe, Keenan, Organick, and Stenberg, Computer Science: A First Course, John Wiley & Sons, New York, 1969.

Instead, let us concentrate on studying a computational method for locating a root precisely within an interval over which the function f(x) changes sign. A very simple algorithm suggests itself. Divide the interval in some way into two subintervals. Choose from the subintervals that one in which there is still a sign change of the function from one endpoint to the other. Continue the process until the desired accuracy has been obtained. There are two important refinements of this sketchily defined procedure that must be made. One is to tell precisely how the division into subintervals is to be made, and the other is to determine a criterion to apply to tell us when to stop the process.

Since the function f(x) must be repeatedly evaluated in the process of searching for a root, it might seem reasonable to use, as a criterion for having located the root, the condition that f(x) is small, say less than 10^{-6} times its value at one of the endpoints of the original interval. There is an objection to be raised to such a condition, however. The precision that is specified in that condition is a precision not on the accuracy of location of the root, but on the value of the function at the approximately located root. These quantities, the accuracy of location of the root and the value of the function at the approximate root, will be related, but how they are related depends on special knowledge about the function, and in general, we will not have that knowledge. In some problems, such as finding a square root, which involves solving the equation

$$x^2 - N = 0,$$

the relation will be a direct one, and the condition that f(x) should be small is a satisfactory way to determine an accurate location of the root. In other cases, the accuracy may not be as good, and it will be preferable to specify the desired precision of root location directly.

One way to accomplish this is to continue subdividing the interval that contains the root until the interval size itself is within the desired precision. This precision may be given as a fraction of the original interval, or it may be given in absolute terms, as a numerical interval.

On the other question, the method by which the interval is to be divided into subintervals, we could, if no better way suggests itself, simply divide the interval in half at each iteration. This is known as the bisection method, for obvious reasons. Another method, which we shall call division by linear interpolation, begins by taking the values of the function at the endpoints, $f(x_1)$ and $f(x_2)$, as points on a graph of the function. Although we do not know as yet precisely what the function looks like between these endpoints, we know that it must cross the zero axis somewhere between them. As a very crude approximation to the function, we might connect the two known points on the graph of the function by a straight line. Solving for the point at which this straight line crosses the zero axis gives an estimate for the zero-crossing point. The actual function is evaluated at that point, and one of the two subintervals is selected for further searching.

The method of division by linear interpolation sounds as if it may produce better estimates of the root location, in fewer iterations, than will the method of bisection, for it utilizes more of the available information, namely, the relative magnitudes of the function at the endpoints of an interval. But in fact, it will only produce better estimates for functions that can be reasonably well approximated by straight lines. For a more detailed analysis, refer to the graph of Figure 11.4. In this graph, the distance between the approximate root and the actual root is $(1 - m(r)/m)$ times the distance of the actual root from the endpoint, where m and $m(r)$ are the slopes of the two lines indicated in the diagram. In very many cases, the slopes of the two lines will be nearly the same, and the process will converge rapidly to an accurate estimate. However, if the slope of the curve at the actual root is nearly zero, as indicated in Figure 11.5, then the process will converge to an accurate estimate more slowly than will the method of bisection.

In addition to its simplicity, the method of bisection assures us of a uniform rate of convergence to a root, independent of the details of the behavior of the function near its root. The uncertainty in the root location, which is the interval width, is always 2^{-N} times the width of the original interval after N iterations of the bisection method. For this reason, the bisection method is often to be preferred over the method of division by linear interpolation, even though the latter method yields more rapid convergence to a root in many typical problems.

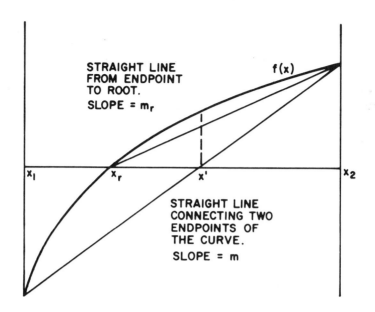

Figure 11.4 Division of an interval by linear interpolation. The interval from x_1 to x_2 will be replaced by the smaller interval from x_1 to x' in the next iteration.

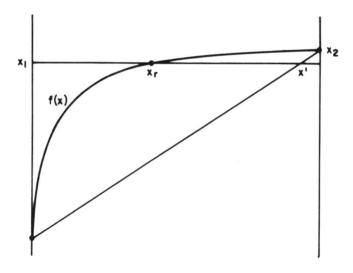

Figure 11.5 Illustrating a case for which division by linear interpolation does not move the endpoint much closer to the root.

315

A combination of the two methods can yield the advantages of both, however. Linear interpolation provides a good estimate of a root location in an interval in which the actual function can be well approximated by a straight line. For smoothly varying functions, which are most frequently encountered in the description of continuous systems, any function is well approximated by a straight line over a sufficently narrow interval. Since the aim of the bisection method is to define a narrow interval in which the root of an equation must lie, this suggests application of the method of linear interpolation to futher refine a root estimate, after the interval has been narrowed by the bisection method. Using linear interpolation as a final step makes it possible to save half the number of iterations of the bisection method that would be required to obtain comparable accuracy without the use of interpolation.

Example 11.3.1 -- Root-finding by binary search

The specifications for our root-finding program are that, when it is given as arguments the endpoints of an interval and a function whose values at these endpoints differ in sign, it will attempt to find the root of the equation $f(x) = 0$ by dividing the interval ten times. This may produce an estimate of the root accurate to one part in 2^{10}, if the numerical accuracy of evaluation of the function is good enough. Following the estimate of the root by iterated bisection, linear interpolation will be applied to further refine the estimate.

Since only the sign of the function at the endpoints of the interval is of interest, the sign is the only information that needs to be recorded. A Pascal program for locating roots of equations is:

```
program Roots (Input, Output);
(* locates a root of F(x) = 0 in the interval End1..End2 *)
    var
        End1, End2, Middle : Real;
        K : Integer;
        Sign1, Sign2, SignMid : Boolean;

    (***** the function whose root is to be found ****)
    function F (X : Real) : Real;
        begin F := X*(X*(X + 3.5) - 3.5) - 6.0 end;
```

316

```
begin
    Read (End1, End2);
    Write ('BETWEEN', End1, ' AND', End2);
    Sign1 := F(End1) < 0.0;   Sign2 := F(End2) < 0.0;
    if Sign1 = Sign2 then
        begin
        Writeln
('THE FUNCTION HAS THE SAME SIGN AT BOTH ENDPOINTS');
        Halt;
        end;
    for K := 1 to 10 do
        begin
        Middle := (End1 + End2) * 0.5;
        SignMid := F(Middle) < 0.0;
        if SignMid = Sign1 then
            End1 := Middle
        else
            End2 := Middle;
        end;
    (**** refine the estimate by interpolation ****)
    Middle := End1 + (End2 - End1) * Abs(F(End1)) /
                        Abs(F(End1) - F(End2));
    Writeln ('THERE IS A ROOT OF F(X) AT X =', Middle);
end.
```

11.4 Solving systems of linear equations

There are many problems in the physical sciences which lend themselves to formulation in terms of a set of simultaneous, linear equations in several variables. This is the analytical technique used in systems involving several variables, and the physical world is full of such systems. For instance, the description of motion in three-dimensional space can be given in such a system. A very important computational problem is to obtain the solution of a system of N linear, simultaneous equations in N variables. Since this is a very old problem, there is a standard method for its solution, originally attributable to Gauss. It involves only the linear operations of addition and of multiplication by a constant, but the objects subjected to these operations are the equations themselves.

Let the N equations each be written in a standard form, illustrated for the ith equation,

$$a_{i1}x_1 + a_{i2}x_2 + a_{i3}x_3 + \cdots + a_{iN}x_N + b_i = 0$$

317

where the a_{ij}'s are coefficients and the x_j's are the variables.

Since the right-hand side of each equation is zero, the system of equations will have exactly the same solutions if any equation is replaced by a constant multiple of itself, that is, if each coefficient a_{ij} of the ith equation (including the coefficient b_j) is replaced by $C * a_{ij}$, where C is any non-zero constant. Also, the solutions will remain unchanged if any equation is replaced by the sum of itself and another one of the equations. To sum the ith and jth equations, the coefficients of common variables in the two equations are added. Finally, these two operations, multiplication by a constant and addition of equations, can be composed without affecting the solutions. Thus the ith equation could be replaced by

$$(a_{i1} + C * a_{j1})x_1 + (a_{i2} + C * a_{j2})x_2 +$$

$$\ldots + (b_i + C * b_j) = 0$$

How can these operations be used to derive a simpler but equivalent set of equations from the system originally given? First, let us observe one particular form that such a system might take, in which a solution can be found directly. In order to study this form, it will be most convenient to represent the equations by a matrix of their coefficients:

a_{11}	a_{12}	a_{13}	$\ldots$	a_{1N}	b_1	x_1
a_{21}	a_{22}	a_{23}	$\ldots$	a_{2N}	b_2	x_2
.	.	.	$\ldots$	.	.	.
.	.	.	$\ldots$	.	.	.
.	.	.	$\ldots$	.	.	.
a_{N1}	a_{N2}	a_{N3}	$\ldots$	a_{NN}	b_N	x_N

In the matrix representation, we have omitted writing the plus signs, the variables, and the right-hand sides of the equations. All these are understood. Now if all of the coefficients to the left of a_{ii} in the ith equation happened to zero, and if this were the case for every equation so that the matrix contained only zero coefficients in the triangle below and to the left of the main diagonal, then the equations could be solved directly, provided that none of the coefficients a_{ii} was zero.

$$
\begin{array}{cccccc}
a_{11} & a_{12} & a_{13} & \cdots & a_{1N} & b_1 \\
0 & a_{22} & a_{23} & \cdots & a_{2N} & b_2 \\
0 & 0 & a_{33} & \cdots & a_{3N} & b_3 \\
\cdot & \cdot & \cdot & \cdots & \cdot & \cdot \\
\cdot & \cdot & \cdot & \cdots & \cdot & \cdot \\
\cdot & \cdot & \cdot & \cdots & \cdot & \cdot \\
0 & 0 & 0 & \cdots & a_{NN} & b_N
\end{array}
$$

The solution procedure would start with the Nth equation, which is independent of the others:

$$a_{NN}x_N + b_N = 0$$

After this equation is solved, the value $-b_N/a_{NN}$ can be substituted for the variable x_N in each of the remaining equations. But when this has been done, then the $(N - 1)$st equation is also susceptible to direct solution, and so the solution proceeds, one equation after the other, until all of the variables have been evaluated. This form, in which the nonzero coefficients lie in a triangle, is one we would be justified in regarding as a simplification.

Returning to the business of replacing equations in the system by linear combinations of themselves and other equations, we now have some motivation to ask if there is some linear combination of the first equation with the ith that will have zero as the coefficient of the first variable. Suppose that we multiply the first equation by $-a_{i1}/a_{11}$, and add the result to the ith equation. We will get the row of coefficients

$$\left(a_{i1} - \frac{a_{i1}}{a_{11}}\, a_{11}\right) \quad \left(a_{i1} - \frac{a_{i1}}{a_{11}}\, a_{12}\right) \quad \cdots \quad \left(b_i - \frac{a_{i1}}{a_{11}}\, b_1\right)$$

of which the first one is seen to be zero. In fact, if we were to apply a similar operation to each equation following the first, choosing a constant multiplier appropriate to each, then the whole first column of coefficients in the matrix would be zero, except for the first one. At this point, the matrix of coefficients would appear as follows, where the primes over some of the coefficients indicate only that they are different from those of the original system of equations.

$$
\begin{array}{cccccc}
a_{11} & a_{12} & a_{13} & \cdots & a_{1N} & b_1 \\
0 & a'_{22} & a'_{23} & \cdots & a'_{2N} & b'_2 \\
0 & a'_{32} & a'_{33} & \cdots & a'_{3N} & b'_3 \\
\cdot & \cdot & \cdot & \cdots & \cdot & \cdot \\
\cdot & \cdot & \cdot & \cdots & \cdot & \cdot \\
\cdot & \cdot & \cdot & \cdots & \cdot & \cdot \\
0 & a'_{N2} & a'_{N3} & \cdots & a'_{NN} & b'_N
\end{array}
$$

where the primes over some of the coefficients indicate only that they are different from those of the original system of equations.

In the matrix above, the 2nd through Nth equations can be solved independently of the first. Ignoring the first equation for the time being, we see that the procedure for putting columns of coefficients to zeros can be applied recursively to the system of equations 2 through N. When the whole process is finished, we will have a system of equations whose matrix is in triangular form. Most importantly, it will be equivalent to the original system, provided that none of the diagonal coefficients that appear in the denominator of any coefficient is zero. In order to see more explicitly the form that a computational algorithm will take, let us compose a Pascal procedure.

Example 11.4.1 -- Solution of simultaneous linear equations by Gaussian elimination

The procedure that we wish to construct will take as its arguments a two-dimensional array containing the coefficients of the equations that are to be solved, a one-dimensional array into which the answers are to be written, and an integer value which is the number of equations and variables. Recall that the matrix of a system of N equations in N unknowns will have N + 1 columns, the extra column containing the constant term of each equation. We have named the main procedure Gauss, and it in turn employs two subordinate procedures, SubtractEquation and Sum.

The procedure to subtract equations determines a constant coefficient by which to multiply the first equation so that when it is subtracted from the second equation, the resulting coefficient of the Ith variable will be zero. Subtraction is then carried out, one column at a time. Notice that it is not actually necessary to carry out the step of

```pascal
procedure Gauss (A : RealArrayType;
                 var X : SolutionVectorType; N : Indextype);
(*******************************************************
 *   The types, which must be declared globally, are:  *
 *   type Indextype = 1..MaxIndex;                     *
 *        RealArrayType = array [Indextype,Indextype]  *
 *                             of Real;                *
 *        SolutionVectorType = array [Indextype] of Real*
 *   N gives the actual number of equations            *
 *******************************************************)
var
    I, J : Indextype;

procedure SubtractEquation (I, J : Indextype);
(*******************************************************
 *   determine a constant multiplier that will make    *
 *   the Ith coefficient in the Ith equation equal     *
 *   to the Ith coefficient in the Jth equation.       *
 *******************************************************)
var C : Real;    K : Indextype;
begin
    C := A[J,I] / A[I,I];
    for K := succ(I) to succ(N) do
        A[J,K] := A[J,K] - C*A[I,K];
end;

function Sum (I : Indextype) : Real;
    (***** sum the products of coefficients with *****)
    (***** variables already evaluated.          *****)
    var RowSum : Real;    K : Indextype;
begin
    Rowsum := A[I, succ(N)];
    for K := succ(I) to N do
        RowSum := RowSum + A[I,K]*X[K];
    Sum := RowSum;
end;

begin        (* Gauss *)
    (***** triangularize the matrix of coefficients *****)
    for I := 1 to N - 1 do
        for J := succ(I) to N do
            SubtractEquation (I, J);
    (***** solve the triangularized equations *****)
    for I := N downto 1 do
        X[I] := -Sum(I)/A[I,I];
end;
```

setting the coefficient of the Ith variable to zero, for it will never be used again in the course of the remaining computations. We can save an unnecessary step by beginning the subtractions at the coefficient of the (I + 1)st variable.

The second subordinate procedure has the task of summing, in the Ith equation, the products of the coefficients with the variables already found. These are the (I + 1)st through the Nth variables. The constant coefficient A[I, N+1] must also be added.

EXERCISES FOR CHAPTER 11

11.1 Compose a Pascal procedure to compute the sine function for an argument given in radians. Test the procedure on argument values of 0, 0.1, 1, 10, 100, and 1000 radians. Compare the results with those yielded by the built-in function Sin( ).

11.2 Evaluate the following finite sum for n = 45 and n = 50:

$$\sum_{r=1}^{n} \frac{n! \ (n - 2r) \ (-1)^{r}}{(n - r)! \ r!}$$

Can it be evaluated for n = 1200?

11.3 Conventional earth-based navigation utilizes the solution of triangles. If only one fixed reference point can be located, then compass directions to that reference point, taken from two ends of a line whose length has been measured, will enable the positions of the ends of the line to be determined relative to the known position of the reference point. The determination involves setting up and solving a pair of simultaneous algebraic equations. Similarly, compass observations of a pair of known, fixed reference points, made from a single observation point, provide sufficient information from which to calculate the position of the observation point. (To obtain a pair of equations that are to be solved, you must apply the techniques for solution of triangles that you have learned in high school trigonometry.)

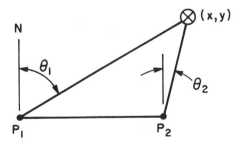

Figure 11.6

(a) Design a Pascal program to give the coordinates of the two observation points when one reference point is observed and the distance between the observation points is known (Figure 11.6).

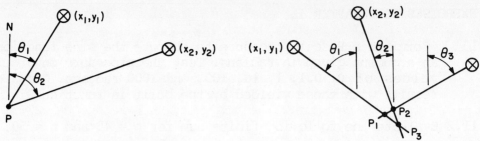

Figure 11.7   Figure 11.8

(b) Design a Pascal program to give the coordinates of an observation point from which two known reference points are observed (Figure 11.7).

(c) Modify the program of part (b) to give the coordinates of the vertices of the smallest polygon enclosing all of the estimates of the observation point, when compass sightings to N fixed reference points are made, for N > 2 (Fig. 11.8).

11.4 In studying the physical properties of a simple crystalline compound having a cubic cell, such as NaCL (Figure 11.9), it is of interest to calculate the binding energy of a single interior ion due to electrostatic attraction and repulsion by all of its neighbors, both near and far. After all of the constants have been factored out of the equation for the energy, it turns out to depend on a mathematical constant (called Madelung's constant) whose value can be expressed by the following triple summation

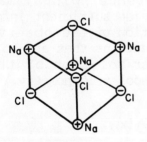

Figure 11.9

$$M = \sum \sum \sum \frac{(-1)^{k+m+n}}{\sqrt{k^2 + m^2 + n^2}}$$

where the sum is to be carried out over all values of k, m, and n, both positive and negative, excepting the single combination $k = m = n = 0$.

Quite obviously, the summation cannot be done over all terms, but must be approximated by a finite number of them. The approximation will be better, the more terms that are included. A careful analysis will show that many terms can be evaluated without recalculation of the square root function, however. For instance, the contributions of the

324

terms for $k = 1$, $m = 0$, $n = 1$ and $k = 1$, $m = 0$, $n = -1$ are identical; each contributes $1/\sqrt{2}$.

Calculate the best approximation to Madelung's constant that you can obtain in 15 seconds of computing time. (Test the built-in Pascal function Clock to limit your execution time. But don't test it too often, for the test itself will cost you some extra time.)

11.5 If we wish to calculate the area of a plane geometrical figure, but we lack an explicit formula for that area, we can compute the area approximately by dividing the figure into narrow bands, computing the area of each band, and summing all of the partial contributions to obtain the total area. Two simple strategies for estimating the area of a band suggest themselves immediately. Suppose the boundary of the figure lies between the line $y = 0$ and the curve $y = f(x)$. and that a typical band is bounded by the lines $x = x_1$ and $x = x_2$. One method of estimating area, called the midpoint rule, is to approximate the area by

$$M = (x_2 - x_1) * f\left(\frac{x_2 + x_1}{2}\right)$$

Another, called the trapezoid rule, is given by

$$T = (x_2 - x_1) * \frac{f(x_2) + f(x_1)}{2}$$

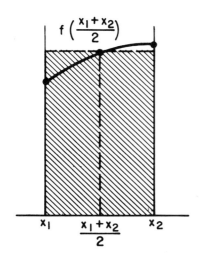 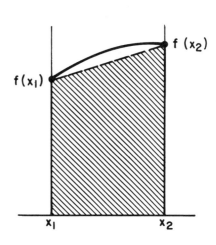

Figure 11.10

Write a Pascal program to compute the area of a figure using all four of the following rules:
1. The midpoint rule
2. The trapezoid rule
3. The average of midpoint and trapezoid estimates, $(M + T)/2$
4. Simpson's rule, the weighted average given by $(2/3)M + (1/3)T$

Use the program to estimate the areas of

(a) a parabola, $y = 1 - x^2$.
(b) a sinusoid, $y = \text{cosine }(\pi x/2)$.
(c) a semicircle, $y = \sqrt{1 - x^2}$;

each extending from $x = 0$ to $x = 1$. Vary the widths of the strips, using widths of 0.1, 0.01, and 0.001 to determine the effect of the width on the accuracy. Compare the results with the exact areas obtained by the use of calculus:

(a) $= 2/3$, (b) $= 2/\pi$, (c) $= \pi/4$.

To obtain a valid comparison, have the computer evaluate the exact values to seven significant decimal places.

12 HOW DOES
THE COMPUTER WORK?

Up to now, we have been dealing with the computer as a device that is capable of interpreting instructions given in Pascal and carrying out the computations directed by those instructions. It accepts input in the form of patterns of small, rectangular holes punched in 3-1/4 by 7-3/8 inch paper cards, delivered to one of its card reading machines, and it generates output by printing messages in capital letters on long sheets of paper folded into a zigzag stack.

A first-hand visual inspection of a computer does not tell us much more than we already know. It consists of a collection of metal cabinets, commonly painted in shades of gray, blue, or coral and having a few switches and neon indicator lights on the front, and large electrical cables issuing from the back. Some of the cabinets contain spools on which magnetic tapes are mounted; some contain stacks of discs vaguely reminiscent of coin-operated juke boxes, and some do not. If you should happen to see one of these cabinets with its covers open, you are liable to see panels of circuit boards and an elaborately organized bird's nest of fine wires. Obviously, you are not going to find out very much about a computer by looking at it.

12.1 Organized complexity

One thing that a look inside a computer should do is dispel any notion you might have had that a modern computer is designed along similar lines as is the human brain. From what is known of biological information processors, it appears that the organization of current computers is quite dissimilar. Nor is there a close parallel between the basic elements. The basic element of the human brain is the neuron, or neural cell, which is in itself an enormously complex unit whose physiology is still not completely understood. The basic element of a computer is an electronically controlled switch, usually realized by one of the many variant forms of a transistor. The physics of these switches is quite well understood, and an individual switching element is simplicity itself. A single computer may contain some number of these switching elements between several thousand and several millions, but it is still a far cry from the estimated ten billion cells that constitute an adult human brain.

It is apparent just from the numbers of basic elements involved that both the human brain and the digital computer are structures of potentially enormous complexity. But since relatively little is known, in detail at least, about how the brain is organized, and the organization of a digital computer is entirely known and documented, we shall cease speculation about the brain as a model and look at the organization of a hypothetical computer. Because of the potential for complexity, one should not attempt to understand the functioning of a whole computer on the level of the operations of its primitive switching elements. We shall approach the computer by looking at successive levels of refinement of details, just as we have learned to approach the design of computational algorithms.

Let us begin by considering the organization of a very simple computer, shown in Fig. 12.1. It consists of three interconnected boxes. The function of the input/output unit is to translate input given in the form of holes in a punched card, or impulses on the keys of an electric typewriter, into electrical signals acceptable to the electronics of the computer. Conversely, it translates a set of these signals delivered to it to activate a printing device.

The function of the memory unit is to store for future reference information delivered to it in the form of electrical signals. The memory is organized as a mammoth array of individual cells, each cell designated by its address, or relative index within the memory array. The information stored in a cell might be an item of data, or an encoded instruction for the computer, or an encoded memory-unit address where another piece of data or an instruction is to be found.

The function of the central processing unit is to decode the instructions it receives, to generate memory addresses at which data or additional instructions are to be found, and to carry out

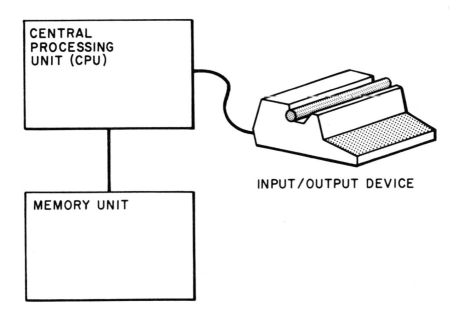

CENTRAL
PROCESSING
UNIT (CPU)

MEMORY UNIT

INPUT/OUTPUT DEVICE

Fig. 12.1 Organization of a simple computer

the primitive computational steps called for by the instructions. The connections between the various units in Fig. 12.1 represent bundles of cables along which signals representing data, memory addresses, orders, and replies are sent.

Each of these units is interesting in its own right, but since we must limit our objectives, let us look only at a very simple central processing unit (CPU) in more detail. Upon ripping off the cover, figuratively speaking, we see that its contents are organized as shown in Fig 12.2. They are divided by function into a control unit and an arithmetic unit. It is the job of the control unit to decode instructions and issue orders. In the course of issuing orders for the execution of an instruction, it will have to assemble two addresses—code words identifying specific locations in the vast space of the memory unit—one of which will tell where to find the data required for the execution of the current instruction, and one of which will tell where the next following instruction is to be found. The control unit must have some temporary memory in which to store these two addresses. The temporary memory is provided by a pair of registers (about which more will be said later) called the instruction address register and the data address register. There must be connections from these two registers to the memory unit, so that the code words they contain can be used by the memory unit to address the contents of the desired memory locations. In addition, the instruction decoder must have a connection to the memory unit by which it receives the code word representing the next instruction to be executed. It must also have connections to the arithmetic unit and to the input/output unit so that it can send them orders and receive their replies.

The arithmetic unit also contains a visible register, called the accumulator, and usually contains another, hidden register, here called the second operand register. There is in addition some special-purpose control circuitry that we call the arithmetic logic control. Connections are required between the arithmetic unit and the control unit to receive orders and send back replies, and to the memory unit to exchange data between the arithmetic unit and the memory location designated by the contents of the data address register.

You can see from the description outlined above that the organization of even a simple computer is rather complex, but not really mind-boggling. At this point it may be well for us to stop and follow the course of execution of a short sequence of instructions. Suppose that a program contains the statement

330

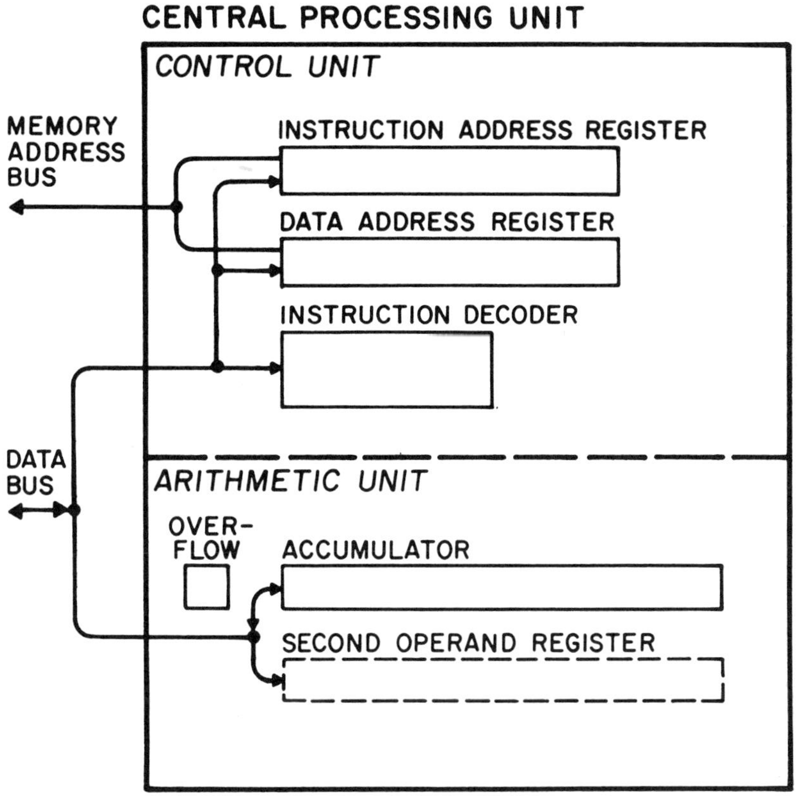

CENTRAL PROCESSING UNIT

Figure 12.2 Contents of the CPU. Internal connections among
the various registers and the instruction decoder
exist but are not shown.

```
A := B + C
```

where A, B, and C have been declared to be scalar integer variables. This Pascal statement might have been translated into the following sequence of instructions for the simple computer:

LOAD B   Meaning fetch the value of B from the memory into the accumulator register.

ADD C   Meaning add the value of C to the number already in the accumulator.

STORE A   Meaning store the value now in the accumulator into the memory location corresponding to the variable A.

Actually, this sequence of primitive instructions could not be presented to the computer in this form. The name that a programmer gives to a scalar variable will not have any meaning for the electronics of the simple computer; the signals that it "understands" can more easily be represented by numbers. The reason is that the transistor switches deliver one of two possible voltage levels onto their attached wires, each of which defines a binary (two-valued) condition that can be represented by a numeral 1 or 0. Let 1 represent the condition that one voltage appears, and 0 represent the condition that the other voltage appears. The actual value of the voltage is quite irrelevant to us (although not to the electronics); what is of significance is the fact that there are just two meaningful conditions. Now if these wires are arrayed in a linear order, the linear array of numerals corresponding to the conditions of voltages on the individual wires forms a binary representation of an integer number. Hence, we claim that the signals understood by the electronics of a computer are quite naturally represented by integer numbers.

Returning to the question of how to represent program variables, the function of a program variable is to store a value for later reference. The computer can store values in its memory unit. The memory unit consists of a large physical array of memory cells, each implemented by some type of electronic or magnetic device. Each of these cells is distinguished from its neighbors by an address. In the commonest types of random-access memory units, the addressing of a memory cell is realized by encoding the address as a set of voltages on a bundle of wires called the address bus, which is connected to the memory unit.

332

The electronics of the memory unit responds by connecting another set of wires, called the <u>data bus</u>, to the particular memory word whose address was specified. A program variable is made to correspond to a particular memory cell by designation of an address. Suppose the following correspondence has been established:

```
A  EQU  001001
B  EQU  001002
C  EQU  001003
```

where EQU stands for "is equivalent to."

The electronics will also not accept English words as the codes of the operations it is to carry out, so the instructions seen by the electronics have numbers substituted for these words as well. Suppose that the codes are:

```
LOAD   EQU  60
STORE  EQU  61
ADD    EQU  71
```

Finally, the program itself will be stored in the computer's memory unit; so the address at which each instruction is to be found must be specified. The stored instructions will look something like this, in numerical representation:

Memory location	Instruction stored here	Interpretation
000100	60 001002	Load the contents of memory location 001002 (corresponding to the variable B) into the accumulator, erasing its previous contents.
000101	71 001003	Add to the contents of the accumulator the contents of memory location 001003 (which corresponds to the program variable C).
000102	61 001001	Store the contents of the accumulator into memory location 001001 (which represents the program variable A) replacing its previous contents.

Now let us see what the computer we have described will do with one of these instructions. Suppose the machine is started in the following state:

instruction address register

000100

data address register

XXXXXX

accumulator

XXXXXXXX

memory unit

address:	000100	000101	000102	...	001001
contents:	60001002	71001003	61001001	...	00000000

001002	001003
00000048	00000120

were the string of X's indicated for some registers indicates that their contents are undefined or irrelevant. When we start the machine, it will seek the first instruction and attempt to execute it. Upon starting, the instruction address, 000100, will be placed on the address bus, activating the electronics of the memory unit, which will then connect the data bus to memory cell 000100. The contents of that cell, 60001002, will then appear on the data bus. Next, the rightmost six digits of the number presented to the control unit on the data bus will be loaded into the data address register for future reference. The leftmost two digits will be accepted by the instruction decoder for immediate processing. The registers of the CPU now look like this, at the end of the fetch phase for this first instruction:

instruction address register

000100

data address register

001002

accumulator

XXXXXXXX

In the next stage, or "execution" phase, of the first instruction, the contents of the data address register are put onto the data bus, and the electronics of the memory unit decodes this address and connects the data bus to memory cell 001002. Meanwhile, the instruction decoder has found out what is meant by he operation code 60. It therefore sends an order to the accumulator to clear itself of any previously held data and accept new data from the data bus. It also signals the instruction address register to increment its current value by 1, since the instruction being executed did not explicitly specify a different instruction address. After hese operations are completed, the registers of the CPU look like this:

instruction address register

| 000101 |

data address register

| XXXXXX |

accumulator

| 00000048 |

The machine is now ready to begin a new instruction fetching cycle.

It may seem a rather complicated job to design electronics that will accomplish all of these functions and will synchronize each activity with the others so that the functions are carried out in the right order. It is a complicated job, but computer engineers approach it by using very systematic design procedures and by breaking down tasks of great complexity into subtasks of manageable proportions.

You may also have noticed that much of the activity in a computer involves shipping small amounts of data from one register to another. This is also true in real computers of conventional design, even very large ones of much greater complexity than has been described here. Let's see how a computer does arithmetic in one of these registers.

12.2 Shift registers

In the simple computer we are describing, all arithmetic operations are done in the accumulator. In this example (typical of early computers), the accumulator incorporates a 'shift register'. By a register, we mean merely a set of identical elements,

335

each capable of holding a single binary bit, that is, of a 0 or a 1 value, and which can be tested or set. The addressable elements of the memory unit are therefore registers. The individual binary elements that make up a register are indexed in a linear order, so that we can refer to the bits held by a register according to their positions in sequence. The bits, taken in sequence, form a binary representation of an integer number. Usually, all the registers in which data are to be held will contain the same fixed number of binary elements, and this length is called the word size (in bits) used in the machine.

A shift register has, in addition to the capability to store a sequence of bits, the capability to shift the pattern of bits that it holds one position to the right or left, upon receiving a signal to do so. At first, this does not sound like a very significant ability. But remember that in the binary representation of a number, a shift of the bit pattern one position toward the left represents a multiplication by 2; one position to the right represents a division by 2 (for positive numbers, at least). Shifting is also useful when data are to be shipped off in packages other than the contents of an entire register.

It may not be helpful to describe the operation of a shift register in terms of electronics (this will depend on your previously acquired knowledge of electronics), but we can describe a shift register that can be constructed by you and your friends, if you can follow instructions. The basic element will be a human being. The shift register consists of several such elements, seated or standing in a line, side by side . As a shift register element, you have two possible states, 0 (left arm at your side) and 1 (left arm raised above your head). Most of the time, you do nothing except remain in a constant state, but upon a given signal (when someone nudges you on your left side) you may change states, according to a fixed rule, and signal the shift register element to your right (by nudging him with your right elbow). The rules for this important activity are also very simple:

(a) Upon receiving a signal (being nudged in the left side), inspect the shift register element on your left and remember his state. Pass the signal (nudge) along to the shift register element on your right.

(b) Upon receiving a second signal from your left, assume the state that you remembered as the state of the element to your left when you got the first signal, and pass the nudge on to your right. Get ready to obey instruction (a) again.

336

To test this shift register, you will need a control element who stands to the left of the leftmost shift register element. The control element can clear the register by nudging repeatedly, the pattern of a single 1 state will be passed steadily through the length of the shift register from left to tight. If you try a few such experiments though, you will probably discover that the reliability of humans as shift register elements is not very great. Electronic devices are better.

One problem that may occur in the shift register described above is that, if the control element gives nudges too quickly in succession, trying to force the shift register to act more quickly, there is a very great likelihood that errors will occur. Also, following the initiation of a signal by the control element, it takes quite a little time for the sequence of nudges to propagate from the first shift register element to the last. Similar problems can occur in the electronics of a computer. There is a design alternative that is sometimes adopted: the use of a cadence caller, or clock, to synchronize the activities of the individual elements. Suppose we introduce this modification into our experimental shift register.

Add a person whose job it is to call out, alternatively, "Ready" and "Shift" at two-second intervals. Also change the rules for a shift register element to eliminate nudging as a means of relaying a signal. The new rules are:

(a) Upon hearing the call Ready, inspect the element to your left and remember his state (1 if his left hand is raised; 0 if it is down).

(b) Upon hearing the call Shift, assume the state you have remembered from (a).

The role of the control element is, as before, to initiate a pattern by raising or lowering his hand in sequence with the cadence, but he does not now have to set the cadence himself by the frequency of his nudging. The modified shift register will very likely be more reliable than the former design.

In the computer, each shift register element has a particular input on which it accepts the cadence count, or clock signal, and the role of the control element is played by an input line, or in some cases by a constant-voltage line. Often, shift registers are designed so that the input line to each element, which normally inspects the state its left neighbor upon a Ready signal, can optionally be switched to inspect the state of its right neighbor for right-to-left shifting operations. It can also be switched to inspect a specific line of the input data bus, in order to load the shift register from the memory unit.

12.3 The accumulator

Our accumulator is a shift register having the capabilities of left- and right-shifting and of being set from the data bus. In addition, it can add, complement itself by having every one of its elements simultaneously change state, and perform the logical operations AND and OR. Obviously, quite a lot of electronic circuitry is required to build such an accumulator. When electronic circuitry was expensive, up until a few years ago, many computers were designed with only a single accumulator, as is the hypothetical one we are now describing. Since integrated-circuit technology has now made electronics relatively inexpensive, many newer computer have a dozen or more accumulators. The most complicated of the functions that an accumulator can perform is addition; so we shall attempt to reassemble our human shift register and give its elements the necessary instructions to become adders. All of you shift register elements, line up!

The basic operation that a shift register element needs is the ability to add 1 to his present state number modulo 2. We will first tell him how to do this, and then tell him when to do it. Whenever you are instructed to HALFADD 1, do the following.

HALFADD: If you are in state 0, then change your state to 1, else if you are in state 1, then change your state to 0 and signal the element to your left by nudging him.

The nudge used to signal the next element to the left represents a carry. One plus 1 modulo 2 is indeed 0, but if numbers larger than 1 are to be represented, a carry bit must be passed along to be added into the next higher binary numeral position. Thus the adder instructions should certainly include the following:

(a) Whenever you receive a carry bit (nudge) from the element to your right, HALFADD 1.

Normally, the number to be added to the accumulator will appear on the lines of the data bus. Each element of the accumulator will have to add to its binary value, the value of the input corresponding line of the data bus. Let us represent the data bus by recruiting another line of humans to sit in front of the shift register elements, and set some constant pattern of bits on the data bus by instructing each of its members to hold his left hand in a fixed (raised of lowered) position. Now we can give a second instruction to our shift register elements.

(b) Upon receiving a signal from the cadence caller, inspect the state of the data bus line represented by the person in front of you. If that state is 1, then HALFADD 1.

Now however, if we attempt a trial of our adder, setting one pattern of bits into the accumulator and another on the data bus, and have the cadence caller give an instruction Start to simultaneously activate all of the accumulator elements, chaos will probably ensue. If the bit pattern initially in the accumulator contained a lot of 1's, then the HALFADD instructions given by rule (b) are going to coincide with those given by rule (a) at some accumulator elements, who will not know what to do, since they were not told to stack up simultaneously arriving HALFADD instructions. Perhaps it was not such a good idea to try to initiate addition simultaneously over all of the accumulator elements.

Suppose the accumulator elements are numbered from one up to the length of the accumulator, beginning at the right. Then, if the cadence caller signals each accumulator element individually, by calling his number in turn, and allows enough time between successive signals for all the HALFADD instructions generated by carries under rule (a) to be completed, no simultaneous HALFADD instructions will be received by any element, and the accumulator will be able to add. In electronic accumulators too, there must be sufficient time lag between the additions of successive bit positions to the accumulator to allow the propagation of carries to be completed.

In most accumulators, the register is equipped with an additional binary element, whose logical position is to the left of the highest-order bit. This element is not used in shifting operations, nor in OR and AND, but it is used in addition. In case the sum of two numbers, each representable by the number of bits contained in the accumulator, is a number too large to hold in the accumulator, the addition will generate a carry bit from the leftmost element of the normal accumulator, a carry bit that has no place to go. The extra accumulator element provides a place in which to put it. The problem remains that the sum is still too large to represent in the fixed-length registers of the

339

machine, but at least hat problem can be detected by testing the extra element of the accumulator. The extra bit is called the overflow bit, and when your Pascal programs produce a carry into the overflow bit during the course of adding two positive integers ot two negative integers, you may receive an error message.

12.4 Other arithmetic operations

We will not go into the operations of floating-point arithmetic, but we can take a look at some other operations of integer arithmetic. Most of them turn out to depend on addition. Before we look at subtraction, however, it is necessary to say a little more about number representation. If the accumulator of our machine is N bits long, not counting the overflow bit, then it seems that we should be able to represent integers modulo 2^N, and to represent a positive integer as large as $2^N - 1$. But we must not forget about negative integers either, and it is going to require one bit of information to represent the sign of a number. There are many possible ways to represent negative numbers in a computer; we will describe just one. The highest-order bit is set aside to represent the sign of a number, with 0 standing for plus and 1 standing for minus. This having been decided, you can see that the largest positive integer that can be represented is only $2^{N-1} - 1$, since the Nth bit must be zero for every positive number. It would seem, then, that the representation is fully decided, the highest bit giving the algebraic sign and the remaining bits giving the magnitude in binary radix representation.

To do subtraction of numbers that are given in this sign-magnitude representation, we must use an algorithm such as the one we are taught in elementary school: subtract digit-by-digit and generate a carry in the number being subtracted or a borrow from the number from which the subtraction is being done. However, if we use a little ingenuity and change the way of representing negative numbers, the algorithm for subtraction becomes exactly that for addition, plus an inexpensive preparation of one of the two numbers before the addition is carried out.

Observe that, when there are just N bits to work with, a complementation of the bit pattern of any positive number gives us a representation of some negative number. For instance, suppose the register length is six bits. Then the number 10 is

340

represented as

001010

Taking its complement gives

110101

which we know to be the representation of some negative number because the leftmost bit, which we have designated the sign bit, is 1. When we add these two together, 10 and its compliment, their sum is

111111

Moreover, this last result is no coincidence, for taking any six-bit pattern and summing it with its complement produces the same result. Would the complement of a positive number make a good candidate for the representation of the negative of that number? Certainly it is a possible representation, for it is unique; we can go back and forth between a number and its complement without losing any information. But one drawback is that the complement of zero gets a different representation than does zero itself: zero is 000000, but the complement of zero is 111111.

The representation we shall adopt for negative numbers is called two's complement representation. It is commonly used in computers, although it is certainly not the only representation in use. To obtain the negative of a number, we take the complement of its binary representation and add 1. Thus the two's complement of zero is

```
 111111
+000001
 000000
```

with a carry generated into the overflow bit. The negative of 10 is

```
 110101
+000001
 110110
```

and when the negative of -10 is taken

```
 110101
+000001
 001010
```

the result is seen to be 10. To do subtraction, A - B, in two's compliment representation, we first take the complement of the binary representation of B, add 1, and then add A. The only capabilities needed by an accumulator are to add and to complement a number.

Multiplication is a little harder than addition or subtraction. Of course, multiplication can be accomplished by repeated additions of the same number, but if the multiplier may be large, this seems inefficient. The algorithm we learned in elementary school is more efficient. It forms a product by taking the sum of partial products, shifted to the left by the number of places that the individual multiplier digit appears from the rightmost place in the multiplier. This algorithm is even simpler when the numbers are represented in binary form, for each partial product is either the shifted multiplicand or is zero. For example, the product of 10 and 6 would be written as

```
      001010
      000110
      ------
      000000
     001010
    001010
   000000
  000000
 000000
 ------
    111100
```

To modify this algorithm slightly for the computer, the sum of the partial products will be accumulated as the algorithm progresses, rather than saving all partial products to be added together at the end. The multiplicand will be kept available on the data bus throughout the multiplication operation. Initially the accumulator is set to zero, the multiplier is entered in the second operand register, and the multiplicand appears on the data bus. The steps of the multiplication shown above, for a six-bit accumulator, would be as follows.

First step: Test the leftmost bit of the second operand register. Since it is zero, no addition of a partial product is required.

accumulator	second operand register	data bus
000000	000110	001010

342

Second step: The contents of the accumulator and the second operand register are both shifted left one position, and the leftmost bit of the second operand register is again tested. Again, no addition is called for.

accumulator	second operand register	data bus
000000	001100	001010

Third step: The accumulator and second operand register are shifted left one position. No addition is called for.

accumulator	second operand register	data bus
000000	011000	001010

Fourth step: The accumulator and second operand register are shifted again. Since the leftmost bit of the second operand register is now a 1, the contents of the data bus are added to the accumulator.

accumulator	second operand register	data bus
001010	110000	001010

Fifth step: An additional shift of accumulator and second operand register indicates another addition of the data bus to the shifted accumulator.

accumulator	second operand register	data bus
011110	100000	001010

Sixth step: Accumulator and second operand register are shifted once more to the left, but no further addition to the accumulator is indicated.

accumulator	second operand register	data bus
111100	000000	001010

The algorithm terminates after a number of steps equal to the length of the second operand register. In this example, we have ignored the sign bit, but if it is included, a very similar algorithm succeeds with both positive and negative numbers in two's complement representation. When both multiplier and multiplicand are of the same sign, a 1 in the sign bit of the product indicates overflow, not a negative product.

Implementing the division algorithm in the arithmetic unit is slightly more complicated than is multiplication, although it too can be done by using only the accumulator, the second operand register, and he data bus. However, by now you should have some idea as to how the arithmetic unit functions, on the level of register operations if not in terms of electronic circuits, and there are some further topics that should now be looked into.

12.5 How the computer communicates with the outside world

So far, our discussion of the operation of a simple computer has avoided mentioning the third principal functional unit, the input/output device. Each input/output device also contains within itself a register, and the connection between the CPU and the register of the input/output device is merely another path for data transfer between registers, using a bus. Communication on the I/O bus does pose some special problems, for the reason that the input/output device is usually much slower than is the CPU. Therefore, it is not practical to synchronize its activity with that of the CPU by using the same cadence caller that synchronizes activity between the CPU and its memory unit.† Instead, synchronization is accomplished by sending messages back and forth between the CPU and the register of the input/output device, using lines of he I/O bus that are specially designated for this purpose.

Many input/output devices are designed to handle information in units of individual characters. Since the electronics of the computer will not recognize characters directly, they are encoded in the form of a sequence of binary bits, using the ASCII or the EBCDIC code. A sequence of bits of the length required to encode a single character is called a byte. In most computers, certainly in all but the smallest ones, the length of a register (in bits) is greater than one byte, often two to eight times greater. Thus, it is common that information stored in the memory unit in the form of characters will be stored with several bytes occupying each addressable memory register. In order to transmit a single byte to the input/output device to be printed, it is necessary to load into the accumulator the contents of the memory location in which the byte is stored, and to shift the contents of the accumulator until the sequence of bits constituting the desired byte occupies the low-order bit positions of the accumulator (those from which connections can be made to the I/O bus).

---

† In some computers, even transactions between the CPU and the memory unit are not synchronized by a cadence caller, but are handled as are input/output transactions.

Returning to the question of synchronization, the CPU must have some way to know when the input/output device is ready to receive a new byte to be printed (or in the case of input, when it is ready to transmit a new input byte). And the input/output device must have some way to know when a byte is to be printed. In Figure 12.3, the connections of the I/O bus to the accumulator are shown. Along with the data lines, which carry the data to be transmitted in either direction, and the order lines, which carry an instruction code to the input/output device, there is another line called the ready line which is used to pass a synchronization signal. The ready line connects a pair of one-bit registers, one in the CPU and one in the input/output device. When the line is in state 0, it indicates that there is an input or an output transaction in progress. It is the responsibility of the CPU to initiate input/output transactions, and so it has the duty to set the ready line to state 1 whenever it wishes to start such a transaction. It is the responsibility of the input/output device to complete these transactions, and so it is obligated to clear the ready line to state 0 when it completes a transaction. Whenever the input/output device is not actually busy processing an I/O transaction it must sit obediently testing the state of the ready line, waiting upon the event that the CPU will set the state to 1, indicating the start of a new request for action by the input/output device.

As for the CPU, when it receives a sequence of instructions to output a byte, it will first be told to load the accumulator with the contents of a memory register in which the byte is located. Then, if the byte is not initially located in the low-order bits of the register, the next instruction in the program will tell the CPU to shift the contents of the accumulator some number of bit positions to the right. Upon decoding the next instruction of the program, the CPU will be directed to put the code for a print order onto the order lines of the I/O bus, to connect the low-order bit positions of the accumulator in which the byte is located to the data lines of the I/O bus, and to set the ready line to state 1. Responsibility for completion of the output transaction now rests with the input/output device, and the CPU must wait until it is done. To do this, the next instruction of the program may be one which instructs the CPU to loop on that instruction, not changing the contents of the instruction address register until a test of the ready line shows its state to be 0.

Now it frequently is the case, particularly in large, fast computers, that the CPU could be put to other work instead of

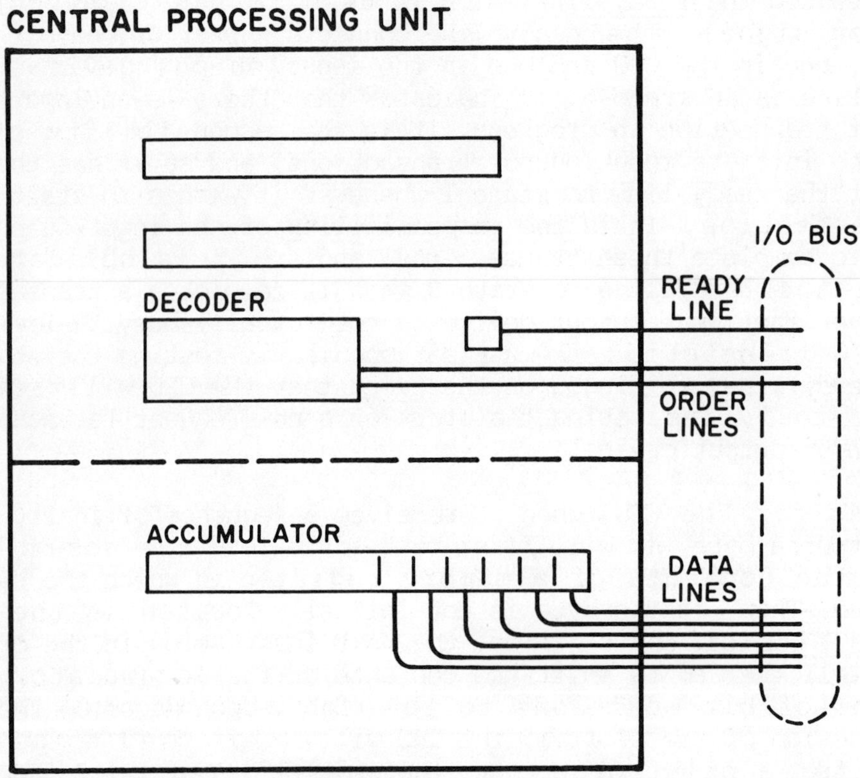

CENTRAL PROCESSING UNIT

Figure 12.3 Connections of the I/O bus to
registers of the CPU

waiting while the print ball of an electric typewriter is spun into the correct position and impacted against a carbon ribbon, paper, and platen. That action may require a very short time on the temporal scale of human activities, but it is long when compared with he time in which the CPU executes an instruction.

The situation can be compared to that of a small businessman who operates a grocery store. He employs a boy with a three-wheeled cycle to make deliveries for him. Each time he assigns the boy a delivery to make, he wants to know when the task has been completed. One way to do this is to send the boy off, then stand at the front door of the grocery until the boy returns. However, this is wasteful of the grocer's time, and so he will occupy himself with other work, such as stocking shelves, marking prices (up), or filling an order for another customer. In order to be notified when the delivery boy has completed his assigned task, the grocer may rely on the telephone, telling the boy "Call me when you have finished."

The grocer in this case will be making a commitment to respond at the request of his employee, interrupting his other activity, important though it may be, to pick up the telephone. He agrees to do this because he knows that the telephone trans-action with his employee will be short in duration, and it will be more convenient for him to have the opportunity to keep busy with other work while the boy makes deliveries, even at the risk of a short interruption, than it would be to waste his own time while awaiting the boy's return.

By analogy, the CPU has the same problem as does the grocer, with the input/output unit playing the role of the delivery boy. In order to adopt the grocer's solution, two requirements must be fulfilled by the electronics. The input/output device must be equipped with a register that can deliver or accept data from the I/O bus in a short interval of time, so as not to cause the CPU to have to wait. The register of the input/output device can then hold the value of the data item for as long as is required to complete the I/O transaction, without requiring that the accu-mulator hold the value on the data lines of the I/O bus during that time. Also, there must be an additional line on the I/O bus, called the interrupt line, to correspond to the bell of the grocer's telephone. Unlike the treatment given to any other line of the I/O bus, the electronics of the CPU must cause it to interrupt execution of a sequence of instructions when a signal appears on the interrupt line so that it can briefly pay attention to an I/O transaction.

347

With an interrupt line, the course of an output transaction is slightly different than before. When the CPU receives instructions to output a byte, it will store in a predetermined memory location, which we shall call Break Address, the location of the first instruction of a sequence that will load the desired byte into the accumulator, shift it, and connect the accumulator to the I/O bus. Having done this, the CPU sets he ready line to state 1, indicating to the input/output device its desire to put it to work. The CPU then goes on to another job, if it has any to do.

The input/output device sits as before, inspecting the ready line to see if there is an assignment for it. If it has completed its last assigned task and finds the ready line again set to state 1, it clears the ready line to state 0 and simultaneously issues an interrupt signal on the interrupt line. Shortly thereafter, it will expect to receive an instruction on the order lines and data on the data lines, signifying the new task it is to carry out.

When the CPU receives an interrupt, it is allowed to complete execution of the instruction in progress, but then is obliged to store the contents of the instruction address register (containing the address of the next instruction in the sequence it has been executing) into a predetermined location, which we shall call Resume Address, and reload the instruction address register with the contents of memory location Break Address. It is suddenly in the business of executing the instruction sequence of the output transaction! When the output transaction has been communicated to the input/output device via the I/O bus, the last instruction of the output transaction sequence will tell the CPU to clear the interrupt line back to state 0 and load the instruction address register with the contents of the memory location we have called Resume Address. Now it is back at executing the normal sequence of instructions that it was doing before it received the interrupt, just as though nothing had happened. What has happened, though, is that a byte of data has been shipped across the I/O bus to the input/output device, which is now busily at work operating the electric typewriter. As a further development in many computers, the input/output devices may communicate a whole sequence of bytes directly to the memory, bypassing the CPU altogether, once the CPU has given a general permission to begin.

In these last illustrations of doing output transactions, you may have noticed that the division between functions done by electronics and functions that must be programmed is becoming fuzzy. It is very difficult, in the case of a malfunction, to tell whether it is due to faulty electronics or a faulty program. Although the interrupt system is made available by the use of electronics, its correct use to synchronize the activities of the CPU and the input/output device depends as much on the segment of the program that handles the details of the output transaction, clears the interrupt line, and recovers the interrupted instruction sequence, as it does on the electronics. For this reason, these program segments are designed by experts, standardized, and made available for use by all users of a computer. Such critical programs form a package known as the operating system of a computer. The computer user is no more welcome to alter these programs than he would be to tinker with the electronics.

12.6 Managing the computer

When you use a large computer, either in batch mode, submitting punched cards to a card reader, or in interactive mode, sitting at a typewriter keyboard, you don't get a chance to see how the operations of the computer are managed. That there is some complex management going on is more apparent when you do interactive computing, because you know that the computer is simultaneously serving several customers at once, although you are usually not made aware of the fact by responses of your own terminal. Even in batch mode computing, however, a large computer will serve several users at once, in the sense that it may not complete the execution of one user's program before it commences the execution of another's. The reason this is desirable is that it allows the computer to make more efficient use of its CPU and its memory. As we saw in the last section, it is possible for the CPU to do other work, if it has any to do, while waiting for the completion of an I/O transaction by an input/output device. A large computer, like a grocery store, may have several employees in the form of input/output devices and secondary memory units, and can keep all of them busy at peak business hours by simultaneously serving many customers. The CPU, which is much faster than the other employees, divides its time among the several customers' jobs and also manages the entire enterprise.

It would be possible, in principle at least, to employ a human to manage the activities of a large computer. But while the human manager was deciding which customer to serve next, and furiously typing his directives on the keyboard of the computer console, the machine would probably have completed all other input and output, all computing, and be quietly resting in a dormant state, awaiting a directive from the tired fingers of its human manager. The solution to this problem is to fire the human and program the computer to manage its own activities. This is accomplished by designing a package of programs is called the operating system, or executive, and is a vital part of a successful computer system. The reliability of the system depends in good measure on how astute were the designers of the operating system in forseeing all contingencies. If a condition occurs for which the operating system does not have an algorithm to tell it how to make a decision, then the computer usually stops, and human intervention is required to sort out the difficulty.

12.7 Compilers

There is probably another gap in your knowledge of how computers work that may trouble you at this point. In the earlier sections of this chapter there were given some examples of how the computer executes primitive instructions by moving data from its memory unit to its accumulator, by executing arithmetic and logical operations on the bit sequence there, and by input/output transactions. But you do not compose algorithms as sequences of the primitive instructions understood by the electronics of a computer, you write Pascal programs instead. How does the computer interpret your programs?

Before the computer can execute one of your programs, it must first read it. When your Pascal program is read by the card reader, it enters the computer as a sequence of characters, each stored as a byte in the memory unit of the computer. The interpretation of a Pascal program begins by analysis of this character string, utilizing techniques such as were described in Example 8.1.1 to determine the identities of constants, reserved words, and the identifiers that are the names that you have given to program variables and procedures. Pascal is a grammatical language, and so the organization of its words and punctuation marks into sentences is described by a grammar. A Pascal program is decomposed into individual phrases, such as statements or expressions. Associated with many of the types of phrases are fixed rules for their interpretation. The parameters to be included in these interpretations can be values of constants, memory addresses that have been associated with program variables in the course of the analysis, or the interpretations that have been made of other phrases of the program. There is a great deal of information that is generated during the analysis phase of the interpretation and that must be referred to in the synthesis phase, when the interpretation finally results in the formation of a list of the primitive instructions that are comprehensible to the machine. (And only to the machine!)

This task, of interpreting Pascal programs and generating a list of primitive machine instructions that can be executed, is directed by a large computer program called a compiler. It gets its name because its function is to compile a list of machine instructions, but it could just as well be called a translator (from Pascal into machine language) or an interpreter. Compilers are very interesting programs in their own right, and you may someday wish to learn more about them, but that will have to be left to other books.

APPENDIX
PASCAL SYNTAX DIAGRAMS

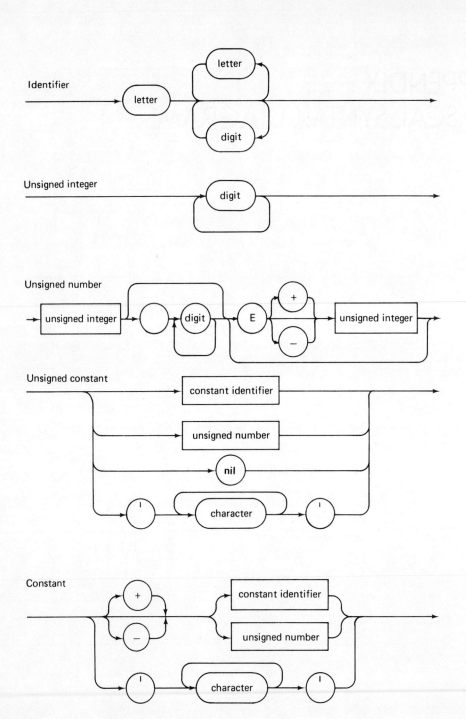

354

Variable

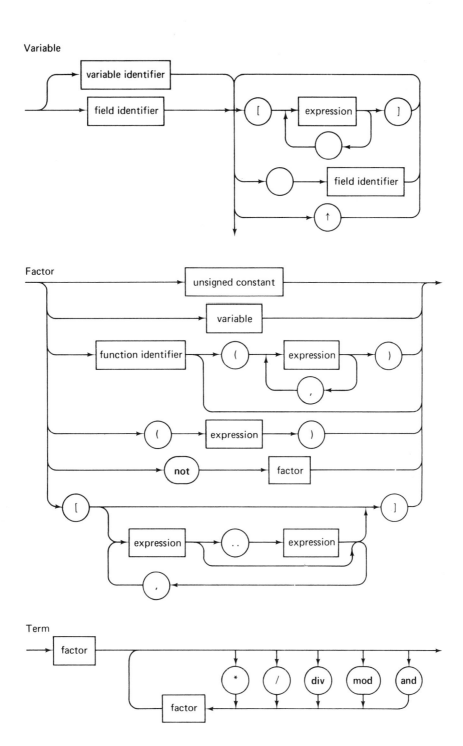

Factor

Term

Simple expression

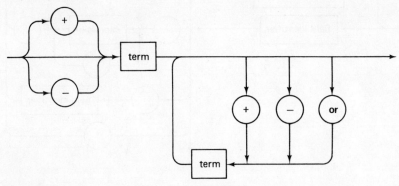

Expression

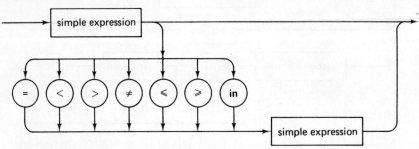

Parameter list

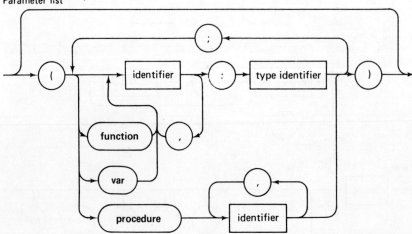

356

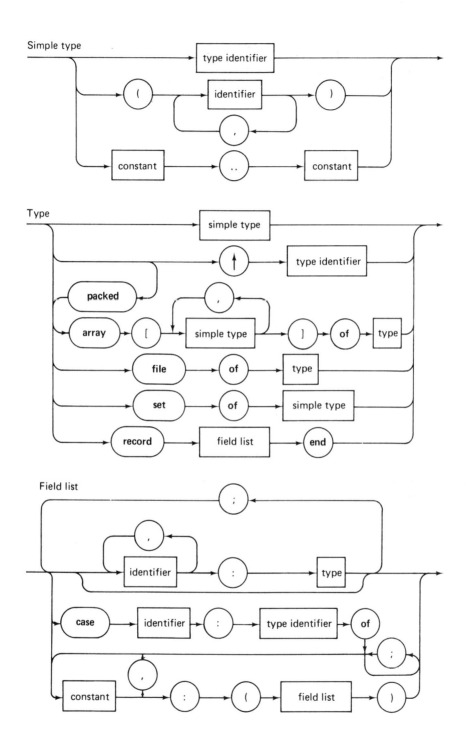

357

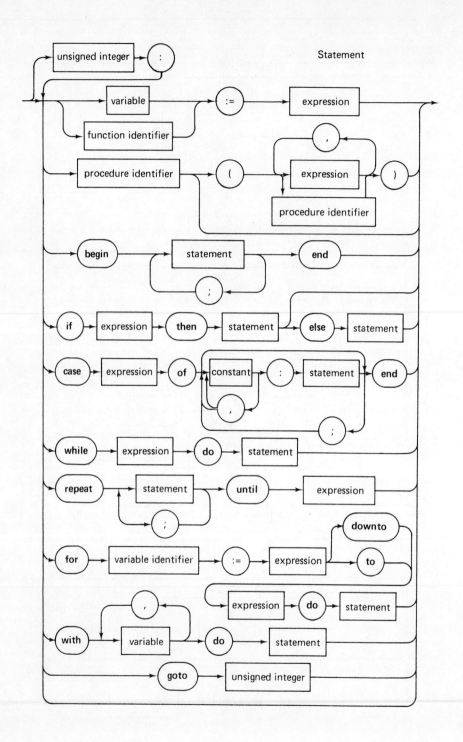

Statement

358

Block

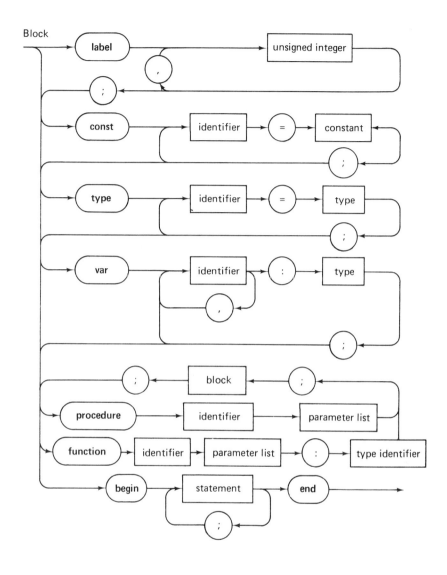

Program

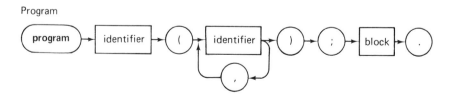

359

INDICES

Index by general terminology

In this index, an underscored page number indicates a definition or explanation of a term; page numbers not underscored indicate use of the indexed term in the text. The reader looking for definitions of terms should also consult the glossary at the front of the book.

Index by keywords and names predeclared in Pascal

This index is to locate definitions and examples of use of the reserved words and predeclared identifiers of the Pascal language. In this index the identifiers are capitalized; the reserved words are not. Words for which no page number is given are not mentioned in this book, but have been included in the index for completeness.

Index to Examples and Exercises
by type of application